Choices and Chances

Sociology for everyday life

Lorne Tepperman
University of Toronto

with the assistance of
John Veugelers

HOLT, RINEHART and WINSTON of CANADA, Limited
TORONTO

Canadian Cataloguing in Publication Data
Tepperman, Lorne, 1943-
 Choices and chances : sociology for everyday life

Bibliography: p.
Includes index.
ISBN 0-03-922564-X

1. Conduct of life.   2. Quality of life - Canada.
3. Social indicators - Canada.   I. Veugelers, John.
II. Title.

BJ1581.2.T46 1988   158   C88-093926-5

PUBLISHER: David Dimmell
EDITOR: Donna Adams
PUBLISHING SERVICES MANAGER: Karen Eakin
EDITORIAL CO-ORDINATOR: Liz Radojkovic
EDITORIAL ASSISTANT: Graeme Whitley
COPY EDITOR: Riça Night
DESIGNER: Jack Steiner Graphic Design
COVER PHOTO: Bertram Brooker (Canadian, 1888-1955), *The Dawn of Man* (L'Aube de l'humanité), 1927. Oil on canvas. 112.2 x 81.3 cm. National Gallery of Canada. Reproduced by permission of Phyllis Brooker Smith
TYPESETTING AND ASSEMBLY: True to Type Inc.
PRINTING AND BINDING: Webcom Limited

Printed in Canada
1 2 3 4 5   93 92 91 90 89

Our only guides are our interests, viewed in the largest possible sense; our interests made as self-aware as possible, since it is unlikely we can attain what we do not want, and impossible to want what is not conceived as attainable.

JACQUES BARZUN*

Darwin, Marx, Wagner: Critique of a Heritage (2nd edition). Garden City, NY: Doubleday Anchor Books, 1958.

Preface

This book urges you to examine your goals and opportunities, then consider the chances that you will get what you want from your education, career, marriage, parenthood, and other parts of your life. It argues that we ought to live with our eyes open, gather evidence about the world, choose in our own best interests (broadly defined), and behave rationally.

People's lives are intertwined with and limited by what sociologists call *social structure*. Our life choices are shaped and limited by the choices and actions of people around us: this is sociology's most central insight. Dominant or popular ideology teaches that people generally get what they want from life, if they want it enough and acquire the right skills and credentials. Supposedly, they alone are to blame if they fail to get what they want. Yet research shows that most people do *not* get what they want, but settle for what they can get. How can we explain this fact, and what does it teach us?

Sociology—the systematic study of social relations—emerged in the nineteenth century as an attempt to understand the enormous social changes caused by the Industrial Revolution and the French Revolution. Even today sociology is, at its core, a prolonged debate about the human ability to improve social life through reason and organized action.

Sociology does not claim that people are entirely rational, or even that sociologists must be, or can be, entirely rational. But it does argue that we must all try to distinguish between beliefs and feelings on the one hand, and facts and reason on the other. That is what I am urging you to do when you read this book.

None of us thinks about life in a completely rational way. Often we find it hard, almost impossible, to change the way we make life choices. We feel almost imprisoned by our fears, passions, and unexamined certainties. We may prefer to consult our feelings on major decisions, do what family and friends advise, go with hunches, or take a shot in the dark. Sometimes we even rely on luck to get us through. Yet deep down we all know that there must be a better way of making important choices.

I cannot claim that the "advice" this book offers is complete or foolproof. It is only a first approximation, and I have found it helpful in organizing my own thinking. Ideally, this book will make you wonder whether some of the things you feel sure about are really so, and it may get you thinking about the ways you make your own life choices. I assume, simply, that whatever your particular life goals may be, you are aiming to get as much satisfaction out of life—that is, *life satisfaction*—as you possibly can. All the analyses that follow are aimed toward that goal.

Research on life satisfaction has developed quite intriguingly in the past decade or two. It now offers sociology rich information about who is most satisfied with life (and various parts of life— work, marriage, and so on), under what conditions, and why. In addition to a growing body of Canadian, American, and European research available in print, we have also had access to a large 1981 survey of life satisfaction conducted at the Institute for Behavioural Research, York University (Toronto). From time to time, analyses of unpublished data from this survey are introduced to complement already published findings.

You may choose to doubt or ignore the conclusions this book has drawn. After all, a sociological conclusion about a category of people to which you belong will not inevitably apply to you. No one knows which characteristics—alone or in combination— will guide or predict a given person's behaviour. But if I can get you to analyse the way you live your life, and the choices you are making, in a different way, the book will have succeeded, whatever you decide to do.

Moreover, this book shows how one sociologist goes about examining some major life concerns. Your own instructor may have a somewhat different approach. This is my personal version of what the American sociologist C. Wright Mills called "the sociological imagination," and it draws upon sociology's central goals, concepts, and insights.

How This Book Relates to Your Textbook

This book was written to supplement, not replace, the large multi-topic textbook you are probably using in your introductory course. How do the two books connect?

First, your textbook may discuss sociological topics in an abstract, general way that you may have trouble relating to your own daily life. You may not see how the theories it discusses—especially those theories attributed to Marx, Weber, and Durkheim (sociology's founders)—bear on life today. This problem has led some students to believe that theorizing is something people used to do but don't do any more; or that only geniuses can make theories. As graduate students, my friends and I used to call the required sociological theory course "Dead Guys 101."

Actually, all sociologists make and test theories. Even you make theories about society. This book uses theories that can be related back to the "dead guys" written about in your textbook. But it does not make the connection with their theories obvious; that is something your instructor may want to do in discussing this book with you. As you learn new things from this book, try connecting them to things you heard in lectures or tutorials, or read in the textbook. Everything should connect.

But theorists may not always agree. Sociology thrives on theoretical debates fuelled by different assumptions about reality, findings that conflict with one another, and disagreements about the quality of certain evidence. Lively debates are the evidence of a living discipline, so do not be frustrated or annoyed if a point made in this book fails to match a point made elsewhere. Ask your instructor about the disagreement; talk about it; and think of ways to resolve it. That is how sociological research begins.

Another way that this book differs from your textbook is that it offers advice, while your textbook does not. You should not take the advice without thinking, but rather use it to sharpen your own investigation of personal goals, opportunities, and experiences. This book simply takes the sociological knowledge found in your textbook and asks, If this theory is true, what should follow? How does this affect me? Nothing will make you take a theory more seriously than if you consider whether to risk your future on its being true. So this book encourages you to think of sociological theories as predictions with important consequences for your life.

Finally, your textbook may not contain as much information about life in Canada as you would like. Some textbooks rely on data from the United States, Britain, or other countries to illustrate their theoretical points. This book uses almost exclusively Canadian data that are as up-to-date as possible. (American data are used occasionally when Canadian data are unavailable and there is reason to believe American and Canadian results would be similar.) As a result, you will learn a lot about life in Canada and the organization of Canadian society from this book. The topics and data are arranged around the concept of *life cycle*, the sequence of stages people typically pass through as they grow older. This further relates sociology to life in Canada in the 1980s, as some textbooks do not.

What you read in your textbook about education is augmented by what you read here about educational decisions you must make; what you read in your textbook about work, by what you read here about career choices; what you read about families in your textbook, by what you read here about marriage and parenthood; and so on. You will find a considerable overlap between this book and your textbook. (See the Appendix for more specific suggestions about pairing this book with a standard textbook.) But remember, this book is all about life in Canada, it is organized around the life cycle, and it turns sociological knowledge into advice.

This book will make your understanding of the course textbook richer and more personal. By showing how theories can apply to your own life, this book will show the ways sociology—a living, growing discipline—can shed light on issues of immense personal and social importance.

Acknowledgements

Many people helped me write this book, and I want to thank them.

Tessa McWatt, then a college editor at Holt, Rinehart and Winston, got me interested in starting the book; Donna Adams, her successor, has helped me finish it. Both have treated me with the courtesy and good humour that every author hopes for. So my first thanks go to them. Thanks are also due to Riça Night for her help at the copy-editing stage, and to Liz Radojkovic for a major editorial overhaul.

John Veugelers, while still a third-year undergraduate, helped me design the book and do preliminary research. He ended up drafting two chapters, commenting on several I had drafted, and generally provided moral support in the early stages. We can expect great things of John, and I thank him for being in the right place at the right time.

My introductory sociology students in 1986–87 gave me information that I needed to plan the book; my introductory students in 1987–88 sat through lectures based on the manuscript draft chapters as they came into being. I thank them for their patience.

A number of fine scholars—some friends and others bare acquaintances—were more than co-operative when I asked them to comment on draft chapters. Their expertise in particular areas helped me avoid some foolish errors and put me onto useful, unfamiliar references and ways of thinking. They are Anne Marie Ambert (York), Paul Anisef (York), Rod Beaujot (Western Ontario), Tom Burch (Western Ontario), Margrit Eichler (OISE), Bonnie Fox (Toronto), Ted Harvey (OISE), Nathan Keyfitz (IIASA), Eugen Lupri (Calgary), Nancy Mandell (York), Alex Michalos (Guelph), Ray Murphy (Ottawa), Robert Pike (Queen's), and Jeffrey Reitz (Toronto).

Reviews were commissioned by the publisher at various stages of the project. Françoise Boudreau (University of Guelph), Ian Gomme (Memorial University of Newfoundland), Hugh Lautard (University of New Brunswick), and René Souery (Centennial College) were all helpful at the early stages of conception. Five reviewers also gave me thorough commentaries on the entire first draft of the manuscript: James Cote (University of Western Ontario), Helen Douglas (Okanagan College), William Hanigsberg (Dawson College), Charles Hobart (University of Alberta), and Nancy Nason-Clark (University of New Brunswick). Their comments were useful and, for the most part, encouraging. I am very grateful for their help.

Other colleagues were willing to read a second draft of the manuscript. Their advice helped me reorganize and fine-tune much of the material. I want to thank Ray Breton, Lorna Marsden, Bill Michelson (all University of Toronto), Jack Richardson (McMaster), and Jim Curtis (Waterloo) for their comments and criticisms at this stage.

Authors always end their acknowledgements by saying that any faults that remain in the book are their own doing, and I shall not break this rule. My reviewers have done *their* best to inform and persuade me; I alone am responsible for mistakes in the pages that follow.

This book is dedicated to my wife Sandra, who has taught me a lot about history, law, and policy-making; and to my children. Andrew, Charles, and Alexander have many important life choices ahead of them; I hope they make them well.

Publisher's Note to Instructors and Students

This textbook is a key component of your course. If you are the instructor of this course, you undoubtedly considered a number of texts carefully before choosing this as the one that will work best for your students and you. The authors and publishers of this book spent considerable time and money to ensure its high quality, and we appreciate your recognition of this effort and accomplishment.

If you are a student, we are confident that this text will help you to meet the objectives of your course. You will also find it helpful after the course is finished, as a valuable addition to your personal library. So hold on to it.

As well, please don't forget that photocopying copyright work means the authors lose royalties that are rightfully theirs. This loss will discourage them from writing another edition of this text or other books, because doing so will simply not be worth their time and effort. If this happens, we all lose—students, instructors, authors, and publishers.

And since we want to hear what you think about this book, please be sure to send us the stamped reply card at the end of the text. This will help us to continue publishing high-quality books for your courses.

Contents

Chapter One

Patterns of Desire: *why you want what you want*

Introduction

Life in a modern society is full of choices. People seem to like having choices, but choosing well is difficult and burdensome. The consequences of a wrong choice can be costly or painful. Taking responsibility for our choices is often unpleasant. We can close our eyes to choice and try to believe that there is only one way to live; but few of us these days can believe that for very long. Evidence of different kinds of lives surrounds us. The more we learn about the world, the more variety we can see, and the more things we learn to desire. We find that we can choose for or against things in a great many situations.

On the other hand, none of our choices is free. Every choice has a consequence. Every choice has a cost, if only the cost of foregoing another choice we might have made. Moreover, every choice is limited by what we know about the situation, who we are in society, what we have to trade for the thing we want. In those respects some people have more choice than others, a better choice of possible lives. But no one has unlimited choice, and no choice is cost-free. That is a condition of living.

Moreover, many major experiences in life are not chosen at all. They may include unwanted pregnancies, marriage break-downs, forced unemployment, disabling accidents, abusive parents, betrayal by friends, the outbreak of war, and economic depression. They may also include passionate infatuation, lucky winnings, devoted friends and family, inborn skills and aptitudes, peace, and prosperity. You are not to blame for the first category of experiences, nor to be praised for the second. These are simply contexts within which you are fortunate or unfortunate enough to live your life.

Within this human condition, we all work out our life's desires. This fact never changes: only situations and desires change. So a book about life choices in Canada today must look at Canada as it exists today and ask, What do people want out of life? What satisfies them? What are people's main concerns? What kinds of people are most satisfied with their lives, and how do they get that way?

These are the kinds of questions this chapter hopes to answer. Philosophers have been discussing these questions, in one form or another, for thousands of years: the answers are important and hard to discover. I hope to begin answering these questions in a different way—a sociological way—using evidence collected from the people around us.

Answering these questions will take the whole book: In relation to life satisfaction, this chapter introduces the questions in their most general form. This chapter will discuss the kinds of people who are most satisfied. The chapters that follow will examine particular aspects of life, and things that contribute to satisfaction in each of those "domains." Finally, we shall examine two theories that attempt to account for what people want and how satisfied they are with what they get.

People are more than a mere sum of social characteristics and psychological drives. They embody a complex mix of motives that defies easy summation. Moreover, people provide exceptions to every rule social science can devise. It is this delicacy and complexity of everyday life that makes social science challenging. But like natural scientists, historians, and novelists, sociologists seek the underlying order in apparent chaos: the laws that govern and predict tomorrow's universe. Let us begin by showing that this goal is at least approachable.

What You Want

Most of us are pretty self-centred. By that I do not mean "selfish," always putting our own interests before anyone else's. I mean we are wrapped up in our own ideas, plans, and values. We rarely take the time to think about other people's thinking. This lets us imagine that our own thoughts are unique, unlike anyone else's. We believe that the things we want to get or do, the choices we plan to make in life, and even the ways we spend our time and money are uniquely our own. We may also feel we have unlimited opportunity to get what we want, and with enough luck and planning, we will get it.

So if I asked you about your own life and what the future is likely to hold, after reflecting on the particulars of your life you might tell me something like this:

> Overall, my life is going pretty well. I'm doing a little better than the average person. Of course, there were times in the past when my life was a lot better; and things might slip a bit more in the next few years— it's hard to say. I know I'm not living the kind of life right now that I deserve to. But I feel pretty certain that some day, my life is going to be far better than it is today, better than my best days in the past, and even better than the best kind of life I deserve right now.

That is what the average Canadian adult thinks, according to the results of a national survey conducted in 1981 (referred to throughout this book as the Quality of Life survey). But I do not mean to suggest that everyone is the same, with the same ideas, desires, and plans. People vary a lot in all these respects, and survey data also show this very clearly.

The Quality of Life survey asked people to rate their lives— past, present, and future—against the worst life and the best life they could imagine. Results show that most people think they deserve a life close to the best one imaginable. Moreover, the best life they can ever expect to have is also very close to the best life they can imagine.

Canadians are fairly upbeat. Most people rate their lives—past and present—in the top half of the rating "ladder": closer to the best life than to the worst life they can imagine. They do the same when they rate their (expected) future lives, believing that they will come close to the best lives they can imagine.

But Canadians are not as optimistic as some other people. A review of Gallup polls conducted in 30 countries during the 1980s reveals that most people in the world are *not* optimists (Michalos, forthcoming). Asked "So far as you are concerned, do you think that [next year] will be better or worse than [the year just ending]?" about two respondents in three indicate that they think next year will be no better, and possibly worse, than last year. By this measure, the world's greatest optimists can be found in

Argentina, Greece, Korea, and the United States, where more than half the respondents regularly expect that next year will be better than this one. Along with Chileans and South African whites, Canadians rank just above the world's average on optimism, with 35 to 39 percent saying that next year will be better (Michalos, forthcoming, Table 2).

So Canadians are not the world's *most* upbeat people. They are, however, twice as likely to express optimism as Germans, Austrians, and Belgians. Some people are less optimistic and more satisfied with life than others. In fact, the two sentiments are connected. What makes people vary in this way? What patterns their views?

We are tempted to say things like "Who knows why? People are just funny that way!" or "Everybody's different. There's no accounting for people's views." But to say this is to fall into the trap of self-centring—claiming that everyone is unique and the variation among people is infinitely great and unexplainable. We have already noted that people assess their lives in similar ways. This uniformity puts the lie to some people's belief that human behaviour is beyond explaining. When people's desires and concerns differ or vary, they do so in patterned, predictable ways. It is on this fact of "patterned variation" that all social science—sociology, psychology, anthropology, and other related disciplines—rests.

Because the issue is so basic, this chapter will devote a great deal of time to showing that people's views about life vary in patterned, predictable ways. Later chapters follow the same theme through particular domains of life: education, career, marriage, child-rearing, and so on. By the end of this book, we will have discovered that people's lives really *can* be understood better with the help of social science concepts and measurements.

Not only are life satisfactions patterned, but so are life concerns: the things that people hope to get out of life. What, then, are the most important life goals of average Canadians? What are they hoping to get out of life?

Two of the three life goals Canadians identify as most important are "social goals" (Atkinson & Murray, 1982). Highest marks are given to relationships with other people. Most important of all is "family security," defined as "providing love and care for family members." One in every two adult Canadians says this is a first or second most important goal of life. Close in importance is "love," or "having the affection and romantic love of a man or woman." One in every three respondents cites that as a most or second most important goal in life.

The only other widely held goal is "economic stability," defined as "having a steady, secure income to provide for your basic needs and those of your family." About one respondent in three says that this is a most or second most important goal in life. Although seemingly different, this goal may not really differ from the first two; it probably expresses a desire for family security through income security, not a desire for income in its own right.

Few Canadians seem to be driven by the desire for great wealth, outstanding achievement, social recognition, or excitement. The average Canadian adult comes across as a kind, loving, sociable person with realistic life goals. No wonder, then, that people are so convinced that, in future, they will attain a life close to the best life they can imagine achieving. The best life they can imagine is what they desire; and the life most Canadian adults desire is within their grasp. They want what they can get.

Equally, few Canadians attach much importance to spiritual understanding, salvation, or—like the Good Samaritan—helping strangers. For example, fewer Canadians than Americans are religious fundamentalists. Rather, Canadians focus their attention on the world of everyday life and the people they commonly see and care about. In this way, today's Canadians are probably quite different from Canadians a century ago, or contemporary Iranians: for both these groups, religious and theological concerns would loom much larger.

Canadians are also not "rugged individualists" or "me-first" types. Few share in the "self-fulfilment ethic" Yankelovich (1982) found so common in the United States. For many Americans, "creativity is a life-style." These Americans spend a lot of time and money in the search for excitement, sensation, new experiences, self-discovery, and self-improvement. They focus their lives on themselves. About one American in six is strongly committed to this kind of personal gratification and self-fulfilment. A majority of Americans (63 percent) pursue similar goals more moderately; another 20 percent pursue completely different, more traditional life goals. By contrast, Canadians are less committed to this self-fulfilment ethic. Only one Canadian respondent in eight—typically younger, more educated, and drawing a higher income than average—cites self-development as a first or second most important goal; one in seven says independence is most or second most important; and for almost no Canadian surveyed is excitement a goal of main importance.

A poll conducted in November 1987 (*Macleans*, January 4, 1988, p. 45) shows that Canadians see themselves just this way, compared with Americans. Respondents were six times as likely to consider Canadians *more* concerned than Americans about the environment and the poor; they were seven times as likely to consider Canadians more honest and fair. They also believed Canadians were somewhat more hardworking, better informed, and sophisticated. On the other hand, respondents were more than twice as likely to consider Americans more competitive and eight times as likely to consider them more violent.

Summing up to this point, Canadians tend to hold similar views of their past, present, and future life. They are generally satisfied, relatively optimistic, and their life concerns largely involve loving and caring for their families. They are not strong individualists, nor much concerned about getting to heaven.

Patterns of Variation

The rest of this chapter will explore the ways desires and satisfactions vary, and theories about that variation. This exploration has two main purposes. The first is to understand better why certain Canadians want what they do out of life, and why some feel more or less satisfied than the average. Bear in mind that the present chapter does not answer these questions fully. Later chapters will answer similar questions about particular domains of life in greater detail. A second and more important purpose is to demonstrate that people's desires and life concerns are *patterned*: they vary in predictable, largely understandable ways among different segments of the population.

Variations in Time   People's satisfaction with life, and their particular desires and concerns, vary over time. That is why we cannot understand what it was like to live in another historical period unless we understand fully the values people held, goals they set for themselves, and satisfaction they felt with social conditions that might not satisfy us today.

These variations are easiest to see when we compare large chunks of time—for example, the Middle Ages and today. An ambitious work of early American sociology studied how people had changed their values over thousands of years (Sorokin, 1941). Data collected from a variety of civilizations showed that, historically, major civilizations of the world had gone through cycles of value change, returning repeatedly to certain key concerns.

People's values change slowly and repeatedly over long periods of time, often returning to earlier concerns and ways of thinking. So historical context is all-important if we want to understand why people want what they do out of life, and how they feel about their lives at any given moment in time.

However, values and satisfactions also vary over periods shorter than millenia. Comparing years closer to the present also allows us to use standard, well-understood instruments to measure changes. For example, Canadian data for the period 1968 to 1977 show a continuing decline in the percentage of people saying they are very satisfied with their lives overall (Atkinson, 1979). More people are indicating moderate rather than great satisfaction with life.

As in a similar study of trends in the United States (Campbell, 1980), the most marked declines in life satisfaction are found among younger Canadians: 43 percent of people aged 20 to 29 were very satisfied in 1968, but only 29 percent were very satisfied in 1977. So part of the reason for declining overall satisfaction is that a new birth group, or *cohort*, born between 1948 and 1957, had entered adulthood by 1977. These younger Canadians, less satisfied with life than people born a decade earlier had been at the same age, are part of the "baby-boom" generation. Much research suggests that this group is passing through life more frustrated and unhappy than earlier cohorts (see, for example, Jones, 1980; Kettle, 1980).

One explanation of this dissatisfaction is demographic—that is, due to population changes. People born at a time of high birth rates, as the baby-boom generation was, must compete more intensely for spaces in colleges and universities, scholarships, entry-level jobs, higher career positions, housing, and other rewards throughout life (Easterlin, 1980). By contrast, people born between 1939 and 1948—who were teenagers in the 1950s and young adults in the 1960s—had it much easier. Since they were relatively fewer in number, they enjoyed smaller school classes, expanding educational opportunities, and more job possibilities when they entered the work force.

But even this relatively small cohort grew less satisfied between 1968 and 1977, as they passed into their thirties. The explanation lies in something that happened to people during that decade: an economic slowdown or recession that started around 1974 and produced its worst effects in the early 1980s. Throughout this period, employment and career opportunities worsened for everyone, but especially for younger people. Young adults' lower life satisfaction in 1977 partly reflects frustration and disappointment with this state of affairs.

With a return to economic growth, everyone's life satisfaction should increase. However, some cohorts, especially the baby boomers, may feel relatively dissatisfied throughout their lives. Their expectations about life—based on the experiences of earlier cohorts who had entered adulthood during periods of economic growth, or were visibly prosperous when the baby boomers were growing up—are too high. Under intensely competitive economic conditions, baby boomers will have to lower their expectations if they are to feel more satisfied with life. And, to some degree, this will happen through aging alone. Data show that aging generally increases life satisfaction by lowering standards, reducing needs, and moderating desires.

Young people born after the baby boom—in the late 1960s and the years since—already show the change of desires that one might expect from people living in a period of economic difficulty. Research from many countries shows that high school and college students today have much more practical goals than baby boomers did in the 1960s and early 1970s.

For example, an American study (*Globe and Mail*, January 15, 1988) reports that three-quarters of college freshmen feel that being financially well-off is an essential or very important goal, and most are attending college primarily to achieve that goal. Fewer than two in every five freshmen attach the same importance to developing a meaningful philosophy of life. Moreover, data collected continuously since 1966 demonstrate that these views are part of a long-term trend: a growing materialism and declining concern with a "meaningful philosophy." Indeed, the two concerns have completely reversed their degree of importance for freshmen in the last 20 years.

Given this growing concern with financial well-being—though weaker in Canada than in the United States—it should come as no surprise to find that young people's life satisfaction declined during the recessionary 1970s. By 1981, satisfaction was even lower than it had been in 1968 and 1977. Only 29 percent of all respondents (compared with 35 percent in 1977) said they were very satisfied with life (Quality of Life survey, 1981).

Since 1981, Canada's economic condition has improved, young people have lowered their expectations and desires, and the baby boomers have aged. For all these reasons we would expect people to be more satisfied, or happier, with life today; and the data bear out this expectation. Statistics Canada (*Globe and Mail*, February 27, 1988) reports that "asked to describe themselves as very happy, somewhat happy, or unhappy, 48 per cent of Canadian adults said they were very happy, compared to only 21 per cent when the same question was asked 10 years ago."

What, then, do we know about the way satisfaction changes over time? Satisfaction changes for a variety of reasons. Basic conceptions of life may take generations and even centuries to change. In the course of a single lifetime, the average satisfaction in a society will be affected by relative numbers of old and young (since older people are more satisfied); the sizes of cohorts (since very much larger-than-average cohorts are less satisfied); the economic conditions of the period (since periods of growth are more satisfying periods); and the length of time people have had to adjust their expectations to an economic decline or other social difficulty.

However, economic and demographic factors are far from the only influences on people's life satisfaction. In fact, they may be among the less important influences. This fact becomes clearer when we examine other variations in satisfaction: for example, variations by country at a given point in time.

Variations from Country to Country   At any given time, people living in different societies will differ in their life satisfaction. One study shows that Canadians, despite having the highest gross domestic product per capita (standard of living) are only fourth-ranked among nine nations where the majority of people surveyed say they are very satisfied with life (Atkinson, 1979). Denmark ranks first in overall satisfaction, despite a third-ranking standard of living. Ireland, with nearly the lowest standard of living among the countries studied, has the second highest proportion of people indicating great satisfaction with their lives.

Income and standard of living are only weakly connected with life satisfaction; people can be poor but satisfied, a point we shall consider later. Satisfaction is largely determined by people's expectations. The greater the gap between what people have and what they expect to have, the more dissatisfied they will be. Accordingly, the less optimistic Danes and Irish average much higher levels of satisfaction than the more optimistic Canadians. High hopes are more likely to lead to great disappointments, hence lower satisfaction with life.

Do people around the world all share the same basic concerns and feel the same amount of satisfaction with life; and if not, why not? Asking the same questions of 14 international samples (which, unfortunately, do not include Canadians), Cantril (1965) found that the people living on Israeli kibbutzim are the most satisfied of all with their present lives. Next most satisfied are respondents in the United States and Cuba. Least satisfied with their lives are respondents in Poland, India, and the Dominican Republic. Using an index of socio-economic development (that is, modernity) that comprises 11 items—including gross national product per capita; number of doctors per 10 000 people; percentage living in cities with populations over 100 000; and percentage of literate people—Cantril found that average life satisfaction is only weakly related to the level of development.

Socio-economic development, or modernization, does not necessarily make people more satisfied with life: it also creates new desires, hopes, and fears. In modernizing countries, people have to adjust their expectations of life to take into account new possibilities. Failure to satisfy these new expectations and desires is dissatisfying. (For Canadian evidence along similar lines, see discussions of Quebec's "Quiet Revolution" by Clark, 1975, and Guindon, 1978.)

Cantril allowed people to speak freely about their hopes and fears, then coded the answers they gave into categories including "personal economic situation," "family references," "health," "personal values and character," "job or work situation," and "social values." People answer in such different ways in different countries that it is difficult to summarize and compare concerns. But personal economic aspirations are mentioned by more people than any other; they outnumber all other concerns in the poorest countries—the Dominican Republic, Brazil, India—and even in some prosperous countries like West Germany, by a considerable margin. Next in frequency of mention are family references: these are more common than, or almost as common as, personal economic concerns in the kibbutzim, Israel generally, Nigeria, Yugoslavia, and the Philippines. References to personal values are extremely common in rapidly developing places (the kibbutzim, Nigeria, Cuba, and Egypt) but less common in countries where modernization has been stifled (India, the Dominican Republic, and the Philippines) or completed (the United States and West Germany).

Health concerns are mentioned somewhat more often than social values, and are voiced most often in the rapidly developing or developed countries. Almost no one mentions health aspirations in India or the Philippines. Jobs and work are the last category of hopes mentioned by large numbers of people. No simple pattern can be detected in the percentages raising this concern: it is no more common in developing or developed, socialist or capitalist countries. On the contrary, if we take into account the fact that respondents in some countries express many hopes while those in other countries express relatively few, the percentage expressing hopes about jobs and work is reasonably constant. About 5 to 15 percent in every country express hopes concerning this issue.

What, then, do we learn about people's desires from such an ambitious comparison of nations? *Do* people all share the same basic concerns and feel the same amount of satisfaction with life? In short, the answer is "No." Except at a very general level, people do *not* share the same life concerns around the world.

We learn most about national differences by comparing countries that are alike in many ways. Such comparisons are most like controlled experiments, the preferred method of research in physical science. By comparing similar societies, we are in effect "holding constant" a great many factors while only one or two possible explanatory factors vary. The few varying factors are, logically, the only possible cause of differences in the thing to be explained.

Atkinson and Murray (1982) compared Canadian data on life satisfaction with similar American data collected by Campbell, Converse, and Rogers (1976). Despite a remarkable similarity between the two peoples, certain key differences in the kinds of satisfactions that best predict overall life satisfaction do emerge.

The most important difference is that Americans "can be described as more diverse in their value orientations" than Canadians. Canadians are rather single-minded. They place much more importance on romance and marriage than Americans do. In fact, their satisfaction with life overall is primarily determined by these relationships. When these relationships are going well, they feel that life as a whole is going well. Further, in Canada, "marital concerns would more often take precedence over material considerations" than in the United States. Among other things, work has much more influence on life satisfaction in the United States than in Canada; but apparently, this is not due to a greater American concern with monetary reward.

The very high value Canadians put on love and marriage supports the claim that Canadians are more "collectively oriented," or attached to groups, than Americans. On the other hand, the greater significance of work for Americans demonstrates that a greater value is placed on achievement, or accomplishment, in the United States. Atkinson and Murray (1982, p. 29) conclude that "the greater value of social relationships in Canada, and of achievement in the United States, reflect long-standing societal differences which will persist in the future."

To summarize, people's satisfaction and life concerns vary among societies in complex ways. Material factors like standard of living are not enough to explain these differences. Even such similar countries as Canada and the United States show different patterns, suggesting long-standing, deep-rooted cultural values that defy easy explanation. (Attempts to understand these differences are found in Bell & Tepperman, 1979, and Marsden & Harvey, 1979; more will be said about them in Chapter 7.)

Variation across Ages   People living in different periods and nations differ, but they are not the only ones. Canadians of different ages also vary in their life satisfaction, with older people being generally more satisfied than younger ones. People's life concerns also change as they get older.

As they age, people pass through a life cycle—a sequence of typical, important stages. At each stage, certain concerns become paramount and others trivial. That is because as people age, they enter and leave social roles (Nicolson, 1980).

In our early lives we are most concerned about relations with our parents. Our childhood home is the culture and society we know best, and we measure everything else—including our wishes, hopes, and self-esteem—against what we have learned there. As we age, all this changes radically. We become acquainted with a much larger world at school. Our peers (and their values) are much more varied than our parents and siblings. Moral certainties are thrown into doubt by the evidence of acceptable variation in the world. In adolescence, needs for peer acceptance increase at the same time as we are searching for an identity and purpose of our very own. We feel torn between the often conflicting goals of finding our own true selves and gaining social acceptance as "one of the crowd."

Asked about their goals in life, or "terminal values," the vast majority of Canadian teenagers sampled say "friendship" is their main concern (Bibby & Posterski, 1985). Compared with only 27 percent of Canadian adults, 91 percent of the teenagers say friendship is "very important." Next in importance to teenagers is "love," then "freedom." "Love" is also a significant adult goal, but only 42 percent of adults (compared with 87 percent of teenagers) indicate that it is of great importance. And while 84 percent of teenagers say freedom is of great importance, only 33 percent of adults agree. Success and a comfortable life also prove to be more important to teenagers than adults. By contrast, family life—the most important goal of Canadian adults—is in seventh position for teenagers.

Teenagers are in the process of rejecting family life and becoming individuals. They want to be loved but not limited: hence, they reject family in favour of friends. As full-fledged adult individuals, they will re-integrate themselves into nuclear family life, which is so destructive of the freedom and privacy they value highly. Our cultural norms invite this rejection and re-integration as part of normal development and the passage from childhood to adulthood.

In a similar fashion we might explain the teenager's greater desire for success and comfort, compared with adults. To Canadian adults, material success and comfort are means of attaining family security. To teenagers, these are means of freeing themselves from family constraints and proof that they have achieved full membership in adult society.

Differences between people of different ages do not end with the passage from adolescence into adulthood. Far from it. "Work and financial situation [occupy] more important positions . . . for those under 30; marital and family concerns [dominate] the child-raising period between ages 30 and 44; while leisure and health considerations become more prevalent for those over age 65" (Atkinson & Murray, 1982, p. 29).

This all makes sense. People create and raise families in their thirties and forties, so family life *should* typically be most important at this time. For the majority, health is not yet a problem at that age, and leisure is limited by career and family duties in a way that it will not be 20 years later, when all the children have left home. Finally, work and financial considerations are less important at that age because, by age 35, a career path has largely been established and financial conditions improve slowly and gradually after that point, if at all.

Not only life concerns change with age: so does overall life satisfaction. Figure 1.1 shows that the proportion of older Canadians (ages 65 and over) who are very satisfied with life is roughly double the proportion of younger Canadians (ages 20 to 40) who are equally satisfied. The younger Canadians belong to a birth cohort—the baby boomers—with too-high expectations, as we noted earlier. As well, people become more satisfied as they age, a pattern we shall see repeated time and again in this book.

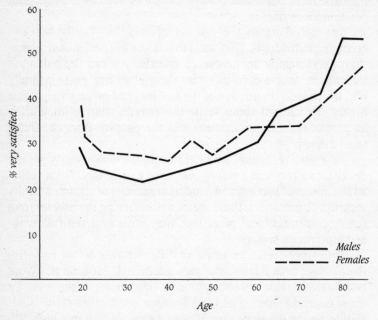

FIGURE 1.1 Percentage very satisfied with life overall, by age and gender: Canada, 1981. *Includes people scoring 10 and 11 on an 11-point scale. A 10-year rolling average is used.* (Source: *Quality of Life survey, 1981.*)

Note, however, that the patterns are somewhat different for men and women. Both show satisfaction dropping in young adulthood, then rising in later adulthood. But the age-based change is more profound for males than females. Young women start out more satisfied than men and end up in old age less satisfied than men. Old age is a lonelier and more economically distressed time for women (who are more likely to have lost their spouse) than men.

The rest of the book will deal with these issues more thoroughly. At this point, note only that life satisfaction and life concerns vary considerably by age and stage in the life cycle, at least in Canada. To know a person's outlook, it is not enough to know his or her age, but age and life-cycle stage certainly make a great difference.

Variations across Status and Income Groups   Social position also influences people's life concerns. Common sense says that it is better to be rich than poor, famous than unknown, and powerful than powerless. But remember, Canadians do not place much importance on material wealth, compared to other sources of satisfaction like love and family. As we shall see in Chapter 7, certain regions of Canada, such as the Maritimes, are particularly unlikely to value riches, despite their relative poverty. Riches bring people satisfaction only if riches are valued, and not everyone values them. Are rich people really more satisfied with life, as lay wisdom tells us?

In an effort to answer this question, Diener, Horowitz, and Emmons (1985) sampled people from *Forbes* business magazine's list of the wealthiest Americans, and compared them with people selected randomly from telephone directories. Those agreeing to participate completed a questionnaire about life concerns.

Wealthy respondents prove to be happy a higher percentage of the time, score significantly higher on two different life satisfaction scales, and report significantly lower levels of "negative affect"—that is, unhappiness. Not all the wealthy are happy, of course; in fact, some are just as unhappy as the unhappiest ordinary person sampled. Further, few respondents, whether wealthy or ordinary, believe that money is a major source of happiness. However, this denial may simply reflect the notion, common in our culture, that "money can't buy happiness."

Wealthy and ordinary people also differ in what satisfies them. Wealthy respondents more often mention self-esteem and self-actualization as sources of their satisfaction, while ordinary people more often mention physiological (food, shelter, and other basic human needs) and safety concerns as sources of satisfaction.

But bear in mind that Diener *et al.* were comparing ordinary people with some of the wealthiest people in the world. What if we compare the poorer 99 percent of the population with one another: does income still make a difference? No; your income quintile (that is, the fifth of the income distribution you are located in) makes little difference in your overall life satisfaction, at least in Canada (see Table 1.1). Income influences people's satisfaction with their *financial* situation; not surprisingly, people with a higher

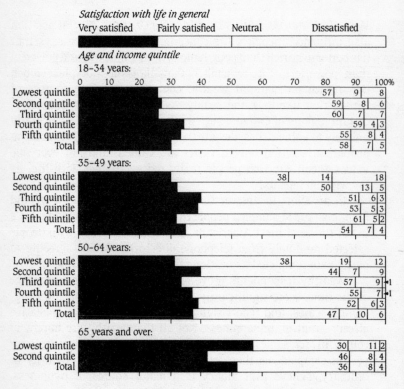

TABLE 1.1 General life satisfaction, by age and income: Canada, 1979. (Source: *Atkinson, 1980, Chart 14.3.*)

income are more satisfied financially. But for Canadians, financial concerns are relatively unimportant, compared with love and family. So, at least in Canada, a large income *does not* buy the average person life satisfaction (Atkinson, 1980).

However, life concerns do vary with socio-economic status. (Socio-economic status, or SES, is a combined measure of education, income, and job prestige.) People with higher SES rate "social values" such as love, family security, and friendship significantly higher than people with low SES; conversely, they rate "material values" like prosperity and economic stability lower (Blishen & Atkinson, 1982). And, just as Diener *et al.* (1985) discovered in comparing the wealthy with ordinary people, high-status people in Canada place a significantly higher value on achievement, self-development, and excitement than do lower-status people.

If we ignore the very wealthiest people, income does not influence Canadian life satisfaction very much, but it does influence Canadians' main life concerns. How can we explain the variations in life satisfaction and concerns we have observed so far? Two main theoretical approaches are considered below: Maslow's theory of a need hierarchy and Michalos's theory of multiple discrepancies.

Two Theories of Satisfaction

Maslow's Need Hierarchy   Psychologist Abraham Maslow put forward a central theory in the study of life satisfactions. It holds that every human being longs and strives for self-actualization, the complete fulfilment of his or her unique potentiality. Attaining such fulfilment is the ultimate and supposedly essential human need. Such fulfilment will bring any person the greatest possible satisfaction.

Maslow's theory is not original. His "essentialism"—which looks for the essential, basic, or universal qualities of human nature—may originate in the thinking of Plato and Aristotle. Moreover, Karl Marx offers sociologists a related, more refined approach. Marx's *Early Philosophical Manuscripts* (1844/1985) discusses "alienation" as stifled self-fulfilment under capitalism. According to this theory, psychological well-being must grow out of social and economic well-being. Individual satisfaction must be achieved through societal change.

According to Marx, alienation results from economic exploitation, most advanced under capitalism, which deprives people of control over their labour and the fruits of their labour. People seek to fulfil their creative impulses in work. But the need to sell their labour for wages denies these impulses and estranges people from their work, their true selves, and others similarly forced to work for wages (see Rinehart, 1987, for a good summary of this theory).

The essentialist theories of Marx and Maslow differ in important ways. For Marx, the end of exploitive wage labour brings self-fulfilment, since it ends alienation. Self-actualization is impossible under capitalism but virtually assured under socialism. Social impulses will be liberated by the ending of capitalist exploitation alone. Presumably, belonging and acceptance will follow easily once people are no longer alienated from themselves and others.

On the other hand, Maslow appears to believe that self-actualization is possible under a variety of social and political conditions. However, the attainment of belonging and acceptance is always problematic: it cannot be assured, any more than the attainment of food, shelter, and physical safety can be assured. These are all goals people have to attain on their way to self-actualization.

The most distinctive feature of Maslow's theory—the one that makes it most *unlike* Marx's (let alone Plato's or Aristotle's) and most *like* theories in developmental psychology—is that it is a "stage theory." It proposes that people must pass through successive stages of fulfilment—survival, security, belonging, esteem—before being able to reach, or even want, total fulfilment or "self-actualization." The failure to complete one stage prevents a person from successfully proceeding to the next stage.

Thus, for example, a person who has not attained physical security cannot hope to attain belonging, and may not even want it yet. A person who has not attained belonging cannot (and will not) hope to attain esteem. The stages must be passed through in order, and all lower-level needs must be satisfied before self-actualization is possible. Even for people who have passed through all the lower stages of fulfilment, self-actualization is not guaranteed: it is merely a possibility.

Few have attempted to test Maslow's stage theory with representative survey data. One exception is a study by Atkinson and Murray (1982), using Canadian survey data. Like Maslow, the researchers find it useful to distinguish between "sustenance values and needs" and higher-level values such as belonging, esteem, achievement, and actualization. The failure to satisfy sustenance needs—needs for physical well-being and economic security—results in a partial fixation on these concerns, while satisfaction reduces their importance, just as Maslow would predict. People with a low income (or poor health) are particularly likely to focus their desires on income (or health) improvement, while other Canadians are not.

Yet even here, the evidence supporting Maslow's theory is weak. Even among people failing to fulfil these basic needs—poor people and sick people—health and economic security are far from dominant concerns and have only a weak influence on overall life satisfaction.

The survey evidence supports Maslow's theory even less when we consider people who *have* satisfied their "basic needs." "Values of belonging, esteem, achievement and actualization . . . do not appear to be stratified as Maslow suggests," say Atkinson and Murray (1982, p. 31). People failing to fulfil any of these secondary needs do not fixate on the unfulfilled need, inflating its importance in their lives. They do the very opposite, and substitute other domains as sources of gratification. Thus, unmarried people with good jobs and high incomes place more than average value on their work, while unmarried people with lower incomes place more than average value on leisure, because other aspects of their lives are not rewarding enough.

Stage-one and -two values operate by different rules and have different potentials for influencing the general quality of a person's life. For example, poverty and poor health can reduce the quality of a person's life, but "high incomes and good physical condition seem to have limited potential for increasing well-being, at least directly." On the other hand, stage-two domains—for example, work, family, and leisure satisfactions—"carry the potential to make life genuinely enjoyable as well as miserable" (Atkinson & Murray, 1982, p. 33).

The researchers conclude that "the substitutability of second-stage values offers some relief from frustrations encountered in particular domains," if optional sources of reward are available.

At least in our society, survival and security needs must be satisfied before people can look to other domains for fuller satisfaction. Incomplete fulfilment of sustenance needs leads to fixation, and starving people cannot substitute love and esteem for a good dinner. In this sense, objective reality sets limits on how people will seek and achieve satisfaction.

Yet for the majority—whose sustenance needs *are* met—higher-level needs can be satisfied in a variety of ways. In general, people make do with what they have at hand. They do not pine after the impossible. Objective reality does not set problems that must be dealt with in a single way.

This means that the young, single person beginning his or her adult life can find satisfaction in a variety of ways. One will find it in a career, another in marriage, and a third in leisure activities or friendship. Even the greater emphasis on fulfilment through family and romance in Canada than elsewhere is no more than a tendency, not an ironclad law. In practice, people will set their goals to capitalize on real opportunities for satisfaction, *given* their personal values.

To summarize, Maslow and other essentialists would argue that your satisfaction in life depends on the size of the gap between what you have attained and what you want to attain. In turn, what you want to attain—whether you know it or not—is a hierarchy of goals culminating in self-fulfilment. According to this theory, everyone wants the same things—call them essential or universal wants—and must attain them in the same sequence if they are to achieve maximum life satisfaction.

Data fail to support this theory. Principally, we have strong reason to doubt that everyone wants the same things. Evidence shows that wants (concerns, hopes, and desires) vary by age, period, country, and social class; they even vary in other ways we have not yet considered. Second, evidence shows that frustrated desires are remedied by the substitution of one satisfaction for another. As a result, researchers find little connection between people's sense of satisfaction with life and their actual material or social well-being, measured objectively. Once people have satisfied the most basic needs for food and shelter, their life satisfaction can be raised by a wide variety of material, social, and cultural "goods."

In conclusion, we find little evidence of a single, essential, and universal set of needs—no one path to life satisfaction.

Multiple Discrepancies Theory   People's needs and desires are not patterned in any simple or rigid way. Rather, they vary according to personal background and present opportunity. Our backgrounds and personal histories present us with images of the "good life." We grow up hoping for a certain kind of future. Often our hoped-for futures are strikingly similar to the adult lives we witnessed as children in the parental home. Sometimes they are strikingly different, as among people who vow they will never turn out like their parents did. What is remarkable is the strength of relationship—whether positive or negative—between what we learn as children and what we become as adults.

Our hopes—what we want and expect—are not only shaped by parents and siblings. They are also influenced by other significant people we encounter in growing up: role models, mentors, idols, good friends, enemies, and so on. We are also influenced by the groups we belong to and by the outlooks, norms, and behaviours they teach us. Finally, there are a number of institutions and groups in our society whose purpose is to influence or manage our wants: the media, advertising agencies, politicians, interest groups, and churches are among them.

Consider the role of the mass media. Young people spend enormous numbers of hours beside their radio and television sets. The media show us imaginary characters being rewarded for certain qualities, behaviours, or values. By identifying with these characters, we receive *vicarious*, or second-hand rewards. The fact that these rewards are vicarious does not seem to lessen their influence on how we think and behave.

So our personal background and the future it has taught us to expect have been shaped by family, friends, and people we "meet" only through the media. Other influences at work or school—agents of "adult socialization"—continue to mold us throughout life. It is the general thrust of Alex Michalos's "multiple discrepancies" theory that our satisfaction with life will be determined by discrepancies between life as it is and life as we thought it should or would be. The more our real life departs from the life we compare it with, the more dissatisfied we will be.

To state the theory of multiple discrepancies more formally, people's life satisfaction is determined by the size of the gap or discrepancy between what they have attained and what they want. But unlike Maslow, Michalos does not argue that everyone wants the same things. Rather, his theory holds that what you want is determined by the sum of six perceived discrepancies: discrepancies between what you have today and (1) what relevant others appear to have; (2) the best you had in the past; (3) what, three years ago, you expected you would have today; (4) what you expect to have five years from now; (5) what you think you deserve; and (6) what you think you need.

All these perceived discrepancies are, in turn, affected by objectively measurable discrepancies. That is, the gaps we perceive have some basis in reality, although no one-to-one relationship exists. "All discrepancies, satisfactions and actions are directly and indirectly affected by age, sex, education, ethnicity, income, self-esteem, and social support" (Michalos, 1985, p. 348). These social characteristics, which influence our opportunities for getting what we want out of life, also influence our perceptions and our sense(s) of having, or not having, what we want.

Life satisfaction is determined as much by our bases of comparison—and the personal histories that shape them—as by objective reality, the opportunities and troubles that face us every day. According to this theory, people are drawn forward by a picture of the future, of life as it "should be" for them, and by a desire to close the gap between what they expect, want, and get.

Each person's picture of the future is the result of self-comparisons with "relevant others" and with his or her own past. It is also shaped by things we feel we need and deserve—undoubtedly all originating in earlier experience but difficult to track to their sources. So for the most part, we are not driven forward by objective need, but drawn forward by the discrepancy between what we have and what we want. (In turn, what we want is, largely, what we had expected to have.)

Typically, the discrepancy between what we have and what we want is measurable: we do not simply fantasize these things. If I want to look like Robert Redford but believe I do not, I am probably right, and dispassionate observers would agree with my assessment of a gap between desire and reality. Sociologists can reliably and validly measure what people do and do not have, and even point to objective, real factors that create the shortcomings. As noted, age, gender, education, ethnicity, income, self-esteem, and social support are factors that influence what we do and do not really have. This list is far from exhaustive, but offers a good starting place.

The factors that influence our opportunities to get what we want also influence or pattern our desires. Traditionally, females have been taught not to want the same things as men, for example.

This kind of training lowers dissatisfaction when opportunities really are limited. When aspirations and expectations rise more rapidly than opportunities (generally, or for particular groups such as women, racial minorities, old people, and so on), dissatisfaction rises rapidly even if opportunities are actually increasing. What is key is the relationship between rates of change in opportunities and desires. When opportunities grow more slowly, discrepancies increase and so does dissatisfaction.

We noted earlier that few people in our society are very dissatisfied with life: most are moderately satisfied. The rarity of dissatisfaction testifies to two facts. First, people lower their expectations and aspirations as they confront limited opportunities; and they substitute attainable desires for unattainable ones. Second, the images of the future that fuel our desires are often remembrances of an even more limiting past.

This theory helps us explain the absence of radical political sentiment among the unemployed and otherwise seriously disadvantaged. In part, some would argue, political inaction results from obstacles to political mobilization. Others would say that it lies in "false consciousness," meaning a false perception of how the world really operates. While both explanations may be right to some degree, multiple discrepancy theory implies a third explanation: namely, people form their visions of the future in a backward-looking, conformist, and moderate way. I do not compare myself with millionaires, then strive to narrow the discrepancy between what I want and what I have, any more than I compare myself with Robert Redford, then try to close the gap. The actual— my everyday experience—forms the basis for my assessment of the possible. Usually, what people want is what they can get, and this becomes ever truer as people age.

The result is social conservatism, especially among adults. It is important to counter this conservatism with a progressive vision and well-founded information about *possible* comparison groups (Michalos, 1987, pp. 44-46). People tend to know most about people a lot like themselves; therefore, they set low standards for their own futures. More and better information about others with whom they might *reasonably* compare themselves will help them strive, personally and collectively, for a better life. This is movement out of a Fool's Paradise (characterized by satisfaction based on poorly founded information) into a Real Paradise (characterized by satisfaction based on well-founded information).

Better information about the present and a commitment to a better future are necessary conditions for self-improvement and social change.

How can we judge what is truly possible for human beings to achieve? Seeking the truly *impossible* is ridiculous and sometimes hazardous. Failing to seek the truly *possible*, when it is desired and known to be possible, is slothful. But people's failure to seek the possible because it is not known to be possible, though desired, is the problem Michalos seeks to solve.

Consider this analogy. An excellent runner has just run a four-minute mile and has to decide whether to shoot for a three-minute mile. Is that truly possible—a worthwhile goal—or truly impossible—a ridiculous and possibly dangerous goal? Without more information, the runner can make no sensible decision. Available information confirms that no one has ever run a three-minute mile. On the other hand, evidence shows that people have been running ever faster miles. Therefore, a three-minute mile may be possible for some runner, some day. The question has now changed form. It is now, Can *this* runner, given his or her particular abilities, hope to run a three-minute mile in his or her lifetime?

Social conservatism is supported by a common failure to investigate the limits of the possible, due to limited information, misinformation, and backward- rather than forward-looking images of the future. In a "Real Paradise," well-informed people journey to the boundaries of the truly possible, then accept the result. Knowing what is truly possible is no easy matter, nor is accepting a less than ideal result. But if multiple discrepancy theory is valid, this is the only sensible and ultimately satisfying life strategy.

Does the theory actually work? If it does, measurable multiple discrepancies should predict people's life satisfaction better than any other variables we can think of and measure. In an early study, Michalos (1985) asked nearly 700 university undergraduates to answer questions about their lives, and measured the strength of relationships between discrepancies and satisfaction.

Multiple discrepancies "explained . . . 53% [of the variance] in global S[atisfaction] and 50% or more in 7 out of 12 domain S[atisfaction] scores." The model was particularly successful in accounting for people's satisfaction and financial security, paid employment, leisure activity, religion, and self-esteem. We conclude that the theory performed very well indeed. Roughly half of all the variation in people's satisfaction—overall as well as in particular domains of life—was "explained" by the variables in the model, leaving another half to be explained by other factors. By conventional standards, this is a very strong finding.

The finding has now been replicated—and, if anything, strengthened—by data collected from over 6000 university students around the world (Michalos, 1987). As researchers' data-sets become larger and more varied, multiple discrepancy theory appears to make even more successful predictions.

The impact of discrepancy variables on satisfaction is indirect. Discrepancies such as the gap between what relevant others appear to have and what you have influence the discrepancy between what you have and what you want. In turn, this discrepancy influences your satisfaction. From this fact Michalos concludes that "the idea of *managing* satisfaction and happiness is plausible. . . . The very same processes that make it possible to rightly persuade people of things that are true, good and beautiful, also make it possible to wrongly persuade people of their opposites, falsehoods, evil, and ugliness" (Michalos, 1985, p. 393).

So, for example, people's satisfaction can be increased by downward comparison with less fortunate others. Moreover, we could inflate people's satisfaction in a number of other ways: by making them want less, misremember the past, and expect little (or less) from the future. This dangerous potential for pacifying discontent is a matter we shall consider further, toward the end of the book.

For Michalos (1987), the solution is a theory of value and a moral theory that will help people identify "good management." As well, "there is a fundamental role to be played by all [informal and formal] educational institutions. People's satisfaction and happiness can be more or less cognitively well-founded, and reasonable people will want to be sure that they are essentially well-founded."

In a nutshell, "cognitive well-foundedness" is the goal behind this book. We want to explore patterns of desire and opportunity in real life, so that we know better what we are pursuing in life, as well as how and why we are doing so. It is only in the context of good information that a reasonable life can be lived. Sociology as well as philosophy has a role to play in that endeavour.

Concluding Remarks

Within our culture today, people share similar life goals and life satisfactions. Most people want what most other people of their own age, gender, and class want, allowing for subcultural variations of certain kinds. However, people's goals and satisfactions are not universal. They vary over time and place. They vary over millenia, and they vary less dramatically over decades. They vary from one civilization to another, one country to another, and even (as we shall see in Chapter 7) one region of Canada to another. That is why we must know the social and cultural context in order to understand people's satisfaction with conditions *we* might not find satisfying.

The effect of socio-economic development on national goals is very much like the effect of maturation on individual goals. Both tend to increase information about choices and raise expectations, thereby diminishing satisfaction; and both tend to increase the potential for real achievement, thereby increasing satisfaction. The two influences tend to offset each other.

Different countries are about as variable as different people in their goals. In a very abstract sense, everyone wants the same things: family, security, peace, a job, and so on. This gives support to Maslow's theory of a need hierarchy, which we discussed at length. Yet countries and individuals order their concerns in different ways. Individuals within a given country (like Canada) are more like others living in the same country than they are like people living in other countries. It may simply not be useful to talk about "essential" or "universal" needs and concerns beyond food, shelter, and physical safety.

A major variable shaping life concerns and life satisfactions is *age*, and we shall return to it time and again. People of different ages see life differently: they have different concerns. As well, aging significantly affects satisfaction, increasing it in most cases. This fact is best proven by longitudinal data—data collected by following the same people as they age over time—not cross-sectional data—data which merely compare people of different ages at the same point in time. Unfortunately, social scientists have drawn most of their inferences about aging from cross-sectional data. So we must recognize that their conclusions are particularly liable to disproof in future.

But most of the findings point in a similar direction, the one we have taken. The reasons for greater satisfaction through aging are numerous and complex, but multiple discrepancies theory helps to identify them. Aging seems to produce low and diminishing expectations, narrower bases for comparison, less (and often worse) information about the truly possible, an increasing tendency to look backward rather than forward, and (for various reasons) an increasing aversion to risk. But older people may also possess a better sense of the truly possible than younger people. They may have learned from life.

People in different income groups also see life differently. Like people in wealthier countries, wealthier people have different concerns from poorer people: more concerns about self-actualization, for example, and fewer concerns about food and shelter. But unlike older people, they are not necessarily more satisfied. Rich people—who have a lot of information, high expectations, and a great opportunity for high achievement—run the greatest risks of disappointment. Paradoxically, the poor—who expect less, know less about what they do not have, and know that they have little chance to get it anyway—sometimes find it easier to achieve satisfaction than rich people.

Above the level of bare subsistence, not only are people's needs, concerns, and satisfactions culture-specific, they are subculture-specific. Our satisfaction is shaped by comparisons with people around us. Further, we are able and willing to substitute attainable for unattainable goals to maximize satisfaction. Where all else fails, we scale down our aspirations to increase our satisfaction. Whether good or bad, a Fool's Paradise or a Real Paradise, it is what people typically do. We want what we can get.

The next chapter discusses patterns of opportunity—why you get what you get.

References

ATKINSON, T.H. (1979). *Trends in life satisfaction among Canadians, 1968-1977* (Occasional Paper No. 7). Montreal: Institute for Research on Public Policy.

_____ . (1980). Public perceptions on the quality of life. In Statistics Canada, *Perspectives Canada III* (Catalogue No. 11-511E, pp. 275-292). Ottawa: Supply & Services.

ATKINSON, T.H., & MURRAY, M.A. (1982). *Values, domains and the perceived quality of life: Canada and the United States.* Toronto: York University, Institute for Behavioural Research.

BELL, D.V.J., & TEPPERMAN, L. (1979). *The roots of disunity: A look at Canadian political culture.* Toronto: McClelland & Stewart.

BIBBY, R.W., & POSTERSKI, D.C. (1985). *The emerging generation: An inside look at Canada's teenagers.* Toronto: Irwin.

BLISHEN, B.R., & ATKINSON, T.H. (1982). *Regional and status differences in Canadian values.* Toronto: York University, Institute for Behavioural Research.

CAMPBELL, A. (1980). *The sense of well-being in America: Recent patterns and trends.* New York: McGraw-Hill.

CAMPBELL, A., CONVERSE, P.E., & ROGERS, W.R. (1976). *The quality of American life: perceptions, evaluations and satisfactions.* New York: Russell Sage Foundation.

CANTRIL, H. (1965). *The pattern of human concerns.* New Brunswick, NJ: Rutgers University Press.

CLARK, S.D. (1975). The post Second World War Canadian society. *Canadian Review of Sociology and Anthropology, 12*(1), 25–32.

DIENER, E., HOROWITZ, J., & EMMONS, R.A. (1985). Happiness of the very wealthy. *Social Indicators Research, 16,* 263–274.

EASTERLIN, R.A. (1980). *Birth and fortune: The impact of numbers on personal welfare.* New York: Basic Books.

GUINDON, H. (1978). The modernization of Quebec and the legitimacy of the Canadian state. *Canadian Review of Sociology and Anthropology, 15*(2), 227–245.

JONES, L.Y. (1980). *Great expectations: America and the baby boom generation.* New York: Ballantine Books.

KETTLE, J. (1980). *The big generation.* Toronto: McClelland & Stewart.

MARSDEN, L.R. & HARVEY, E.B. (1979). *Fragile federation: Social change in Canada.* Toronto: McGraw-Hill Ryerson.

MARX, K. (1985). *Early philosophical manuscripts.* Harmondsworth: Penguin. (Original work published 1844)

MICHALOS, A.C. (1985). Multiple discrepancies theory (MDT). *Social Indicators Research, 16,* 347–413.

_____ . (1987). *Final progress report on Global Report on Student Well-Being: Applications of multiple discrepancies theory.* Guelph: University of Guelph.

_____ . (forthcoming). Optimism in thirty countries over a decade. *Social Indicators Research.*

NICOLSON, J. (1980). *Seven ages.* London: Fontana Paperbacks.

QUALITY OF LIFE SURVEY. (1981). Unpublished raw data from large survey of life satisfaction conducted at the Institute for Behavioural Research, York University, Toronto.

RINEHART, J.W. (1987). *The tyranny of work: Alienation and the labour process* (2nd ed.). Toronto: Harcourt Brace Jovanovich.

SOROKIN, P.A. (1941). *The crisis of our age: The social and cultural outlook*. New York: E.P. Dutton.

YANKELOVICH, D. (1982). *New rules: Searching for self-fulfillment in a world turned upside down*. New York: Bantam Books.

Chapter Two

Patterns of Opportunity: *why you get what you get*

Introduction

Some of the things that will happen to you in life, or have already happened, have little to do with social inequality or your social class. A good friend dies, your mate falls out of love with you, you lose interest in your work: these things happen to people of every social class. They have happened in every society throughout history. In our society, the risks of these occurrences may vary slightly by social class, but other factors besides class also influence them.

However, many important things that will happen to you in life, or have already happened, *are* results of social inequality and social class. Poor people risk unemployment, poverty, illness, and a host of other unpleasant experiences. The rich and powerful can look forward to comfort, income security, and better than average health. Moreover, social inequality will not only influence what happens to you by chance: it will also influence your range of choices and the kind of choices you actually make.

Social inequality is any inequality between people that arises out of social relationships. For example, the inequalities in job recruitment, earnings, and chance of promotion for men and women are social inequalities. They arise out of social patterns of discrimination, not biological differences *per se*.

Likewise, the inequalities between people who hold different kinds of jobs—for example, factory workers and top managers—are social. They include inequalities of income, job security, working conditions, authority, and deference, and they arise out of different relationships to the means of production. One person controls the hiring and firing of workers; the other is controlled. One has only his or her labour to sell for wages; the other will often own a block of stock in the company.

Social inequalities fall into two main categories: inequalities of condition and inequalities of opportunity. Inequalities of *condition* include differences of wealth, authority, and prestige that translate directly into differences of physical and material well-being: food, shelter, physical security, good health, and so on. Indirectly, they translate into differences of mental health and happiness, as we shall see later in this chapter when we discuss "incapacitation."

Inequalities of *opportunity* are differences in the chance that people (or their children) will get to enjoy a different social condition: more wealth, authority, prestige, and so on. Some people, groups, and classes are more "socially mobile" than others, meaning that they have more opportunity to improve their social position. Some people will have a greater chance to get what they want out of life than others will.

Inequalities of condition and opportunity are not randomly distributed among members of society; rather, they are distributed among people primarily by social class. A *social class* is a relatively stable grouping whose members share common conditions and opportunities because of their common relationship to the means of production. Class boundaries remain from one generation to the next, separating a "working class" from a "capitalist class." The membership of social classes is also fairly stable. Although many people are socially mobile—moving out of their class of birth into another in adulthood—for many others class position is inherited—passed from parent to child over generations. As generations pass, certain families remain in the working class and other families remain in the capitalist class.

Most people know *something* about social classes and social inequality; they view these as problems with which Canadian society must deal. Social inequality is so important to people that the constitutions of many nations specifically refer to opportunities that society owes its citizens. One of the earliest written constitutions, the American Constitution of 1787, pledges the government to ensure citizens the opportunity for "life, liberty and the pursuit of happiness." Happiness is viewed as a natural, universal goal that the state must help its citizens attain more easily.

Canada's present constitution, which came into effect in 1982, reflects a different way of thinking about government's obligations to the people. Today's government recognizes a widespread longing for greater, more certain opportunity. Constitutionally, our government has three kinds of obligations. The first is to avoid interfering with civil and political rights. The second, which is a more contentious obligation, is to further the cohesion and stability of Canada's subgroups: Francophone society, the various ethnic groups, and, with the Meech Lake Accord of 1987, Canada's regional and provincial subsocieties.

Third, Section 36(1) of the Constitution commits the federal and provincial governments of Canada to promoting equal opportunities for the well-being of Canadians, furthering economic development to equalize opportunities, and providing essential public services of reasonable quality to all Canadians.

This statement does not tell us precisely what "equal opportunities" means, nor how the government intends to make opportunities equal. It suggests that reducing inequalities requires economic development and adequate public services (such as good-quality education). But this formula may underestimate the difficulty involved. Equalizing opportunities may actually require wide-ranging, profound changes to Canada's social and economic organization.

Two general assumptions guide the analysis that follows. The first is that the processes creating inequality are similar whether we consider individuals, groups, or nations. The same kinds of factors limit opportunity between groups or nations as between pairs of people.

Second, the two kinds of inequality discussed in this chapter—inequality of condition and inequality of opportunity—are connected. People cannot have an equal opportunity to get what they want if they start out with vastly unequal wealth, power, and respect. People who start out with more wealth, power, and respect *always*—in our society and every other—find it easier to get even more wealth, power, and respect. This is because wealth, power, and prestige can be exchanged for one another and "invested" for further gains. Thus, a society cannot equalize opportunity without greatly reducing the range of unequal starting points. If everyone were born with the same wealth, social position, and social connections, a great many people would have much more chance of getting what they want out of life than they do today.

The connection between types of inequality has two more implications. First, getting the most out of your own opportunities in life may mean taking part in collective action to reduce the range of inequality in our society. You can achieve only so much by yourself. Your own life chances are tied up with those of other

Canadians. Accordingly, this chapter will discuss collective as well as individual remedies to limited opportunity.

Second, we all live in the short run. In the long run, society may offer everyone more equal opportunity than it does today. But as the British economist John Maynard Keynes said, in the long run, we are all dead. So we must pay attention to the short run as well. Getting as much as you can out of life will mean more than collective action: it will also mean making sensible life choices within the context of unequal starting points and unequal opportunities.

Four Limits on Opportunity   Four processes limit people's opportunities to get what they want out of life, or to get an equal return on their investments of effort and talent—closure, incapacitation, decoupling, and scarcity.

Closure is the ability of certain groups to control access to certain rewards or opportunities. For example, closure can be exercised by a group of large organizations within an industry; an ethnic group within an occupation; a social class; or even, in small communities, by key individuals or families. It prevents people from entering contests they might win, or rewards people unequally for equal performances.

Through *incapacitation*, certain categories of people are persuaded not to compete for widely desired rewards. Our society's dominant ideology, or world view, teaches us that everyone has an equal chance, but in practice many kinds of people are discouraged from thinking themselves equal and competitive. Women, the poor, the old, the physically disabled, and young people have all been taught that certain kinds of behaviour are inappropriate—unladylike, undignified, hopeless, and so on—or cannot succeed. The incapacitated "choose" not to compete.

Decoupling disconnects certain groups from rewards and key institutions. This lack of connection leads to a lack of information about available opportunities and ways of taking advantage of them. It also keeps people from first-hand acquaintanceship with others who could support or recommend them for rewards. People who are decoupled are not forced out of competition, nor do they eliminate themselves: they simply do not "know the ropes" or "have the contacts."

Scarcity is a shortage of desired goods or opportunities. While a shortage does not determine who will get the available opportunities, it does affect how many opportunities will be shared out in total. Often, people confuse scarcity with a poor distribution of desired goods due to closure, incapacitation, or decoupling. *True* scarcity can be reduced by producing more of the desired goods. Most often, scarcity makes itself felt in declining returns on investments; an example is the "underemployment" of recent postsecondary graduates. We will discuss this problem at length in the next chapter.

Closure

What we commonly call "power" is exercised by certain groups who create rules—for instance, laws and structures of authority—that allocate desirable goods within society (Murphy, 1982). Research on Canadian society by Porter (1965), Clement (1975), and Newman (1979) reveals that a person's social class largely determines his or her access to the most powerful (or "elite") positions in the economy and government. People born into the higher social classes are more likely to enter elite positions than people born into the middle class. Almost no members of Canada's economic and political elite come from a working-class background. This class-based difference in access is due partly to the decoupling of working-class people, as we will see shortly, and partly to closure. The upper class has traditionally closed its ranks to outsiders. Moreover, access to high-paying jobs in industrial societies **has** increasingly required a credential, often in the form of an educational degree, that the possessor has qualified for selection. Degrees from medical schools are particularly valuable credentials: virtually no doctors are unemployed or poorly paid. Who determines how these scarce degrees will be handed out: who will get them, and in return for what sacrifices?

Without a degree in medicine, no one is permitted to practice medicine. This limitation protects doctors by preventing competent nurses, paramedics, and other health professionals from breaking the medical monopoly on certain practices that generate high incomes. How did doctors achieve this unusual degree of closure over health care? This question interests many who study the professions and *professionalization*.

Closure and Professionalization   We see closure at work in the continuing battles over health care—debates about who shall pay and who is entitled to receive how much; and the exclusion of such competitors as chiropractors, homeopaths, and midwives from public recognition and coverage under public health plans. We also see lower-status educated groups—for example, social workers and psychologists—trying to "professionalize" themselves in hopes of higher status and better pay.

In some ways, we learn most about professionalization from the attempts that have failed. Mitford (1963) tells about the attempts undertakers have made to upgrade their status. Not content with being viewed (and paid) as technicians or business-people, undertakers seek greater credibility as "funeral directors" or "grief management consultants." So far their attempts have largely failed to persuade the public.

In North America, professionalization has been part of the general rise of the middle class through its own efforts. The notion of "career" is a relatively new idea tied to the growth of a new middle class, the expansion of higher education, and the spread of a new demand for more credentials for more people (Bledstein, 1976). Professionalization has fed the American hunger for stable sources of authority in a rootless democratic society.

In other countries—France, Germany, Russia, and Italy among them—professions were brought into being by the state. For example, Napoleon instituted national schools of engineering as breeding grounds for higher-level civil servants (Larson, 1977). In these countries, the state, not an autonomous middle class, brought about modernization of the society. There, the professions—their training, credentials, and career paths—were shaped from the top down, not created by practitioners and sold to the state and public. In the older European societies professionalization was part of national economic and political planning. Canadian professionalization has been somewhat closer to the European pattern than to the American pattern of self-initiated upward mobility.

This difference in origins may help to explain why, in America, the professions are neither part of an overall social plan, nor easily ruled by any state authority. American professionals largely set their own income and social status in the absence of imposed controls.

In many respects, professional associations are little different from trade unions: both aim to protect and promote the economic interests of their members. They differ in only two important respects. First, professional associations help middle-class people protect middle-class incomes, while unions help working-class people protect working-class incomes. Because of the higher social origins of professionals, people more willingly believe that professional associations really act in the public interest rather than in the private interest of their members.

Yet the public health movement in North America has *not* been championed by leaders of medical associations. The reduction of illness and mortality in our society has historically owed more to public works (sewage and garbage management, clean water, and so on) than to the work of practicing physicians. Even today, medical associations show little interest in workplace safety, environmental pollution, anti-smoking campaigns, or any other fights against major causes of illness and death. Instead, medicine—especially American medicine—increasingly addresses itself to high-tech, high-cost remedies that benefit only a very few: for example, the recipients of organ transplants.

Second, professional associations and unions, as movements, have used different means to protect their members. Unions typically threaten or use strikes to increase workers' incomes, employing collective means to pursue collective guarantees for their members. Professional associations occasionally do this. Instead, they rely on political lobbying and the manipulation of public sentiment through the mass media to control the public "image" of their members. They aim to protect their members from political interference and personal liability in dealings with the public. Associations help their members earn whatever the market will bear in private dealings with customers. Professionalization provides some consumer protection, but far from the amount the public believes it is receiving.

Medicine may be an exceptional illustration of the professionalization process. Because of the nature of the service provided—a matter of life and death—medicine has an almost unlimited market. Also, its scientific basis seems to produce desired results. The general lesson we learn from professionalization is that closure—in this case, control over public and private spending on specialized services—arises under certain kinds of historical, political, and economic conditions. It is a form of collective upward mobility that perpetuates and redistributes inequality. Professionalization advances primarily private interests by capitalizing on our fear of harm, belief in education, and inability to evaluate and control the people who serve us.

Closure and Institutional Completeness   Another kind of closure is based on ethnic or racial origin. The job recruitment of people with similar ethnic backgrounds can be found in many workplaces. As a result, people of the same ethnic origins control specific organizations and even entire industries. When an ethnic group captures and monopolizes an economic activity, allowing access to that activity only or primarily on the basis of ethnic background, it is practising closure.

Ethnic communities differ as much from one another as they do from the dominant Anglo-Saxon community. "Institutional completeness" is the main condition making ethnic closure possible (Breton, 1964). It is the degree to which an ethnic group has created a set of social, cultural, and economic institutions sufficiently complete to allow near-total isolation from the rest of society.

A community's degree of institutional completeness determines the proportion of individuals who conduct most of their personal relations within the ethnic group. Ethnic organizations such as schools, camps, churches, business associations, social clubs, and mutual societies or credit unions provide a context within which community members can meet and do business with other community members. These organizations make people more conscious of their ethnic origins. Like professional associations and unions, these organizations press for group interests.

In Canada, the degree of a community's institutional completeness is largely determined by the extent of problems immigrants face on arrival. Immigrants may not be able to speak English (or, in Quebec and parts of several other provinces, French). They may be unaccustomed to urban, industrial life or lack relevant job skills and job contacts outside their own community. On the positive side, they can speak in their native tongue; often have social contacts brought from their homeland; and may use their friendship or kinship contacts to develop job and business relations (see, for example, Li, 1982). So immigrants create a community that plays to their strengths and covers up their weaknesses.

Certain groups also face serious discrimination on their arrival in Canada and for some time afterward. Living in a situation of institutional completeness can protect immigrants in an actively hostile social and economic environment. This self-protective strategy has been historically practised by Jews and Chinese in Canada, both victims of serious discrimination.

However, a community's institutional completeness tends to persist even after the discrimination that created it has diminished or disappeared (Reitz, 1980). Institutions formed within an ethnic community generate a demand for the services they provide. Thus, the mere survival of ethnic communities does not prove ethnic discrimination is occurring. Institutional completeness may also be fed by continuing fears of discrimination. For example, memories of the Holocaust and Israel's ongoing problems have undoubtedly strengthened the Canadian Jewish community.

Conversely, some discriminated-against groups have little opportunity to practise closure in their own interest, despite good reason to do so. For example, Canadian blacks are in a worse position than either Jews or the Chinese. They suffer severe discrimination, yet lack the institutional completeness that would help them prosper as a community. The reasons for this are complex, but the fact that blacks come from a variety of different continents and sociocultural backgrounds is important. Unlike the Jews and Chinese, Canadian blacks share little except their skin colour. Like Canada's native people, blacks have a common social and economic disability thrust upon them despite their heterogeneity.

What we usually mean by the term "discrimination" is just closure practised by the majority against a minority group. In one study of discrimination, sociologists surveyed nearly 2000 Toronto workers representing the "majority Canadian group" and seven ethnic minorities. In the part of the labour market controlled by Anglo-Saxons, incomes for members of various ethnic groups vary directly with Anglo-Saxon attitudes toward those ethnic groups. All other things being equal, Anglo-Saxons earn more than anyone else in work settings controlled by Anglo-Saxons. Next-ranked earners are Germans, followed (in descending order) by Ukrainians, Italians, and Jews, with Chinese, Portuguese, and West Indians at the bottom of the ladder. This rank-ordering of incomes is identical to the rank-ordering of Anglo-Saxon ethnic preferences (Reitz, Calzavara, & Dasko, 1981).

Given the average levels of education they have attained, Jews are underpaid in work organizations that other ethnic groups control. As a group, Jews have avoided such discrimination and moved ahead by working hard, getting educated, and establishing themselves in certain well-paid occupations, especially business and the professions. Yet in large part, they have achieved their success by isolating themselves from work situations that would make them vulnerable to discrimination by Anglo-Saxons. French Canadians, by similar criteria also discriminated against by Anglo-Canadians, have adopted a similar strategy in Quebec.

Today, ethnic minorities (other than Francophones and Jews) are still largely absent from the economic elite, but they are doing well economically. As ethnic communities have prospered, so have ethnic individuals. Certain key institutions—for example, universities—appear to have broken traditional barriers of discrimination against ethnic and racial minorities, but others—such as the oldest financial institutions—remain firmly in the hands of WASP (White Anglo-Saxon Protestant) males. Human rights legislation is aimed at preventing discrimination, but it has been far from successful to date.

The decision you make about your career should therefore take into account the strengths and weaknesses of your own ethnic, racial, or status group. If you choose a career within your own community, ethnic or class closure will work for you, not against you. Whether working within that community is likely to satisfy depends on your own skills and aspirations, and on the institutional completeness of your community: the range and number of opportunities it offers. In the long run, more satisfactory solutions are needed; we will discuss those solutions in later chapters.

Incapacitation

As adults and children, we learn to live effectively in the real world. Socialization teaches us how and why to conform to cultural values and social norms. But socialization also teaches us how to *not* function in the real world. This crippling socialization, which we all receive, is *incapacitation*. For many people, it means learning ways of thinking about ourselves that make us less than what we might otherwise be. Incapacitation is any socialization that induces low self-esteem, a low sense of mastery or control, alienation, and distrust. Generally, incapacitation makes people believe that they *cannot* and *should not* do what they hope to do. This socialization leads to lower aspirations, lack of assertiveness, and even withdrawal from competition.

So, for example, youngsters are taught that there are a great many things they cannot understand and discuss reasonably with their elders, because they lack the necessary experience, wisdom, or insight. They are told to wait until they are older; then, presumably, they will understand and see their elders were right. Age is held against youngsters; their ability goes untested.

More often than not, old people are treated like children, as if they lack common sense, humour, and insight. They are typically pampered or ignored, but not treated as adult equals. From the moment of their forced retirement from the work force, they are taught "We think you *can't*! We think you *can't*!" For older Canadians, too, age is held against them; ability goes untested.

However, the old and young are not alone in their incapacitation. Among adults, women make up the largest number of incapacitated people. Women are not only denied the chance to try a great many things, they are also taught that they cannot do them and should not want to. For example, until a recent Supreme Court decision, Canadian females were prevented from trying out for male hockey teams. Further, women continue to play a more limited role than men in the Canadian Armed Forces. Traditional notions of "feminine" behaviour are as limiting to women as the bustles and other ridiculously encumbering clothes they used to wear in the name of fashion.

However, we must avoid the error of "exceptionalism" when studying the incapacitation of young people, old people, women, the poor (see, for example, Lewis, 1966; Sennett & Cobb, 1973), the unemployed (Grayson, 1986; Schlozman & Verba, 1979), and the stigmatized (Goffman, 1963; Lemert, 1972). As Mills (1943) pointed out, these social problems (and others) are connected by a common thread, and we cannot understand the individual case without understanding that common element. The unifying element in cases of incapacitation is our society's *dominant ideology*. This ideology teaches people who are victimized—by the class structure and otherwise—to blame themselves (Ryan, 1976).

What do average Canadians think about their opportunities? Survey results suggest that Canadian adults are confused. On the one hand, nearly two Canadians in three say that people should reduce their desires in order to prevent disappointment in life. Almost as many feel that people should be content with what they have, since you never know the future (Quality of Life survey, 1981). People are largely resigned to the limits on their opportunity. This is what Mann (1970) has called "pragmatic acceptance" of the facts of social inequality.

On the other hand, nearly half feel that people should set goals that are hard to achieve. Over two-thirds say that what you get out of life is your own doing, not the result of luck or chance. Accordingly, eight in every ten respondents feel that people should try to improve their position, rather than accept it, and that people's problems are never too big to keep them from running their lives the way they want to (Quality of Life survey, 1981). These statements suggest a belief that nothing can stop a committed person.

These are not the views of two distinct groups. Rather, a large proportion of Canadians are ambivalent or confused about their opportunities for life satisfaction. In a sense, everyone knows about such constraints as closure, decoupling, and scarcity. But people rarely confront such knowledge consciously and rationally, and take appropriate action. Our thinking is largely "ideological," and ideology is primarily a system of beliefs—untestable by reality—and only partly a system of ideas and knowledge.

Moreover, the idea that people can make the lives they want is rooted in an old philosophical outlook that political theorist C.B. Macpherson (1962) has called "possessive individualism." Macpherson summarizes this outlook—which developed out of seventeenth-century English political debates—in seven propositions:

(i) What makes a man human is freedom from dependence on the wills of others.

(ii) Freedom from dependence on others means freedom from any relations with others except those relations which the individual enters voluntarily with a view to his own interest.

(iii) The individual is essentially the proprietor of his own person and capacities, for which he owes nothing to society.

(iv) Although the individual cannot alienate the whole of his property in his own person, he may alienate his capacity to labour.

(v) Human society consists of a series of market relations.

(vi) Since freedom from the wills of others is what makes a man human, each individual's freedom can rightfully be limited only by such obligations and rules as are necessary to secure the same freedom for others.

(vii) Political society is a human contrivance for the protection of the individual's property in his person and goods, and [therefore] for the maintenance of orderly relations of exchange between individuals regarded as proprietors of themselves. (pp. 263-264)

What Macpherson has called "possessive individualism" is at the root of what others have called "laissez-faire capitalism," "liberal democracy," or the "liberal ideology." It emphasizes the rights of individuals against government interference, and protects people's rights to carry out economic exchange any way they want to, so long as they do not break laws.

Liberal democracy rests on free choice, free competition and, as a result of the other two, a free market in labour, goods, and ideas (Macpherson, 1965). These freedoms are usually found in societies with a capitalist economy, universal suffrage, and two or more political parties. But given social inequality—unequal starting points—freedom comes into conflict with fairness. That is because liberal democracy holds people responsible for protecting their own interests in exchange with others. It denies that any collective interests may be more important than individual interests: for example, environmental protection and world peace, as against unlimited resource use or weapon-selling. It also forgets that some people are less able than others to protect their own interests.

The assumption that people can protect their own interests and that no one else—including government—needs to do so, is completely unfounded. Even during the heyday of laissez-faire capitalism (the nineteenth century), governments regularly interceded on behalf of business and hereditary wealth (Polanyi, 1944). Increasingly, governments also came to realize that widespread poverty endangered the social order. This problem called for more and more-comprehensive "poor laws" and, eventually, social welfare legislation after 1830.

During the worldwide Depression of the 1930s, governments learned to intercede more comprehensively. British economist John Maynard Keynes showed that capitalism could not survive without large-scale government intervention in the economy; government needed to "prime the pumps" and stabilize earning, spending, and saving.

Today, modern economies operate through an extremely complex mechanism of government legislation and assistance to both business and private citizens. Virtually no sphere of life goes unregulated today. In this sense, the assumptions of possessive individualism are quite unfounded.

However, our "institutions of information"—the mass media, churches, and even schools—continue to promote the belief that people are free to make their lives whatever they want to. Hard work and merit are rewarded. Sloth and crime are punished. Moreover, government and other collective bodies—especially trade unions—interfere with people's right to choose. These kinds of ideas, trumpeted by leaders of business through the mass media they own or control, are attractive enough to survive year after year.

But we witness the falsity of these ideas much more often than we see their truth (see, for instance, Marchak, 1987). People we know are often *not* rewarded for hard work and merit. Conversely, the upper classes inherit enormous wealth, generation after generation; this tells us that hard work and merit have little to do with rewards. Moreover, corporate crime, government patronage, and tax laws that favour the rich over the poor all prove that the cards are stacked against ordinary people.

What keeps our society together in the face of this systematic inequality and demonstrated untruth? Surveying studies of public opinion from several capitalist countries, Mann (1970) concludes there is little evidence that people generally agree with the beliefs and values of liberal democracy: there is neither consensus nor consistency in their views. This accords with the ambivalence we found in Quality of Life survey (1981) attitudes cited above. To a large degree, it is this ambivalence that makes the system work. "Cohesion in liberal democracy depends on the lack of consistent commitment to general values of any sort and on the 'pragmatic acceptance' by subordinate classes of their limited roles in society" (Mann, 1970, p. 423).

But Mann also finds evidence of *false consciousness*; this too may produce order and social cohesion. False consciousness is a perception of society that incorrectly describes everyday reality to disadvantaged people. For example, it holds the disadvantaged person responsible for circumstances beyond his or her control, and in that way incapacitates.

So, for example, a person who is laid off or unable to find work will be led by false consciousness to focus attention on personal failings as the explanation, rather than on a high unemployment rate, discrimination, business mismanagement, or bad government handling of the economy. A two-earner family that is struggling unsuccessfully to meet all its financial, occupational, spousal, and parental obligations may turn its aggression inward— spouse against spouse, parent against child (and vice versa)— in this way destroying the family, rather than blame exploitive or inflexible employers, inadequate legislation, and uncontrolled prices.

Mann (1970) finds evidence that false consciousness does exist, incapacitating workers. Workers are indoctrinated—by the mass media and in other ways—to subscribe to vague political philosophies that contradict their everyday experience and support the status quo. (Appeals to patriotism, tradition, harmony, and national greatness are among the stated goals of such philosophies.) In this way, workers are incapacitated by the inconsistency of their beliefs.

They are further incapacitated by failed attempts to alter their circumstances. Consider the case of workers who lost their jobs when two Canadian factories closed down. Grayson (1986) shows that former employees and their spouses were not radicalized by the experience: they did not reject accepted ways of influencing the government that had failed to save their jobs. They simply felt more powerless than ever. Grayson (1986, p. 347) writes, "If people are to be mobilized to save jobs resulting from closure of viable operations, they must be mobilized *while they still have something to lose* [emphasis in original]. . . . Because of the sense of inefficacy that afflicts the victims of plant closures, unions and politicians will have to fight even harder" to prevent and remedy shutdowns.

In such situations, incapacitation is due less to false consciousness or a sense of personal fault than to a feeling of powerlessness that is rooted in reality. But often the origins are more pervasive, harder to see, and harder to change. For example, Baldus and Tribe (1978) studied perceptions of inequality among schoolchildren. By Grade 6, a high proportion have learned to consistently match social class indicators such as clothing, type of housing, and quality of car with one another: fancy clothes, a nice house, a new car, and so on "go together." Moreover, people with good clothes, houses, and cars are believed to care more about their appearance, to be trying harder. Finally, and most worrisome, the richer people are supposedly nicer and "better" people: more honest, better behaved, and harder working.

Children from poorer families are just as likely as children from wealthier families to make these assessments. Moreover, these beliefs grow stronger and more consistent with age. The result is what Sennett and Cobb (1973) have called "hidden injuries of class." Ordinary people who are not rich, not powerful, and not respected cannot easily live with such a negative image of themselves, so they find ways of salvaging their dignity and sense of personal worth.

One way is by dominating others who are even less powerful: poor whites dominating blacks, native people, or other minorities; poor men dominating their wives and children; children tormenting other children or pets. Another way is by imagining that the poor are morally superior to the rich. Both ways are documented in a landmark study of the "authoritarian personality" (Adorno, Frenkel-Brunswik, Levinson, & Sanford, 1969).

According to Sennett and Cobb (1973), people also employ "dreams and defences" to heal these hidden injuries. People who feel worthless dream of becoming "worthwhile" through their own (or their children's) upward mobility, winning a lottery, or some other stroke of good fortune. Women's romance books and magazines are about just this: Cinderellas who—as nurses, secretaries, or other male-helpers—meet and marry their Prince Charming through a combination of good luck, virtue, and wile.

Defenses against incapacitation by feelings of worthlessness include splitting the "real person" from the "performing person." People try to avoid feeling like they belong to the despised or menial role they play. They think, "In reality, I am someone else: not Clark Kent, but Superman. I possess enormous hidden powers that I will reveal at the right moment, winning deserved admiration." This theme of the dual, split, or hidden personality runs throughout mass entertainment because, for so many, it is a necessary escape from daily indignity.

This defense offers most people a (temporarily) constructive adaptation to a destructive social order: "constructive," because it allows people to continue functioning; temporary, because it fails to solve the problem. "It stills pain in the short run, but does not remove the conditions that made a defense necessary in the first place" (Sennett & Cobb, 1973, p. 219).

People live with this kind of incapacitation and the others we have discussed. Defenses they erect against feelings of worthlessness and powerlessness allow life to proceed. But these defenses also sap people's ability to fight the prevailing system of inequality and in that way get more opportunity for themselves and others.

Decoupling

Often without knowing it, even people who are not victimized by closure and incapacitation will suffer restricted opportunity if they are *decoupled* from major sources of opportunity and power in society.

The word "decoupling" suggests a disconnected railway or subway car that has been left unused on a side track. Like train cars, people are connected to one another and often pull one another forward or back. Contrary to the dominant ideology that holds each of us personally responsible for our own fate, much of what happens in life actually results from the actions of others, many unknown and distantly connected to us.

Consider how the careers of church ministers are shaped by very distant events. The job vacancy created by a minister's death or retirement often sets off a chain reaction resulting in the upward movement of dozens of other ministers (White, 1970). For this reason, social mobility is as much the result of "vacancy chains" as the accomplishment of individuals.

Under varying economic conditions, an initial move may produce longer or shorter chains of reaction. Retirement or death may not always lead to a long chain reaction of replacements. Sometimes the departed person's job is eliminated, taken on by someone holding a second job, or filled by a newcomer brought in from outside. These kinds of reactions are probably most common in organizations "downsizing" in response to economic difficulty.

Yet even when a vacancy chain fails to operate, your opportunities are still tied to formal and informal contacts with other people. This fact is compellingly demonstrated by studies of the Canadian upper class (for example, Clement, 1975; Newman, 1979; Porter, 1965). Members of the upper class are tied to one another by a variety of common associations and experiences: marriage; kinship; attendance at the same private schools, summer camps, and universities; membership in the same social clubs; and service on the same boards of directors. Upper-class people are much better acquainted with others in their class than middle-class or working-class people are.

The size of a group affects mutual acquaintanceship. The upper class is small, which makes knowing most other members easier. Another factor is institutional completeness: upper-class institutions and activities are just as exclusive as ethnic institutions, and for the same reasons. Upper-class people have property interests to protect against encroachment by the government and by the lower classes. Class-based institutions and shared experiences produce mutual acquaintanceship, a basis upon which closure can be exercised against outsiders. Similarly, wide contacts among upper-class people form the basis for job recruitment into elite positions.

Social contacts are also important in the middle class. A survey of managers showed that people typically find good jobs through personal contacts (Granovetter, 1974). Yet most people believe that others *do not* find jobs in that way. Most of us are swayed by the ideology that people succeed or fail through their own efforts, so that we think our own experiences are unusual when they are not.

When an employer has a position to fill, many people have suitable qualifications. If the job opening is advertised, many applicants will have to be screened or interviewed. Investigating every applicant to find the best would be very expensive. So employers often ask their personal contacts—people they know and trust—to recommend someone good enough for the job. In this way, the employer can find someone with the right qualifications at relatively little cost. That person may not be the single most qualified individual in the whole country, but will be qualified enough to do the job. Employers want a *satisfactory*, not an *optimal*, solution to their problem.

This method of hiring also gives the employer information about a candidate that is unlikely to surface in a résumé. The candidate recommended by a trusted friend or acquaintance probably has the right attitude as well as credentials.

People find jobs in the same way as employers find job candidates. Job-seekers want to know if the job is a good one, the boss a good boss, the prospects for advancement good, and so on. They will find out more by talking to an acquaintance with first-hand knowledge of the organization, the job, and the boss than in any other way. Impersonal sources of information (for example, organizational brochures and formal interviews) are unlikely to reveal as much about these matters.

So on both sides of the job market—among people who are hiring and people who want to be hired—"networks of personal contact" provide the best information about jobs or candidates. As a result, many jobs find people, or people find jobs, through networks of personal contact. In fact, the best-paying jobs are filled in this way.

Granovetter found that valuable job information is most often passed on by acquaintances, not close friends or relatives. "Acquaintances" are people you can call by their first name, but who are not (emotionally) close friends. We have a great many more acquaintances than close friends, so the likelihood is simply greater that we will get useful information from an acquaintance. Beyond that, close friends tend to have the same information about jobs. Their total information is limited because it is duplicated. By contrast, a person's acquaintances are less likely than his or her friends to know one another, and conversely, they are more likely to know many other people. Acquaintance networks can become very large indeed, numbering hundreds or even, in some cases, thousands of people.

Job referral chains *could*, therefore, be enormously long, but in practice they are not. People do not trust information that comes from someone at five removes from the job or candidate any more than they would trust information a stranger provided. This is because we live in a "small world," as psychologist Stanley Milgram's studies of social networks have shown (Travers & Milgram, 1969). Most people have thousands or tens of thousands of "acquaintances" at five removes; at ten or fifteen removes, every pair of people in the country is likely to have *someone* in common. Therefore, in practice, only acquaintances or acquaintances of acquaintances are likely to pass on valuable job information.

Each acquaintance brings you information and connections that other acquaintances are unlikely to duplicate. So acquaintanceships prove enormously valuable in getting a job. Your chances of hearing about a job or having an employer hear about you are best if you have many acquaintances. But how can a person maximize these chances? Granovetter does not believe that people ought to purposefully "network" in order to increase the number and variety of their acquaintanceships. Few people respond favourably to that kind of overture. They quickly see it for what it is: crass opportunism.

However, one strategy *is* likely to increase opportunities. People who have changed organizations the most times will have the most acquaintances. Beyond a certain point, of course, job-changing becomes counterproductive. If you changed organizations every day, no one would learn what you can do. But a person changing jobs three or four times over 15 years might end up knowing people in 30 or 40 different companies, since usually his or her acquaintances are also changing companies. People with an average job tenure of three to five years seem to do best.

Further, people who begin moving between organizations early in their careers seem to benefit most. This process creates a "snowballing" of career opportunities. People who remain with the same organization for much of their working life have a lot of trouble finding another job when forced to do so.

How far to generalize these findings is hard to say. At least in higher-status jobs, making many contacts, then moving on to another organization, seems to pay the greatest dividends. You get the maximum benefit from this process when your entire network is expanding through your acquaintances' actions as well as your own actions.

This implies that maximum career benefits are to be gained by investing your time in acquaintanceship, not friendship, kinship, or other relationships. However, research on closure suggests that this strategy will work better for some people than for others. First, some organizations consider stability and loyalty very important, and view with suspicion people who have moved every three to five years. Second, for people seeking careers within ethnic communities, involvement with old friends and kin may be much more beneficial than acquaintanceships.

The value of acquaintanceships for finding good jobs *within* ethnic communities will vary according to the kinds of jobs the ethnic community controls. For example, acquaintanceship will be much more likely to uncover a good job in the prosperous and economically diverse Jewish or Italian communities than in the more limited Portuguese or West Indian communities.

The process Granovetter describes may also be more characteristic of middle-class than working-class jobs. Working-class people are far more likely to find their first job through friends and relatives in a similar line of work; later in life, they start finding jobs by answering advertisements and other formal means. Middle-class people do the opposite: namely, they use their educational credentials to find a first job, then they find later jobs through people they have met at work.

This process works against groups that are underrepresented in better jobs or socially decoupled from the dominant group. For example, whites more often make the acquaintance of other whites, and men the acquaintance of other men. When asked to recommend people for jobs, whites will accordingly tend to recommend other whites, men other men. Even without intending to discriminate, the process produces a discriminatory outcome, in that the organization remains racially or sexually unbalanced.

The process is hard to change by appealing to employers' finer instincts. Acting otherwise would be very costly for the individual employer. For example, hiring a qualified black or woman could mean instituting a time-consuming and costly employee search; the employer will avoid doing this unless obliged to by affirmative action laws. Such laws, therefore, will be important in forcing all employers to bear the costs of a wider than usual employee search.

Higher-status people tend to have much larger, more varied, and more valuable networks of contact than lower-status people. Higher-status people have more time and money to travel, meet people, and interact socially: this helps in forming acquaintance-ships. Second, because they have higher status and more access to scarce resources, higher-status people are likely to receive more of other people's attention. Lower-status people will seek them out for advice, encouragement, and help. This will give the higher-status people a great many contacts even without making an effort. Finally, as noted earlier, elite and upper-class institutions bring higher-status people together on a regular basis.

At least in the beginning of their careers, people can do little to attain high status and thereby receive many helpful contacts. But people *can* make the best possible use of their network of acquaintances. People should keep up their contacts, even if it means taking time away from other activities they value. If you are looking for a job, let your acquaintances know it.

Further, people should not be incapacitated by the ideology that teaches us applicants get the best jobs because they are the most qualified. Skills and credentials are certainly important to get you into the race. But after that, the competition for jobs and rewards has a lot to do with interpersonal relations. Unless you are among the ablest in your age group, hundreds and perhaps thousands of other potential job candidates share your qualifications. To the stranger filling a position, you look the same on paper as many others do. So do not ignore the opportunities that can come through your personal network if you use it wisely. (For reasons of space, I will leave questions of how to use your network wisely to the many recent popular books on "networking.")

On the other hand, do not blame yourself if you fail to get the job you want when you want it. Remember that the job may have gone to someone who is no more deserving, but who had the good fortune to link into the organization. Your lack of connection has deprived you of valuable information about available opportunities, ways of taking advantage of them, and first-hand acquaintances who could advance your interests. You were "decoupled."

Scarcity

A fourth reason people often give to explain limited opportunity is that there is not enough to go around: the desired good is in short supply, or *scarce*. Scarcity varies with the ratio of competitors to desired goods. Scarcity can be reduced by eliminating competitors (through closure, incapacitation, or decoupling) or by increasing the supply of goods.

We see scarcity all around us. But not only the poor suffer from scarcity. The middle class is increasingly victimized by scarcity, as witnessed by the growing inability of its young adults to own homes as their parents had done (Berljawsky, 1986). A gap is widening between the rich and everyone else, so as the rich get even richer, the rest get poorer and the traditional middle ground disappears.

Beyond this material deprivation—which, presumably, could be remedied by economic growth and redistribution—we find "social limits to growth" (Hirsch, 1978). Increasingly, people value rare or scarce items—the unique vacation, the unusual home, designer clothing, and so on—*because* they are scarce. People want something that is all their own in a society of growing uniformity. Yet the sheer growth in our numbers makes this goal ever harder to attain.

Often we adapt by giving up something that we have long valued or even loved. We give up going to a beach that was once secluded, a perfect refuge, and is now packed with portable stereo players. We give up going back to our home town, where everyone once knew everyone else; now it is a bedroom suburb full of strangers. We give up a restaurant that used to be wonderful; today, it is full of plastic, junk food, and Walt Disney decor. Can we replace these lost pleasures?

It is becoming ever more difficult to enjoy the truly scarce such as good craftsmanship, privacy, and politeness. We cannot bring the old things back, and only if we have a lot of money can we replace them. So like the employers discussed in the last section, we must seek satisfactory, not optimal, solutions. This may mean looking at our choices in a new way and giving new value to things we had not valued before. Consider the problem in scarcity demographers have called the "marriage squeeze."

Between 1945 and 1957, more babies were born each year than in the year before. Of these, roughly half were male and half were female. But women tend to marry men who are a few years older. A woman about 30 years old in 1987 would find a shortage, or scarcity, of men between 33 and 35 years old. Men of this age would have been born between 1952 and 1954, and fewer men were born in each of these years than were born in each of the years 1955 through 1957, when the woman in question was born. This is the "marriage squeeze" from the standpoint of single women over 30 years old in 1987.

As you might imagine, the situation eventually reverses. Women about 25 years old in 1987 would find no shortage of men several years older, since more males were still being born in each of the years 1959 through 1961 than females in 1962 through 1964. So there is a shortage of brides, a marriage squeeze, for single men under 30 years old in 1987. What creative strategies do people use to deal with such scarcity?

In response to these marriage squeezes, many traditional constraints on mate selection are disappearing. First, people are marrying mates who, in the past, might have been considered too old or too young. Others are marrying outside their own racial and ethnic groups. More often than before, people are marrying previously married people or people from other social classes.

Many who do not solve the mating problem in these ways find alternative solutions such as unmarried motherhood or sequential cohabitation. Still others adjust to a single life by putting their energies into work, leisure, and friendship. Singles today are less stigmatized than they were in the past.

Adjustments to the marriage squeeze are both personal and cultural, and include a new conception of adult life, family, and marriage. Similar adaptations have been made at other times in history and in other countries, where mates have been in short supply due to war or migration.

Making adjustments always helps in the face of scarcity. Scarcity is a normal state of affairs for many reasons, not only demographic. More often, it is due to closure: the monopolization of desired goods by people powerful enough to control access to them. The powerful are able to get far more than their share of what everyone wants: money, good housing, respect, and so on. Moreover, as Marx and Engels (Meek, 1954) argued—against prevailing contemporary beliefs in "overpopulation"—capitalism itself tends to produce scarcity. Capitalists want a large "reserve army of the unemployed" to keep down wages, and shortages to keep up prices. Moreover, under capitalism, investment in technology rises continually and the capital invested in workers' wages falls. According to this theory, capitalism creates too few, indeed ever fewer, jobs; prices rise; and inequality increases steadily.

The best long-term answer to this problem is to break monopolies on production and prices, and a political revolution may be needed to do so. However, most North Americans reject this solution. While some people see revolution as a creative solution to the problem of scarcity, many others see increased productivity as a better solution. Typically, high rates of economic growth give most people more of what they want without breaking the existing monopolies. Such growth does not narrow the range of social inequality, but it makes inequality less visible and less painful.

Often Canada's prosperity has been achieved by making less-developed countries the source of cheap resources and labour power. We have solved the problem of local scarcity by exporting it, worsening someone else's economic situation in order to improve our own. For many today, primary needs for food, shelter, and physical security are simply not being met. At best, greater economic growth is only part of the solution. The Third World remains largely locked out of the benefits of overall economic growth. Beyond that, too much of the world's economic growth is devoted to arms production and warmaking.

In our own society, professional associations, workers' unions, ethnic groups, and other groupings use monopolization to their own advantage. In the long run this strategy cannot succeed. If every collectivity in the world mobilizes to gain a greater advantage, inequality will persist in more aggressive forms. Compare the situation to a parade people have gathered to watch. First a few people stand on their toes to see the parade better, then a few more, and so on. When everyone is standing on tiptoe, each person's ability to see the parade is as unequal as it was before, but everyone has sore toes.

Long-run solutions to the problem of unequal opportunity must be worldwide and co-operative. Anything less will work for only a short time, or will result in economic, political, and military warfare.

What the human race has working against it is greed, extreme and widening inequality, and rapid population growth. Working in its favour is a demonstrated capability to use knowledge and science creatively, adapt to new circumstances, and occasionally co-operate for mutual benefit.

Concluding Remarks

We started by asking why you will not get everything you want out of life, and why some people will get more of what they want than you will. The answer to both questions is the same: class structure. Class structure means unequal opportunity to get what you want. A few will enjoy enormous benefits and privileges, and the majority will not. So in one sense, your situation is not only *unlike* other people's, it is *opposed* to other people's. As they grow richer, you grow poorer, and vice versa. Yet this view is partly an illusion.

Your opportunities are actually tied up with everyone else's. You share common problems with other people in your own social class. Personal, individual remedies have been discussed in this chapter, and they are important; but in what Canadian social philosopher Marshall McLuhan called the "global village"—the planet Earth—they have limited value. Your opportunity is tied to almost everyone else's. The class structure must be changed to achieve maximum benefit for you and almost everyone else.

We shall discuss remedies to your problem of unequal opportunity in the last chapter. They fall into two main categories: individual and collective. The collective remedies, as we shall see, take longer but do a better job.

Why you get what you get is the result of an extremely complex set of arrangements sociologists call *social structure*. The processes of closure, incapacitation, decoupling, and scarcity maintain that social structure by limiting what you get, but also by limiting what you want. Moreover, they limit your ability to close the gap between what you want and what you get, when such a gap develops.

Not only do these processes limit your opportunity and your desires. They also limit your conception of the truly possible. Most people feel that they are less than they should be or can accomplish less than they actually might. People blame themselves for forces beyond their control and understanding: the laid-off worker, the job applicant without connections, the politely excluded, the searcher for a scarce mate. People who solve their problem in an ideologically "wrong" way—for example, the "unladylike" woman, or the person who finds a job through acquaintances—think they are deviant and wonder if they deserve the rewards they get.

Social inequality structures the way we think about our problems. It makes people believe that their common problems are actually individual problems, for which they alone are to blame. For this reason, people try to find individual, not collective, solutions to their problems; hold themselves responsible for what they get out of life; and try to close the gap between what they want and what they get by wanting less.

In the rest of this book we will examine the ways that social structure affects your aspirations and opportunities in a variety of everyday domains.

References

ADORNO, T.W., FRENKEL-BRUNSWIK, E., LEVINSON, D.J., & SANFORD, R.N. (1969). *The authoritarian personality.* New York: W.W. Norton.

BALDUS, B. & TRIBE, V. (1978). Perceptions of social inequality among public school children. *Canadian Review of Sociology and Anthropology, 15*(1), 50–60.

BERLJAWKSY, A. (1986, Winter). Mortgage rates and the housing market. *Canadian Social Trends,* pp. 30–33.

BLEDSTEIN, B.J. (1976). *The culture of professionalism: The middle class and the development of higher education in America.* New York: W.W. Norton.

BRETON, R. (1964). Institutional completeness of ethnic communities. *American Journal of Sociology. 20*(2), 193–205.

CLEMENT, W. (1975). *The Canadian corporate elite.* Toronto: McClelland & Stewart.

GOFFMAN, E. (1963). *Stigma: Notes on the management of spoiled identity.* Englewood Cliffs, NJ: Prentice-Hall.

GRANOVETTER, M. (1974). *Getting a job: A study of contacts and careers.* Cambridge, MA: Harvard University Press.

GRAYSON, J.P. (1986). Plant closures and political despair. *Canadian Review of Sociology and Anthropology 23*(3), 331–349.

HIRSCH, F. (1978). *The social limits to growth.* Cambridge, MA: Harvard University Press.

LARSON, M.S. (1977). *The rise of professionalism: A sociological analysis.* Berkeley, CA: University of California Press.

LEMERT, E.M. (1972). *Human deviance, social problems and social control.* (2nd ed.). Englewood Cliffs, NJ: Prentice-Hall.

LEWIS, O. (1966). The culture of poverty. *Scientific American, 215*(4), 19–25.

LI, P. (1982). Chinese immigrants on the prairie, 1910–1947, *Canadian Review of Sociology and Anthropology 19*(4), 527–540.

MACPHERSON, C.B. (1962). *The political theory of possessive individualism: Hobbes to Locke.* Oxford: Clarendon Press.

_____. (1965). *The real world of democracy.* The Massey Lectures, (4th Series). Toronto: Canadian Broadcasting Corporation.

MANN, M. (1970). The social cohesion of liberal democracy. *American Sociological Review 35*(3), 423–439.

MARCHAK, M.P. (1987). *Ideological perspectives on Canada* (3rd ed.). Toronto: McGraw-Hill Ryerson.

MEEK, R.L. (Ed.). (1954). *Marx and Engels on Malthus.* D.L. Meek & R.L. Meek (Trans.). New York: International Publishers.

MILLS, C.W. (1943). The professional ideology of social pathologists. *American Journal of Sociology, 49*(2), 165–180.

_____. (1959). *The sociological imagination.* New York: Oxford University Press.

MITFORD, J. (1963). *The American way of death.* New York: Fawcett, Crest Books.

MURPHY, R. (1982). The structure of closure: a critique and development of the theories of Weber, Collins and Parker. *British Journal of Sociology, 35*(4) 547–567.

NEWMAN, P.C. (1979). *The Canadian establishment* (Vol. 1). Toronto: McClelland & Stewart.

POLANYI, K. (1944). *The great transformation.* New York: Farrar & Rinehart.

PORTER, J. (1965). *The vertical mosaic.* Toronto: University of Toronto Press.

QUALITY OF LIFE SURVEY. (1981). Unpublished raw data from large survey of life satisfaction conducted at the Institute for Behavioural Research, York University, Toronto.

REITZ, J.G. (1980). *The survival of ethnic groups.* Toronto: McGraw-Hill Ryerson.

REITZ, J.G., CALZAVARA, L., & DASKO, D. (1981). *Ethnic inequality and segregation in jobs* (Research Paper No. 123). Toronto: University of Toronto, Centre for Urban and Community Studies.

RYAN, W. (1976). *Blaming the victim.* (Rev. ed.) New York: Vintage Books.

SCHLOZMAN, K.L., & VERBA, S. (1979). *Injury to insult: Unemployment, class and political response.* Cambridge, MA: Harvard University Press.

SENNETT, R., & COBB, J. (1973). *The hidden injuries of social class.* New York: Vintage.

TRAVERS, J., & MILGRAM, S. (1969). An experimental study of the small world problem. *Sociometry, 32*, 425–443.

WHITE, H. (1970) *Chains of opportunity: System models of mobility in organizations*. Cambridge, MA: Harvard University Press.

Chapter Three

Education: *what you want and what you get*

Introduction

This chapter and others that follow examine specific areas—domains—of everyday life. There are four basic components to this and each analysis that follows: an examination of (1) the system of social institutions relevant to a domain; (2) demographic trends bearing on those institutions; (3) the choices people make in relation to that institutional structure, given their demographic characteristics; and (4) the impact of the choices they make, especially on life satisfaction. Each chapter will end by considering whether people typically get what they want in a particular domain, or grow to want what they get.

Later chapters will discuss careers, marriage, child-raising, and other issues about which you will have to make choices as your life progresses. This chapter will discuss educational choices you are already making, and their likely consequences. Specifically, we will look at two educational issues that concern many students: How do people come to choose the education they get? and How do the choices they make affect their employability, job satisfaction, income, and social status?

Education benefits both individuals *and* society. The outcomes of educational decisions we will examine most closely—employability, job satisfaction, income, and social status—are not the only or even the most important benefits of a higher education; but students are keenly interested in questions of employment and pay following graduation. For this reason we focus mainly on these outcomes.

Some readers may want to skip this chapter. After all, they have already made their educational choices. In fact, older students may already be on their second set of educational choices, returning to school for new training and career. Moreover, many students may feel that, whatever the reason for their choice and whatever the outcome, they will have to live with it: so the less said, the happier they will be. Others may think that they looked into their educational options well enough before making a choice, and do not expect to learn anything new here. These seem like good reasons for not reading any further.

On the other hand, Chapter 2 showed that people often think about their life choices in narrow or mistaken ways. Some readers may even want to reconsider their educational choices in the light of new information.

The Promise of Education

In North America we often hear claims about the benefits of education. Such promises are not new. British philosopher James Mill wrote in the nineteenth century that "if education cannot do everything, there is hardly anything it cannot do" (quoted in Michalos, 1981, p. 94). School reformer Egerton Ryerson promoted free schooling for children of all classes in Upper Canada, arguing that common schools for the rich and poor would create social harmony (Prentice, 1977, p. 126). Today, many continue to believe in the promise of education. Many believe that education can help solve major social problems like crime and poverty. Others feel that combating ignorance through schooling will lead to social progress. For many Canadians, education promises personal success: they consider schooling a ticket to greater opportunity, a better job, and a more enjoyable lifestyle than their parents had (Michalos, 1981, pp. 95-96).

A modern bureaucratic society like ours uses schools to channel, train, and select young people for society's most important roles (Sorokin, 1957). This makes the effective functioning of the educational system—its openness to all, even-handed application of standards, reward for merit, and relevance to the society of which it is a part—central to the effective functioning of society. A good school system is important for the people who need educating, the labour market that employs their skills, and those whose prosperity and well-being ultimately depend on knowledge and expertise: in short, everyone. How far has our society moved toward an "effective" school system?

No one can deny that higher education changed radically in Canada after World War II. One reason for this change was the role of education promoters like John Porter (1979), whose impact on policymakers and educators alike is hard to exaggerate. Another was the launching of Sputnik by the USSR in 1957. This technical coup alerted the West to the need for more scientific research and training, if capitalist countries—particularly the United States and its closest allies—were to compete effectively for world power. A third factor was the baby boom, which resulted in the arrival of huge numbers of children at the primary and secondary schools in the 1950s and 1960s, and postsecondary schools in the 1960s and 1970s. These three factors largely account for the institutional changes that occurred in Canadian education between 1960 and 1980.

A good indicator of the change is the growth in scientific and technical education. A new kind of postsecondary institution, the community college, was created to offer larger numbers of students technical and semiprofessional training. Within universities, technical and scientific programs expanded and received more funding from the government.

Increases in the numbers of students graduating from Canadian bachelor-degree programs in physical science, mathematics, and engineering show the extent of this change. The years between 1960 and 1980 saw a threefold increase in the numbers of students awarded engineering degrees; likewise, the years between 1970 and 1980 saw a one-third increase in the numbers of students awarded bachelor degrees in mathematics and physical science. Undergraduate enrolments increased nearly threefold in engineering courses and fivefold in mathematics and science courses between 1960 and 1980 (Education in Canada, 1960–84).

So over this period, the numbers majoring in mathematics, science, and engineering increased dramatically. As well, the numbers studying mathematics and science but not majoring in these subjects also swelled. Further, the proportions studying science part-time also swelled, from 11 percent to 24 percent in the science group between 1970 and 1984.

Finally, women broke the traditional male monopoly on these fields of study. Between 1970 and 1984, the proportion of women enrolled grew from 2 percent to 11 percent in engineering, and from 25 percent to 39 percent in mathematics and physical science. Not only the numbers, but also the "types" of students had changed; higher education had become more accessible to working and older students through an increase in the availability of part-time studies.

These trends are not unique to engineering, mathematics, and science. Indeed, enrolments expanded and programs and students became more varied throughout the postsecondary system. Moreover, students came to enjoy more freedom in putting together study programs. The traditional standardized university program of study was overhauled.

Not everyone was pleased by these changes. Even today, many feel that postsecondary education has been watered down. Some believe that "Canadian universities no longer take only the best students and no longer give their students the best education" (Bercuson, Bothwell, & Granatstein, 1984). Critics complain that recruitment and grading standards have fallen, and new kinds of disciplines and programs now offered for study (for example, Women's Studies, Canadian Studies, and other interdisciplinary courses) have no standards, intellectual tradition, or justification. (For a similar American commentary, see Bloom, 1987.)

Recent years have seen a slow return to more highly structured programs and stiffer grading in many Canadian postsecondary institutions. But as yet, little effort has been made to dismantle the interdisciplinary programs. Moreover, part-time and remedial programs have continued to expand, reaching out to ever larger numbers of previously excluded students. And women increasingly enter and graduate from programs leading to traditionally male-dominated professions (Marshall, 1987). This institutional change has provided more-varied students with greater educational choice. Women, older students, and members of previously excluded ethnic and racial minorities are particular beneficiaries of these changes.

The impact of this technology revolution on education has never abated since Sputnik. During the days of "flower power" on campuses—the late 1960s and early 1970s—radical students voiced their hostility to science and technology, which they viewed as accessories to the North American "military-industrial complex." But even during that period, science and engineering enrolments continued to grow. Since the demise of "flower power," enrolments in these programs have skyrocketed.

It is unlikely, then, that colleges and universities will return to limited course offerings, limited program choice, limited student recruitment, and domination of the postsecondary curriculum by the traditional humanities: languages, history, philosophy, and classics. Educational change has occurred, but is it the change people had hoped for? Does postsecondary education in Canada today deliver on its promise of more opportunity for the traditionally disadvantaged? Does postsecondary education give people more opportunity and higher economic returns, the way reformers thought it would?

Who Gets a Postsecondary Education?

Even if postsecondary institutions admit applicants without bias, more students of some kinds will gain admission than others. They are just more likely to apply. This "self-selection" begins long before the end of high school, and it is based on gender, place of residence, social class and SES, and ethnicity, as well as ability. Let us examine each of these influences in turn.

Gender More females than males enter secondary school academic programs. However, females who complete such programs more often go on to a terminal (that is, non-transfer) community college program, while males more often go to university (Anisef, Paasche, & Turrittin, 1980, Table 4.1; Guppy, 1984, Table 4).

There are signs that gender differences in education are starting to disappear. In 1961, women represented 69 percent of non-university postsecondary enrolments. By the mid-1970s, the attendance patterns of males and females had equalized and they have remained equal into the 1980s. While in 1961 only one-quarter of Canadian university undergraduates were female, today half are female. Gender-related differences in enrolment levels among graduate (M.A. and Ph.D.) students have not disappeared yet, but they have diminished (Pike, 1988, p. 269).

Many traditional barriers to female postsecondary education have fallen in recent years, but males and females continue to enter different fields of study in what Anisef *et al.* (1980, p. xxiv) has described as "internal tracking based on sex." In Canadian community colleges, far more males than females study architecture, engineering, natural resources, electronics, and transportation. For their part, females predominate in secretarial, community and social services, nursing, and medical treatment technology programs. In universities, female undergraduates outnumber males in education, nursing, pharmacy, and household science, while more males than females specialize in commerce and business administration, dentistry, medicine, engineering, science, and applied science (Statistics Canada, 1985).

Canadian postsecondary students often follow traditional gender roles when selecting a field of study. Stereotypically male occupations are generally better paid, so males cannot be expected to switch their educational plans toward traditionally female-dominated fields. Female enrolments have changed substantially in recent years, with greater enrolments in such traditionally male-dominated fields as veterinary medicine, agriculture, commerce, and law. In particular, women from higher socio-economic backgrounds have been making these inroads (Guppy, 1984). Still, gender imbalances persist in many disciplines (Marshall, 1987).

Location and Residence Like gender, location influences students' postsecondary educational plans. Some provinces produce a higher proportion of high school drop-outs—people who consequently lack the credentials normally needed for admission into postsecondary education—than others. And just as high school completion rates vary by province, so do enrolments in postsecondary institutions. Even the balance of community college and university enrolments varies among provinces. In theory, young people from provinces with low participation rates could travel elsewhere to study, but the trouble and cost discourages many.

Students in the Atlantic provinces generally pay higher tuition fees and carry higher loans than other Canadian students. High school graduates there may calculate that the returns from postsecondary education do not justify the costs involved (Canada, 1976, p. 90).

Just as residence in some provinces reduces student postsecondary opportunity, so does residence in rural instead of urban areas. Anisef *et al.* (1980, Table 4.2) found that postsecondary enrolment rates for Ontario high school graduates vary sharply by size of community. Nearly three-quarters of the young people sampled in Toronto, and 67 percent in other cities, but only 52 percent in Ontario towns and rural areas, attend some postsecondary institution after finishing high school.

Moreover, the larger the community, the more likely a high school graduate will attend a university. Students from smaller communities are more likely to stop studying altogether or enrol in a terminal community college program. They also depend more on government assistance to finance their education, with fewer relying on summer employment earnings or parental support (Anisef *et al.*, 1980, Table 4.24).

Small-town and rural students are discouraged from studying past high school by the prospect of accumulating large debts and the possible scarcity of good summer jobs in their community. Further, young people from smaller communities have to leave home to get a postsecondary education. The cost and trouble of moving away increases the disadvantage of poorer small-town and rural youths.

On the other hand, the poverty of a region may influence educational plans more than its population density. Rural areas contain a higher proportion of poor people, and children of the poor are less likely to get a higher education, however close to a postsecondary institution they may live (Anisef *et al.*, 1980, pp. 148–149).

Social Class and SES   Educational choice is also heavily influenced by social class and socio-economic status (SES). It is hard to tell which aspect of SES—parental income, occupational status, or educational background—makes the most difference to student plans (Guppy, 1984, Tables 2, 3, Zur-Muehlen, 1978, p. 42).

Parents influence educational attainments most by shaping the educational plans their children make, and in turn, how far they go in school. Of course, many students do not carry through their original plans (Porter, Porter, & Blishen, 1982, p. 314). Students who have prepared to go to university sometimes decide not to go. These students can change their plans about education without further preparation. However, students who have not prepared to go to university will find that the decision to continue is a difficult one. Because of streaming, early decisions *not* to go to university are more likely to stick than early decisions to go.

The desire to graduate from university is related to both social class and gender, assuming the same level of ability. "Of the Grade 12 students with high mental ability, 75 per cent of upper-middle-class boys but only 42 per cent of lower-class boys wanted to graduate from university. The equivalent percentages for girls were 61 and 36" (Porter *et al.*, 1982, p. 312).

Students with higher-status fathers (especially if they are boys) are most likely to receive encouragement and feel able to handle university. As a result, middle-class children are more likely than lower-class children to enter the high school program for

students who are university-bound. According to the Porter *et al.*
findings, mental ability surprisingly has no direct influence on
aspirations and only a moderate influence on school grades.

By the time they enter high school, students have usually
established a sense of their own ability, an inclination or disin-
clination to study, and a desire to take or avoid courses that can
lead to postsecondary education. "Parents who do not understand
the consequences of courses that their children take in the early
years of high school will very likely acquiesce when their children
decide to take undemanding courses" (Porter *et al.*, 1982, p. 317).

When parents fall down on the job, teachers and guidance
counsellors must try to create and reinforce higher aspirations.

> They must see their task as providing a bridge between
> the family environment and the educational and occu-
> pational world. Social workers employed by school
> boards could also increase awareness of opportunities
> by going into lower-income homes, especially those
> whose children [have] high mental ability, and explain-
> ing to parents the opportunities that exist. Other pos-
> sibilities are enrichment programs for lower-class chil-
> dren at an early age, introducing children while they
> are still in elementary school to the university and
> explaining its role and its value both for the individual
> and the society. (Porter *et al.*, 1982, p. 317)

Socio-economic barriers to higher education have lowered in
the last few decades, but they are far from gone. Capable young
people from less privileged backgrounds are still more likely to
enrol in terminal community college programs than in universities
(Guppy, 1984, p. 88). Such differences in access to postsecondary
education, especially university, reduce the chances that children
will have substantially different jobs, incomes, or statuses than
their parents. Postsecondary education still tends to transmit social
status from one generation to the next.

Race and Ethnicity   Canadian society includes many ethnic (or
ancestral) groups: the native peoples (Inuit, Indian, and Métis),
the English and the French, and a variety of more-recent immigrants and their descendants. Access to postsecondary education
in Canada varies almost as much for ethnic and racial groups as
by gender, residence, and socio-economic status. Although some
minority groups have benefited considerably from Canada's

growing educational opportunities, others, especially native peoples and French Canadians, have benefited far less (Martin & Macdonell, 1982, p. 238).

Most native people do not come close to getting the high school diploma needed to qualify for postsecondary education. Nearly 80 percent have less than a secondary education, and only 5 percent ever enter postsecondary education (Anderson & Frideres, 1981, p. 181; Statistics Canada, 1980, Table 10.7).

When religious missions ran native schooling prior to World War II, academic subjects formed only a small part of the instruction given. Later, the federal government's greater involvement boosted enrolments, but large numbers of native students fell behind and dropped out. Formal education seemed foreign to them because it ignored traditional native culture and local concerns (Martin & Macdonell, 1982, p. 239). Happily, the past 20 years have seen a strong increase in postsecondary school attendance by native Indians between 18 and 24 years old. Native Indian participation has risen from less than 1 percent to 12 percent; still, the current participation rate for all young Canadians is 20 percent (Task Force on Program Review, 1986a, p. 396).

Further in 1983 only one-quarter of native Indians enrolled in university were expected to graduate, compared with three-quarters of all Canadians enrolled in university (Task Force on Program Review, 1986b, p. 154). In Ontario, a province with relatively high educational participation, the percentage of native males between 18 and 21 with at least some university education actually *declined* between 1971 and 1981 (Anisef, 1985, Figure 4.3).

Blacks were among Canada's earliest immigrant groups. For many years, like the native peoples, they attended racially segregated schools, if any at all. As a result, 94 percent of the 319 blacks in a 1973 Nova Scotia study achieved Grade 11 education or less, and only one person held a university degree. Although these people placed a high value on education, their drop-out rate was also high. Many quit high school for jobs to help support their families. Others quit because their parents could not afford to keep them in school (Henry, 1973, cited in Martin & Macdonell, 1982, p. 242). More recent statistics will be needed to determine whether greater educational opportunity has benefited this group.

French Canadians are another ethnic group with traditionally low rates of postsecondary education. In schools outside Quebec,

Francophones have often been forced to adjust to English, the language of the majority. However, other ethnic groups facing similar problems have managed to get more education than Francophones. In explaining this disparity, many social scientists have emphasized the role of French Canadian cultural values, which discourage high educational attainment and promote family "togetherness and belongingness . . . at the expense of personal ambition and competitiveness" (Rocher, 1975, p. 151).

The gap between French Canadians and other groups has narrowed slightly in recent years. But as recently as 1983, only 11 percent of Quebec youths aged 18 to 24 were enrolled in university full-time, compared with a rate of 15.6 percent in Ontario and 13.5 percent for the entire country (Anisef, 1985, Table 5.3). Admittedly, the province's remarkably high rate of part-time education partly offsets this inequality. Quebec universities are no longer the preserve of the privileged, but full-time university attendance remains low (Anisef, 1985, p. 35).

Of all Canadian ethnic groups, people from Jewish, Chinese, or Japanese backgrounds are most likely to attend school full-time between the ages of 19 and 24. They are also more likely to attend university than other groups. By contrast, youths of British ancestry enjoy surprisingly little advantage in gaining access to university education.

Educational data collected for the Census Metropolitan Area of Toronto show that the proportion of people with at least some university education increased considerably between 1971 and 1982 in every ethnic and gender category. Increases are far greater for females than for males of the same generation and ethnic origin. The most dramatic increases in university education have been made by British- or American-born women and Canadian-born women with Canadian-born parents: both groups more than doubled in university experience. Moreover, the wide educational gap between second-generation Canadians of British and non-British origins observed in 1971 had narrowed considerably by 1982 (see Kalbach, Lanphier, Rhyne, & Richmond, 1984, Tables 1, 2, 4, & 5).

At least in Toronto, with its numerous immigrants of many ethnic origins, and its many postsecondary educational institutions, those traditionally excluded are getting more education as educational institutions expand.

Is Education Becoming More Accessible? Access to post-secondary education has slowly become more democratic (Guppy, 1984). A young person's language and socio-economic background matter less today than in the past, and women now participate as much as men. Many changes occurred because large numbers of *non*-university institutions—community colleges—were built, creating more postsecondary spaces. Community colleges are "a major postsecondary alternative for lower social and economic strata" (Guppy, 1984, p. 89).

However, massive government spending on higher education has not increased university access proportionally (Pike, 1988, p. 271). Part of the reason may be found in Australia's experience. University tuition fees were abolished there in 1974, yet lower-class attendance did not increase significantly. In Canada, "the [Standing Senate Committee on National Finance] believes that when a student is unsettled or lacks motivation, educational costs are often stated as the reason for dropping out after high school. . . . [However,] even if tuition fee levels fell to zero, the percentage of high school graduates who fail to go directly to college or university would not be affected substantially" (Standing Senate Committee, 1987, p. 47).

Cultural and motivational factors may better account for differences in educational choices. Parents' (and their children's) values, not their financial means, continue to determine educational achievement. Those students with higher-status, better-educated parents and those from ethnic groups that strongly value education develop with more of the motivation and know-how necessary for educational success. "The offspring of the 'cultured classes' know better than the children of working-class background how to deal with the social and academic demands of the educational system, and are more aware of the long-term consequences which their programme and course choices entail" (Pike, 1988, pp. 271–272). Accordingly, "in order to increase participation [by children from lower-income families], programs would have to be targeted to helping them much earlier in their educational careers" (Standing Senate Committee, 1987, p. 49).

Children from the higher classes seem to have something extra, which Bourdieu (1977) calls "cultural capital." Its measurable traits include a knowledge of music and literature; frequent attendance at cultural events such as concerts, museums, and plays; interest in reading books and listening to music; and, equally important, the tendency to think of oneself as educated, artistic, or "cultured." Students with the most "cultural capital" are most likely to complete a postsecondary education and gain a high-status job, regardless of parental social status or education (DiMaggio & Mohr, 1985).

Despite student aid and reduced tuition, lower-income students continue to feel pressed to give up studying and contribute financially to the family, or to their own support. Lower-income students are more reluctant to take out student loans, fearing difficulty in repaying these loans. But however the economic and motivational issues are mixed, earlier assistance and encouragement will be needed to influence educational decisions in the future.

As we have seen, gender, region, community size, social class, and ethnicity all play a role in streaming young Canadians into (or away from) postsecondary education. But these patterns are not entirely rigid and unchanging. Government policies have made postsecondary education somewhat more accessible to women and certain ethnic minority groups. Some change has occurred. "These changes would not have occurred unless accompanied by specific *value changes* [italics added] and institutions' willingness to make accommodations" (Anisef, 1985, p. 11).

Even the ideology underlying education has changed. In the 1960s, postsecondary education for the largest possible number was viewed as a societal responsibility that would bring societal benefits. Now, postsecondary education is viewed as yielding the greatest benefits to the individual graduate, not society as a whole. This view justifies passing an increasing proportion of educational cost back to the "user."

An awareness of the factors that influence other people's postsecondary plans may lead you to examine your own educational choices—past, present, and future—with greater clarity. People may realize that their upbringing has limited their educational horizons, or "incapacitated" them. Alternative educational choices actually available to them might yield greater fulfilment.

The Returns on a Postsecondary Education

When asked what concerns them most about their education, today's postsecondary students usually mention job opportunities first. This section will look mainly at how your postsecondary education will affect employability, income, and job satisfaction. However, you should balance the emphasis here on job-related returns by also examining how higher education will influence the overall quality of your life.

Non-monetary Returns   Anyone who has received a good education, in whatever field, will say that education can bring many benefits that cannot be measured in dollars. Just like strenuous physical exercise, strenuous mental exercise—the regular exertion of learning, debate, and new ideas—can be exhilarating and fulfilling. Often people find themselves filled with excitement and admiration by what earlier thinkers have accomplished.

With more education, people also feel a sense of greater mastery as they become more able to understand complicated arguments and create their own. Further, by increasing our knowledge through education, we increase our sense of control over our own lives. This is satisfying and reassuring, though it is often daunting as well (for education also teaches us how much we do not know and cannot control).

Education in the sciences gives people more insight into the logic of the universe and the technological revolution that is sweeping everyone's lives. Education in the humanities puts people in touch with the vast variety of human cultures and ideas. It gives us a sense of the continuity of the human race, and allows us to admire how much people have achieved that is good and beautiful. Education in the social sciences helps us understand why we live the way we do and how we can change ourselves—individually and collectively—before we suffer disastrous consequences.

Higher education is more than a ticket to a job. In the space of three or four years, students gain in critical ability, aesthetic sense, and tolerance for divergent values (Bowen, 1977). College graduates are better informed and more politically active citizens. They even make better parents. Along these lines, Bowen (1977, p. 201) writes:

> The effects of college education on the family are numerous and strong—so much so that these effects may be among the most significant outcomes of higher education. . . . Among the familial impacts are the following:

1. Narrowing the traditional differences in attitudes and behavior between the two sexes.
2. Selection of college-educated persons as marriage partners.
3. Delay in age of marriage.
4. Slight reduction in the divorce rate.
5. Reduction in the birth rate.
6. More thought, time, energy and money devoted to the rearing of children.
7. Influences on parents, spouses and siblings of the college educated.

These kinds of non-monetary benefits are not confined to American undergraduates, nor even to people receiving a postsecondary education. Generally, education is a good thing. In a comparative study of six developing nations, sociologist Alex Inkeles (1973) showed that the amount of education a person has received is the single best predictor of how "modern" he or she is likely to be. By "modern," Inkeles means all the characteristics Bowen has mentioned; he also means "capable of living in a modern world." So the more education you get, the better off you will be.

To narrow our sights somewhat, what are the career benefits for students who manage to get a postsecondary education? Is today's general arts degree a ticket to a good job, or to unemployment-office lineups? Do non-transfer community college programs really give more marketable, job-oriented training? Do recent graduates feel that their postsecondary education was a waste of time?

Job Status Returns Education is an important "intervening variable" between the social characteristics you start out life with and the rewards you end up with. Although access is largely restricted by factors beyond your control—gender, place of residence, and SES among them —it is possible to break free from your past by using higher education as a lever. By seizing the opportunity for higher education, you can get on a somewhat more equal footing with people who started life with more advantages.

Let us begin by examining the effects of postsecondary education on social mobility. Education has an important impact on your social status and upward social mobility (Ornstein, 1981).

Calculations based on Ornstein's (1981) results suggest that each additional year of education moves a student's expected first-job status 2.5 points up the widely used Blishen scale of occupational prestige.

Sample SES scores displayed in Table 3.1 show that Canada's most prestigious and best-paying jobs are typically those that require the most education. The prestige, pay, and educational requirement associated with a job are highly correlated. In other words, higher education is the ticket to higher prestige and pay in Canada, just as it is elsewhere.

Thus, the student with 20 years of formal education can expect occupational prestige that is 30 points higher than that enjoyed

Occupation	Index score
Dentist	74.6984
Physicians and surgeons	74.2246
University teacher	72.2955
Chemical engineer	70.8910
Accountants and auditors	67.4100
Elementary/kindergarten teachers	65.8531
Writers and editors	62.8184
Sociologist/anthropologist/other soc. sci.	60.5728
Radio and TV equipment operator	56.5194
Electronic data processing equipment operator	55.8252
Secretaries and stenographers	52.4465
Bookkeeper	50.7098
General office clerk	46.4416
Typists and clerk typists	45.4604
Receptionist	40.6897
Cashiers and tellers	40.4164
Retail sales clerk	38.3541
Electrical equipment assembler	35.4749
Paper product fabrication worker	35.2914
Food and beverage processor	32.2390
Truck driver	29.7365
Guards and watchmen	28.7070
Carpenter	28.0382
Waiter/waitress	28.0074
Chefs and cooks	26.8068
Bartender	26.4920
Janitor	24.9784

TABLE 3.1 The Blishen Socio-economic Index: scores for selected occupations, based on 1971 occupational data. (Source: *Blishen & McRoberts, 1976, Table 1.*)

by the average person who quits school after Grade 8. A 30-point spread on the Blishen scale is equivalent to the difference between a dentist and a typist, an elementary school teacher and an electrical equipment assembler, or a TV equipment operator and a bartender. Which end of the 30-point spread do you prefer?

Of course, the status benefits of education are *discontinuous*. For example, completing the final year of a B.A. degree is worth far more in prestige and earnings than completing the second-last year and dropping out.

Moreover, university graduates vary regionally in the extent of their upward mobility. Quebec has the highest percentage of upwardly mobile graduates; British Columbia has the lowest (Harvey, 1984). This is partly because Quebec has the lowest percentage of parents with high occupational status, and British Columbia the highest. Lower average origins give Quebec graduates a greater chance of surpassing their parents' status. As well, Quebec's "Quiet Revolution" created a large number of white-collar, middle-to-high-prestige jobs for postsecondary graduates. No other province has transformed opportunities as dramatically as Quebec.

Thus, if you want to increase your job status and income, education appears to be a pretty good "investment" of your time and money. However, since 1964 the upward mobility of Canadian university graduates has declined. "While a university degree has declined [in value] as a path to upward mobility, it would still appear to be important for persons from low occupational status backgrounds and, for persons from higher occupational status backgrounds, it may serve as a hedge against downward mobility" (Harvey, 1984, pp. 282–283). University graduates of 20 years ago may have gotten slightly better jobs than they would today, but opportunities for people without a postsecondary education have also shrunk appreciably over this period. A B.A. may now have more value than ever because it provides even greater protection against low-status work and unemployment. But what kind of job security does postsecondary education provide? Will more education reduce the likelihood of your being unemployed?

Employability Returns   With very few exceptions over the past 15 years, the more education a person has attained, the lower his or her likelihood of unemployment. Even though national unemployment rates have fluctuated over this period, people with more education have always been more likely to hold a job than people with less education, all other things (such as gender and place of residence) being equal. This pattern holds true for people of all ages, including youths (aged 15 to 24), who typically have the highest unemployment rates.

Between 1969 and 1977, unemployment rates for people with a university degree were always lower than for any other group (Zsigmond, Clark, & Picot, 1978, pp. 168 & 170, Chart 28). Even during this period of rapid growth in the numbers of postsecondary graduates, the "employability" of people with a university education did not change.

Unemployment rates among the highly educated remained low because postsecondary graduates were willing to take work that had not traditionally called for a postsecondary education (Zsigmond *et al.*, 1978, p. 170). Highly educated people are increasingly doing work below their levels of skill and ability (Berg, 1970; see Hunter, 1987, for an opposing argument). As more postsecondary graduates enter the labour market, employers demand higher qualifications simply because they prefer to hire the highly educated, and more highly educated people are available today.

Fitting a highly educated person into an undemanding job risks employee boredom, loss of motivation, and rebelliousness. But for several reasons most employers are willing to take this chance. University graduates lend the organization an air of professionalism and credibility. Further, employers assume that postsecondary graduates in general, but university graduates in particular, learn new things faster, have better interpersonal skills, and come from a higher class of family. This makes them more desirable employees.

Beyond this, postsecondary education teaches people to be ambitious and career-oriented (Bowles & Gintis, 1976). Doing work that cannot be closely and continuously supervised, the employee with a postsecondary degree must be relied upon to see personal well-being as linked to the well-being of the organization. The employee must believe that merit will be rewarded and continuous hard work is a worthwhile investment in the future. These views are learned and rewarded in postsecondary institutions, then carried into the work world.

In this way, postsecondary institutions both instill job traits employers desire and select for a good background and high motivation. The evidence an educational credential provides saves the employer a lot of trouble in identifying good candidates for independent work. This is why postsecondary graduates are so rarely unemployed, even if often "underemployed."

Postsecondary education not only influences employability; for women, it also influences the degree of labour force participation. Nearly all working-age men, whatever their level of education, work full-time. But the situation is quite different for working-age women: higher-educated women are the most likely to take full-time paid work, instead of part-time work or full-time work as unpaid family workers (Boyd, 1985, Table 7.5).

Income Returns   Throughout the 1960s, university graduates earned well above the industrial average in their first job. Since then, they have earned relatively less, at first. However, workers with more education catch up soon, and in the long run their earnings surpass others' (Zsigmond *et al.*, 1978, Chart 31, Table V–15). Further, the salary of a university graduate (B.A. or B.Sc.) two years after leaving school averages $5000 higher than that of the community college graduate. The effort is worth it, if higher income is your goal.

As we noted earlier, the financial benefits of educational attainment are, with some exceptions, discontinuous. For most people one more year of pre-graduation training does not bring the same reward as one more year of training that completes a degree. Degree completion is very important. An individual who completes all but the last year of a medical degree is not "nearly a doctor" in the work world, entitled to *nearly* the same rewards as doctors. That person must seek non-medical jobs on a roughly equal footing with high school and community college graduates and with other university drop-outs. Such jobs will not be found in the highly protected (or price-controlled) market for medical services, but in the more competitive market for technical or personal services.

Moreover, *which* degree you complete is also important. Different degrees not only make you eligible for different jobs, they also make you competitive in different job markets.

Still, incomes increase more or less steadily with the amount of education you attain. Jencks *et al.* (1977) tried to isolate the effect of education on earnings from that of other factors such as work experience, family background, and cognitive ability (that is, I.Q.). In the job market that prevailed up to 1970, completing four years of high school raised average earnings by at most 15 to 25 percent. Completing four years of university could add up to 40 percent, because a bachelor's degree provided access to higher-status occupations—that is, better job markets. The economic downturns of the 1970s and early 1980s, along with the continued supply of university graduates, have probably decreased the size of this income advantage; but graduates are still ahead of the rest.

The income value of a postsecondary education also varies by gender. For every type of education, men earn more on average than women. Many women earn less because they enter poorer-paying traditional female occupations (Clark & Zsigmond, 1981, p. 141). However, even if we compare men and women of the same ages (say, 25 to 34) in well-paying, traditionally male-dominated professions such as engineering, the physical sciences, medicine, and dentistry, "women [in 1981] . . . had average employment incomes that were only 77% those of comparable men" (Marshall, 1987, p. 11).

Predicting income returns on education in the future is difficult. The growing number of young B.A.s seeking jobs increases the competition, thereby driving down the price that an employer must pay to hire a B.A. The spillover of postsecondary graduates into lower-status jobs probably limits the potential of high school graduates for career advancement. In the long run, college and university graduates will still push ahead of the competition, though probably not by as much as in the past (Olneck, cited in Jencks *et al.*, 1977, pp. 183-184, 188-189).

Satisfaction Returns   Satisfaction is a more complicated matter. Among Canadian men and women, the proportion claiming to be "very satisfied" with their job drops as level of education increases. Moreover, we find this same pattern within every job category (Statistics Canada, 1980, Charts 14.7 & 14.8).

For several reasons, these findings should surprise us. More highly educated people generally get higher-paying, more secure jobs. Further, past studies have indicated that job satisfaction is greatest in occupations allowing the greatest autonomy and creativity. These are typically the best-paying and most prestigious jobs, and require the most education. Thus, a very high proportion of doctors, mathematicians, and top executives can be expected to say they would choose the same job if they had to choose over again; salespeople, assembly-line workers, and clerk-typists would say the opposite. Why, then, are the most highly educated workers not the most satisfied today?

The better-educated may be less satisfied than expected because they have broader horizons, a richer sense of alternatives, and a wider basis for comparison. Take mathematicians, who may love their work, but be deeply dissatisfied with their own achievement in comparison with Nobel laureates'. No such dangerous comparison is available to assembly-line workers, who neither love their work nor evaluate themselves against an almost impossible career standard.

An American study of happiness concluded that people with higher education and income levels may be more sensitive and psychologically responsive to their environment. This would help to explain why "better-educated and higher-income groups, although happier, [have] greater feelings of social inadequacy and more problems" (Bradburn & Caplovitz, 1965, p. 24).

Certainly, the Canadian Quality of Life (1981) data offers no evidence that higher education makes people more satisfied with life overall, or with their jobs in particular. Among people over age 25, life satisfaction is usually greatest for those with a high school diploma or less. Postsecondary education is slightly more likely to give people job satisfaction, but here too the evidence is very mixed. One cannot conclude from these data that satisfaction—with life or with your job—will increase if you get more education.

Highly educated respondents are particularly dissatisfied with their jobs (and lives) when "underemployed" in work that makes only partial use of their training and skills. Eight out of ten university graduates and nine out of ten community college graduates feel it is important that their job be related to their field of study (Clark & Zsigmond, 1981, Tables 6 & 7). Since job satisfaction varies little among different types of graduates doing what they were trained to do, underemployment and income make a difference.

Indeed, Lambert & Curtis (1979) show that people "treat education as an investment in the interest of future economic rewards." Highly educated adults who are dissatisfied with their economic status are more likely than others to express non-confidence in major Canadian institutions such as schools,

Parliament, the Supreme Court, and newspapers. On the other hand, highly educated people who are economically satisfied are no more likely to do this than less-educated people. Thus, higher education is "radicalizing" when it does not pay off financially, but not otherwise.

The match-up between job requirements and education affects job satisfaction most. Differences in earnings hardly affect the job satisfaction of people doing the job they were trained to do. But when a job is not education-related, differences in earnings affect job satisfaction to a much greater degree (see Figure 3.1).

From the standpoint of satisfaction, postsecondary education is a high-risk, potentially high-yield undertaking. Risks include income lost while in school, large debts, and the chance of having to accept work unrelated to one's education. After unemployment,

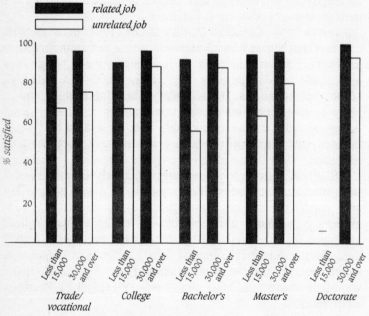

FIGURE 3.1 Job satisfaction of graduates employed full-time, by salary, relationship of job to education, and educational level: Canada, 1984. (Source: *National Graduate Survey, 1984; reported in Clark, Laing, & Rechnitzer, 1986, Chart 18.*)

the worst possible scenario is low-paying work outside one's area of training. The best possible scenario is full-time, high-paying work in one's chosen field. Between these extremes the range of employment outcomes—and satisfaction—is immense.

Education versus Work Experience   Compared with work experience, how important is formal education in ensuring employability and a good income? When postsecondary graduates are asked the reason they were hired for their current full-time job, they say "personality" was the single most important reason (Anisef, 1985, Tables 6, 17, & 19). "Educational qualifications" is the second most common answer, and "qualifications obtained elsewhere" (that is, work experience) is third.

For a great many applicants, hiring *is* based on personal characteristics, supported by educational qualifications. People with high school or some postsecondary education tend to believe that work experience matters most, and they may be right about the jobs that are open *to them*. In a world with ever more college and university graduates available to employers, high school or some (uncompleted) postsecondary training is worth little: it is like having no educational qualification whatever. No surprise, then, that for these youths, educational qualifications counted for little!

The earnings for people with a postsecondary degree increase more rapidly with age than the earnings of those with less education (Featherman & Hauser, 1978, Table 5.27). Attending college initially lowers a person's income; work experience yields more income than education does for people under age 30. But after age 30 the situation changes: the relative advantage of work experience declines and the growth in earnings of those without a degree slows considerably. Work experience yields immediate and impressive dividends for those without postsecondary education, but the benefit is short-lived. In the long run, higher education is the better investment of youthful energy (Featherman & Hauser, 1978, pp. 306–308).

However, this is not to deny the value of work experience. The combination of education and experience is unbeatable. For every type of postsecondary education, having prior work experience increases a graduate's income (Clark, Laing, & Rechnitzer, 1986, Chart 13).

Payoffs to Different Kinds of Education   Between 1976 and 1982, the chance of full-time employment worsened slightly for college graduates and B.A.s. The proportion of graduates working full-time two years after graduation dropped between 1976 and 1982 for all postsecondary graduates, but the drop was least for people with the most education—M.A.s and Ph.D.s (Clark *et al.*, 1986, Table 4).

Even with their supposedly more practical and job-oriented education, community college trade/vocational graduates had more trouble finding a job than any other group. Not only were they most likely to suffer unemployment, but their periods of unemployment were on average much longer: 10 months out of the 24 elapsing since graduation, compared with only 7 months for other postsecondary graduates (Clark *et al.*, 1986, Table 8).

Less often unemployed than community college graduates, B.A.s are most likely to become underemployed. The 1978 economy apparently failed to generate anywhere near enough jobs for recent B.A.-holders. It did, however, absorb most new M.A.s and Ph.D.s into appropriate jobs (Clark & Zsigmond, 1981, Tables 6 & 7). Recent data reveal a somewhat changed pattern: the underemployment of B.A.s has declined slightly and risen for community college graduates. But on the whole, underemployment remains quite high for both groups. Instead of becoming unemployed, graduates are increasingly accepting work for which they are overqualified.

Between the late 1950s and early 1970s, the average status of postsecondary graduates' first jobs also declined. But university degrees consistently led to more prestigious first jobs. In terms of job status attained, an incomplete university education was worth about the same as a community college diploma. The job status a bachelor's degree earned gradually broadened from the mid-1960s through the mid-1970s, meaning that a B.A. could lead to a wider variety of outcomes—good or bad—in 1975 than a decade earlier (Goyder, 1980, Table 4; Harvey, 1984, Table 1).

Currently, highest-status occupations tend to go to university rather than community college graduates, and disproportionately more to males than females (Anisef *et al.*, 1980). Male community college graduates experience the most unpredictable job outcomes of all: they hold a very wide range of jobs, from low to high status.

Eight out of ten graduates with jobs related to their education would take the same educational program over, but only four out of ten with unrelated jobs would repeat. Among people who would change their program, nine out of ten university graduates would enrol in university again, but only four out of ten community college graduates would return. Most would attend university instead.

Satisfaction remains lowest for those who majored in fine and applied arts and the humanities. Surprisingly, in many fields, job satisfaction is greater for those who took three-year instead of four-year degrees. Many four-year graduates may have discovered that an extra year of university at the B.A. level yields no advantage in the job market, and no higher income (University of Toronto Career Centre, n.d., Table 8).

The credentialling function of a university education should not be underestimated. "Although a job may not require particular skills or knowledge gained in university, the possession of a B.A. is evidence of an applicant's maturity, motivation and aptitude for further learning, and thus provides the employer with a means of selecting suitable candidates who will then acquire additional training on the job" (Selleck, 1980, pp. 36–37).

Concluding Remarks

Investments in higher education will have different values for different people. Some people will place a low value on the non-monetary benefits of education. Others find ways of achieving employment security and social status without a higher education; for example, by entering the family business. Higher education is not for everyone, then.

Higher education is not certain to increase life satisfaction or work satisfaction. On the one hand, it gives people the many benefits—financial and non-financial—that Bowen (1977) described. On the other hand, it gives people too much information about the rewards available in life that other people may be getting. Education raises your standards of comparison, and while it increases your chances of achieving job and income rewards, it may not do so as much or as quickly as you would like. There is a real risk that education will raise your expectations more quickly, and higher, than you are able to satisfy them.

Today, postsecondary education is still a worthwhile investment of time and money. In terms of employability, earnings, socio-economic status, and potential job satisfaction, a university degree brings the greatest rewards. Even terminal community college graduates are better off than people with a high school education or less, but the university degree provides the highest overall benefit. And from the standpoint of non-monetary benefits, the more education you get, the better off you are.

Where education is concerned, do people get what they want or learn to want what they can get? On the one hand, people get what they want: how much postsecondary education people get is *primarily* shaped by how much they want (their aspirations), not by tuition costs or other economic concerns. Likewise, the kind of postsecondary education people get is also the kind they want, in most cases. Choices between university and terminal community college programs, between one course of study and another, are "free," subject to limits on the total number of students who will be admitted to any given program.

On the other hand, the amount and kinds of education people want are socially patterned by gender, place of residence, and socio-economic status, and to some degree by other factors like ethnicity and race. As children we have been programmed to want what we (or our parents) expect we can get. If so, educational "choice" is an illusion. Choices and outcomes are predetermined. Social position is inherited from one generation to the next.

Do people learn to want what they get? Not entirely. If they did, people would not change their choices, as increasing numbers of older students do when they return for additional education or new kinds of training. Further, large numbers of graduates are dissatisfied with their educational decisions, particularly when these decisions do not result in the expected employment and remuneration, or when their training does not prove useful on the job.

The educational decision process starts early. People receiving little encouragement for their educational goals at home would do well to find mentors who could advise them about their goals and help to increase their cultural capital. In many ways, your educational choices will become clearer once you have made some career choices. The next chapter takes us a little further through the life cycle. It will discuss likely changes in the world of work and factors that influence the rewards—the pay, security, status, intrinsic interest, and job satisfaction—people get out of their jobs.

References

ANDERSON, A.B., & FRIDERES, J.S. (1981). *Ethnicity in Canada: Theoretical perspectives*. Toronto: Butterworths.

ANISEF, P. (1985). *Accessibility to postsecondary education in Canada: A review of the literature*. Ottawa: Department of the Secretary of State.

ANISEF, P., PAASCHE, J.G., & TURRITTIN, A.H. (1980). *Is the die cast?: Educational achievements and work destinations of Ontario youth*. Toronto: Ontario Ministry of Colleges and Universities.

BERCUSON, D.J., BOTHWELL, R., & GRANATSTEIN, J.L. (1984). *The great brain robbery: Canada's universities on the road to ruin*. Toronto: McClelland & Stewart.

BERG, I. (1970). *Education and jobs: The great training robbery*. New York: Praeger.

BLISHEN, B.R., & MCROBERTS, H.A. (1976). A revised socio-economic index for occupations in Canada. *Canadian Review of Sociology and Anthropology 13*(1), 71–79.

BLOOM, A. (1987). *The closing of the American mind: How higher education has failed democracy and impoverished the souls of today's students*. New York: Basic Books.

BOURDIEU, P. (1977). *Reproduction in education, society, and culture*. Beverly Hills, CA: Sage.

BOWEN, H.R. (1977). *Investment in learning: The individual and social value of American higher education*. San Francisco: Jossey-Bass.

BOWLES, S., & GINTIS, H. (1976). *Schooling in capitalist America*. New York: Basic Books.

BOYD, M. (1985). Educational and occupational attainments of native-born Canadian men and women. In M. Boyd, J. Goyder, F.E. Jones, H.A. McRoberts, P.C. Pineo, & J. Porter (Eds.), *Ascription and achievement: Studies in mobility and status attainment in Canada* (pp. 229–295). Ottawa: Carleton University Press.

BRADBURN, N.M., & CAPLOVITZ, D. (1965). *Reports on happiness: A pilot study of behavior related to mental health*. National Opinion Research Center Monograph in Social Research. Chicago: Aldine.

CANADA. Department of the Secretary of State. (1976). *Some characteristics of post-secondary students in Canada*. Ottawa: Supply & Services.

CLARK, W., & ZSIGMOND, Z. (1981). *Job market reality for postsecondary graduates: Employment outcome by 1978, two years after graduation* (Statistics Canada, Catalogue No. 81–572E). Ottawa: Supply & Services.

CLARK, W., LAING, M., & RECHNITZER, E. (1986). *The class of '82* (Statistics Canada, Catalogue No. S2–168/1986E). Ottawa: Supply & Services.

DIMAGGIO, P., & MOHR, J. (1985). Cultural capital, educational attainment, and mate selection. *American Journal of Sociology, 90*(6), 1231–1261.

EDUCATION IN CANADA: A STATISTICAL REVIEW. (1960–1984). Statistics Canada, published annually. Ottawa: Supply & Services.

FEATHERMAN, D.L., & HAUSER, R.M. (1978). *Opportunity and change.* New York: Academic Press.

GOYDER, J.C. (1980). Trends in the socioeconomic achievement of the university educated: a status attainment model interpretation. *Canadian Journal of Higher Education, 10*(2), 21–38.

GUPPY, N. (1984). Access to higher education in Canada. *Canadian Journal of Higher Education, 14*(3), 79–93.

HARVEY, E.B. (1984). The changing relationship between university education and intergenerational social mobility. *Canadian Review of Sociology and Anthropology, 21*(3), 275–286.

HENRY, F. (1973). *Forgotten Canadians: The Blacks of Nova Scotia.* Don Mills, ON: Longman.

HUNTER, A.A. (1987). *Formal education and initial employment: Unravelling the relationships between schooling and work over time.* Hamilton, ON: McMaster University, Department of Sociology.

INKELES, A. (1973). Making men modern. In A. Etzioni (Ed.), *Social change: Sources, patterns and consequences.* New York: Basic Books.

JENCKS, C. *et al.* (1977). *Who gets ahead?: The determinants of economic success in America.* New York: Basic Books.

KALBACH, W.E., LANPHIER, M., RHYNE, D., & RICHMOND, A.H. (1984). *Ethnogenerational factors in socio-economic achievement in Toronto: The second generation during the 1970s.* Toronto: York University, Institute for Behavioural Research.

LAMBERT, R.D., & CURTIS, J.E. (1979). Education, economic dissatisfaction, and nonconfidence in Canadian social institutions. *Canadian Review of Sociology and Anthropology, 16*(1), 47–59.

MARSHALL, K. (1987, Winter). Women in male-dominated professions. *Canadian Social Trends,* pp. 7–11.

MARTIN, W.B.W., & MACDONELL, A.J. (1982). *Canadian education: A sociological analysis.* Scarborough, ON: Prentice-Hall.

MICHALOS, A.C. (1981). *North American social report: A comparative study of the quality of life in Canada and the USA from 1964 to 1974. Vol. 3: Science, Education, and Recreation.* Dordrecht, Holland: D. Reidel.

ORNSTEIN, M. (1981). The occupational mobility of men in Ontario. *Canadian Review of Sociology and Anthropology, 18*(2), 183–215.

PIKE, R.M. (1988). Education and the schools. In L. Tepperman & J. Curtis (Eds.), *Understanding Canadian society.* Toronto: McGraw-Hill Ryerson.

PORTER, J. (1979). *The measure of Canadian society: Education, equality and opportunity.* Toronto: Gage.

PORTER, J., PORTER, M., & BLISHEN, B.R. (1982). *Stations and callings: Making it through the school system.* Toronto: Methuen.

PRENTICE, A. (1977). *The school promoters: Education and social class in mid-nineteenth-century Upper Canada*. Toronto: McClelland & Stewart.

QUALITY OF LIFE SURVEY. (1981). Unpublished raw data from large survey of life satisfaction conducted at the Institute for Behavioural Research, York University, Toronto.

ROCHER, G. (1975). Formal education: the issue of opportunity. In D. Forcese & S. Richer (Eds.), *Issues in Canadian society: An introduction to sociology*. Scarborough, ON: Prentice-Hall.

SELLECK, L. (1980). *The university graduate and the marketplace*. Toronto: Council of Ontario Universities.

SOROKIN, P.A. (1957). *Social and cultural mobility*. New York: Free Press. (Original work published 1927)

STANDING SENATE COMMITTEE ON NATIONAL FINANCE. (1987). *Federal policy on post-secondary education*. Ottawa: Supply & Services.

STATISTICS CANADA. (1980). *Perspectives Canada III* (Catalogue No. 11-511E). Ottawa: Supply & Services.

_____. (1985). *Education in Canada: A statistical review for 1984-1985*. Ottawa: Supply & Services.

_____. (1987, Spring). Low educational attainment in Canada, 1975-1985. *Canadian Social Trends*.

TASK FORCE ON PROGRAM REVIEW, STUDY TEAM REPORT. (1986a) *Indian and Native Programs* (Catalogue No. CP32-50/12-1985E). Ottawa: Supply & Services.

_____. (1986b). *Education and research* (Catalogue No. CP32-50/16-1985E). Ottawa: Supply & Services.

University of Toronto Career Centre (n.d.). *Report on university of Toronto 1982 graduates*. Toronto.

ZSIGMOND, Z., PICOT, G., CLARK, W., & DEVEREAUX, M.S. (1978). *Out of school—into the labour force* (Catalogue No. 81-570). Ottawa: Statistics Canada.

ZUR-MUEHLEN, M. VON (1978). *The educational background of parents of post-secondary students in Canada*. Ottawa: Statistics Canada.

Chapter Four

Career Choices: *what you want and what you get*

Introduction

This chapter answers questions about jobs and careers: specifically, What are the long-term employment prospects for different occupations? and What makes a job satisfying? To answer the first question, we will evaluate the forecasts social scientists have made about the future job market. Which kinds of jobs are on the rise, and which on the decline? To answer the second question, we will examine data on job and career satisfaction. These data tell us not only which kinds of jobs seem to satisfy people most, but also which kinds of people seem hardest to please.

The kind of job a person gets will be largely determined by personal contacts (see "decoupling") and community resources (see "closure"), both discussed in Chapter 2, and by educational attainment. The kind and amount of education a person takes will be largely determined by factors discussed in Chapter 3: these include gender, place of residence, SES, race, and ethnicity. Taken together, these factors have a powerful effect on the first job you get—which, in turn, influences your later work life (Blau & Duncan, 1967; Boyd *et al.*, 1985).

The kind of job you get is also influenced by forces far larger and even more beyond your immediate control than closure, decoupling, and educational choice. These currently include technological changes and changes in the national and local economy; in the future, you may also feel the effects of free trade with the United States.

Chapter 3 noted a new and growing element in the educational system: older students. Increasingly, people who have already "completed" their formal education are returning to school to get additional or different education. Many attend classes part-time, while holding down job and family responsibilities the rest of the time. They are often 10 or 20 years older than the average undergraduate. This may be the first opportunity some have had to get a higher education. Others have returned to school in hopes of, ultimately, supporting themselves or entering another, more rewarding line of work. For these mature readers, what this book has to say about careers may be old hat.

As before, we will close this chapter with a brief consideration of whether people get what they want or learn to want what they get in the domain of work and careers. Occupationally, many have found the 1980s very uncertain, frustrating, and even chaotic. To predict the future with any degree of confidence, we must assume that many career trends are part of a long, slow pattern of change that began before the 1980s, and will reach their completion long afterward.

The Future Job Market

Among the many changes affecting the job market, free trade is likely to have a major but, as yet, undetermined effect on the readers of this book. Changes resulting from technological innovation dominate current discussion. The microchip has already eliminated many jobs, though it also holds the potential to create many new ones. Most Canadians probably know that, for better or worse, computer technology will continue to evolve and spread. Will today's job skills become outdated in the near future? Will new technology lead to mass layoffs and firings, or will employers retrain their workers? Will entire industries disappear? These are questions career-choosers should be asking themselves.

Other important changes to the recent job market have centred on specific regions. For example, during the 1970s, popular wisdom held that with Alberta's oil boom, places like Calgary, Edmonton, and Fort McMurray would overflow with good jobs. Eager job-seekers poured into the West from across the country. Many were disappointed, and left soon after arriving. Others remained in Alberta, their careers no further ahead than before as they participated in a game of occupational "musical chairs" (Tepperman, 1985).

Other changes have centred on particular occupations. As Chapter 3 showed, the 1960s and the 1970s saw a sudden growth in the size of the school-age population. New government policies made higher education more accessible. Because of educational expansion, graduates trained as teachers found positions waiting for them. In the late 1970s, the size of the school-age population declined, and cuts in government funding limited hiring. Many newer teachers lost their jobs, and many would-be teachers had to choose an alternative career path. But with the recent "baby boom of the '80s" (the result of baby boomers giving birth to offspring of their own) signs already point to a growth of new opportunities for elementary and secondary school teachers.

Faced with these examples, common sense says you are better off knowing the employment prospects for an occupation before preparing to enter it. Choosing systematically will help you make better choices, but it cannot guarantee the results you desire. Even though a great deal of social change is slow and gradual, revolutionary changes do occur. Back in 1940, who was predicting the hydrogen bomb, personal computers, a baby boom, or declining American power in the world? No one. Changes that break old trends and set new ones in motion take us by surprise. We would be wrong to consider history an infallible guide to the future. But we would be even more wrong to ignore signs of change that can affect our lives.

Social scientists have devised three ways of "reading" these signs; we will discuss each one in turn.

Three Ways of Guessing the Future   The first method, *linear extrapolation*, assumes recent trends will continue without significant change for some time to come. The recent past is held to be our best measure for the future. This approach assumes historical continuity: no sharp breaks will alter the patterns witnessed up to now.

In Canada, the most ambitious job forecasts of this type have been made by the federal government as part of the Canadian Occupation Projection System (COPS). This method predicts high growth between 1985 and 1992 in the demand for service managers, dentists, denturists and dental technicians, photographers and camera operators, producers and directors in the performing and audio-visual arts, coaches and trainers in sport and recreation, chefs and cooks, food and beverage preparation supervisors, and sound and video recording equipment operators.

On the other hand, it predicts declining growth in the demand for teachers in universities, community colleges and secondary schools, and for farmers (Employment & Immigration Canada, 1986). Prospects are uncertain for lawyers and notaries, optometrists, community planners, various types of engineer, and power station operators.

Such linear extrapolation tends to overstimulate labour supply. Many readers of the COPS forecast in 1989 may decide to train for the currently predicted "high-opportunity" industries and occupations. Readers of the same COPS forecast a year later will make plans without knowing what the 1989 readers had decided; and so on. By 1992, not only are all the vacancies filled, but enormous numbers of recruits are caught in the middle of training for the very positions that have since been filled. This is one danger of following the advice offered by a linear extrapolation.

Another danger lies in its short time horizon. Journalistic accounts of the labour market are often unscientific and based on short-term trends. For example, a newspaper article headlined "Headhunters big winners as job market picks up speed" (*Globe and Mail*, August 27, 1987) claims that "it's a good time to be an accountant or finance expert but a lousy time to be in medicine, dentistry or most kinds of engineering." Allegedly, the demand is "hot" right now for marketing specialists, health-care administrators, and finance executives, but cooler for "many middle-management corporate jobs and in-house public relations positions."

Job-placement experts and spokespeople for various professional groups usually cite short-term changes in the business cycle, or recent oversupplies of labour power, as reasons for these trends. Sometimes factors like improved foreign trade, growing corporate size, or changed consumer spending are cited, but writers admit that many of these explanations are speculative. General theories of social and economic change are rarely put forward to explain these changes, nor are longer-range predictions attempted.

Such journalistic accounts make interesting reading over breakfast and usually contain some insight, but they share all the weaknesses of systematic linear extrapolation and none of the strengths. Avoid basing your future plans on what you read in the newspaper.

Demographic projection—knowing the changing size and composition of the nation's population—can supplement information on future job opportunities gained by looking at recent trends. Job opportunities are influenced by the ratio of jobs to people seeking jobs. Opportunities will grow with *either* increases in the total number of jobs *or* decreases in the total number of workers. Demographers, who study population scientifically, are particularly interested in the factors that increase and decrease rates of labour force participation and the numbers of working-age people.

Historically, Canada has depended on immigration to provide settlers, skills and, most recently, capital that native-born Canadians were failing to provide. The rate of immigration has been severely limited in the last two decades. Immigration may grow again in the near future; but for the time being, immigration is not an important factor affecting your employment opportunities.

Demographers estimate that until the baby-boom generation passes away, around the middle of the next century, the average age of Canada's population will continue to rise. If childbearing trends continue, the proportion of children in society will continue to fall throughout your lifetime. At the same time, the proportion of working-age people in Canada will grow slightly until around 2011, then start to drop. The 65-and-over age category will change most, more than doubling (from 10 to 21 percent) between 1981 and 2031. In 1981, half the population was under 30 years old; by 2031, half will be over age 42 (Foot, 1982, Tables 3-9 & pp. 107-108).

How will changes in the age composition of Canada's population affect your employment opportunities? First, consider that many occupations aim their services and products at specific age groups. We have already noted the effect of demographic change on one such service: the effect of baby boomers (and their children) on jobs for teachers. When children born during the 1950s and early 1960s were at school, teaching was a secure and growing occupation. As the baby boomers graduated from school, enrolments dropped and fewer new teachers were hired. A demographic shift had affected the need for teachers at the primary, then secondary, and then postsecondary levels of education. During the late 1970s, teachers seeking employment experienced great frustration and disappointment. Now, the "baby boom of the '80s" is starting to revive teaching opportunities.

Other industries catering to baby boomers' young children will also thrive until the mid-1990s. By the second half of the 1990s, industries with products and services directed at teenagers should grow more rapidly (Casale & Lerman, 1986, pp. 237-238; Woods

Gordon, 1986, p. 3) and the universities may start to hire significant numbers of new faculty once again.

Industries catering to the aging baby boomers themselves will become increasingly large employers of labour. As the numbers of middle-aged people grow, more service workers in health, leisure, recreation, and travel will be needed. As the same people reach old age, the demand for nursing-home workers, gerontologists, and funeral directors will swell.

Population composition also affects the supply of appropriately aged workers. Currently, there are too few young workers compared to middle-aged workers. A great many jobs in our economy—low-paid, unskilled or semiskilled, and often part-time—are normally held by teenagers. The current shortage of teenagers and people in their early twenties, relative to people aged 25 to 45, has strengthened the demand for young workers, increasing pay and improving working conditions (Easterlin, 1980).

On the other hand, there are too many middle-aged workers relative to older workers, resulting in a "promotion squeeze." Because of their large numbers, baby boomers have worse chances than earlier generations had of getting into upper-management positions (Kettle, 1980, 192-193). In the 1960s and 1970s, many managers were promoted to top positions while they were still young. Until these managers retire or die, there is little room for career advancement by workers below them; and these managers have many more years to go before retiring. The result is stifled opportunity for advancement among baby boomers.

Attrition—the movement of workers out of particular occupations—increases younger workers' chances of moving up from below; and it occurs for a number of reasons. Some attrition is peculiar to particular career paths. For example, annual attrition is great in occupations where physical strength and agility (for example, professional sports) or youthful good looks (for example, rock music or various "hospitality" occupations) place a premium upon "juniority" rather than "seniority."

In occupations with large numbers of older workers, attrition due to retirement will likely be high in the foreseeable future, therefore creating many new opportunities for younger workers. Occupations with especially high proportions of workers over 54 years old include physicians and surgeons, dentists, pharmacists, optometrists, osteopaths and chiropractors, health-care administrators, and tool-and-die makers. Occupations with low proportions over 54 years old include teachers (at various levels), psychologists, sociologists, anthropologists, denturists and dental hygienists, radio and television announcers, pilots, and commercial artists (Employment & Immigration Canada, 1986).

Many of the occupations just named are traditionally male-dominated professions (Marshall, 1987, pp. 10, 11). Proportions of women in these occupations have increased since 1971, though men continue to constitute the vast majority. It is hard to predict whether job opportunities created by attrition will continue to go primarily to young men, or will be shared more fairly between males and females. Likewise, it is impossible to predict how fairly these jobs will be shared among young people from different class, racial, religious, or regional backgrounds.

Demographers use the "life table"—a technique for analysing age-specific probabilities of dying—to predict retirement patterns almost as accurately as they can predict mortality patterns. But they are unable to predict the creation of job vacancies by economic growth, or the filling of job vacancies by automation (the substitution of machines for people) and immigration (the substitution of people who are somewhere else today for people who are already here). In periods of economic stability and low immigration, this method predicts the future reasonably well.

However, the present is not very stable. Impending changes like free trade with the United States, liberalized immigration laws, and increased workplace automation make demographic projection useful but incomplete. A fuller theory of change is needed: one that meaningfully addresses all of society's parts—social, economic, political, technological, and demographic. That is precisely what futures researchers try to provide.

Futures research predicts changes to work as part of societal change in technologically advanced societies. Sociologist Daniel Bell's (1973) thesis of post-industrial society argues that in today's most advanced societies the economic base is shifting from industrial manufacturing to the production and processing of information. Types of jobs associated with industrial production are disappearing with the rise of information technology and new forms of social organization based on this technology.

According to the post-industrial thesis, the economic emphasis in society will change from producing goods to providing services. Therefore, manual work will decline as a greater portion of the work force engages in cleaner, more interesting white-collar work. Automation will improve the factory jobs that remain; new jobs will require more training and allow workers greater scope for autonomy and creativity.

Many advanced societies (such as Canada) have already entered the post-industrial stage. Just as Bell would predict, the proportion of workers employed in Canada's service sector has steadily increased in the last few decades. Between 1951 and 1981, the proportion of Canadians employed in the service sector grew from 47 percent to 66 percent of the total labour force (Picot, 1987, p. 8). Canada has also seen a significant increase in the proportion of the labour force performing white-collar work. From 15.2 percent at the beginning of this century, the proportion of white-collar workers rose to 52.2 percent by 1981.

However, large increases in the service sector and white-collar work have *not* required large decreases in industrial jobs. The percentage of blue-collar workers in Canada's labour force was not much lower in 1981 than in 1941. Agricultural, not industrial, work has declined as the post-industrial occupations grew: the percentage of Canadian workers employed in agriculture has fallen from 40.3 in 1901 to 4.1 in 1981.

The post-industrial thesis holds that future jobs will offer more creativity and stimulation by drawing more on people's skills. Yet many of the rapidly growing occupations—for example, truck-driving—are blue-collar jobs, and few among the rest require a higher education. Finally, none is outstandingly creative or stimulating. "Many of the growth occupations have little impact on training volumes. For many of them, there are numbers of unemployed people who can take the jobs without major training. Others involve low skill levels" (Canada, 1984, p. 4). Post-industrial jobs may not really improve Canadians' working lives in the foreseeable future. Furthermore, they are relatively low-status, low-paying jobs (see Table 4.1 for currently projected job opportunities).

An interesting finding in relation to the post-industrial thesis is that for only a small minority of respondents (about one in five) does the introduction of new technology pose a "serious problem" at work. Most workplaces have integrated the new technology painlessly.

Surveyed workers are twice as likely to believe that electronic technology has made their work more interesting, less hazardous to their health, less stressful, and better paying than to believe the opposite (Harvey, 1988, Table 8). By a smaller margin, they also believe it has made their work more challenging (rather than less). On the negative side, workers are slightly more likely to feel that technology has reduced their job security than to feel it has increased it. But note that 20 to 30 percent of respondents in each case deny that technology has had any impact whatever.

The post-industrial thesis holds that the refinement and spread of new technology—especially information technology—will radically change work and career prospects. But, in fact, nearly two

Rank	Code*	Occupational Title	Projected Employment 1983 1992 (000s)		Requirements (1983-92) Total (000s)
1	4111	Secretaries & steno	351.3	438.8	87.5
2	4131	Bookkeepers	368.2	448.5	80.3
3	9175	Truck drivers	238.0	310.0	72.0
4	1171	Financial officers	140.9	180.0	39.1
5	6191	Janitors	223.6	261.4	37.8
6	4133	Cashiers & tellers	229.6	263.8	34.2
7	8781	Carpenters	107.3	138.1	30.8
8	4197	Gen. office clerks	136.4	165.3	28.9
9	6125	Waiters	252.4	281.0	28.7
10	6115	Guards & oth. security	76.9	101.5	24.6
11	4113	Typists, clerk/typists	95.7	118.4	22.7
12	4171	Receptionists	90.4	112.0	21.6
13	1137	Sales mgmt. occs.	169.9	191.1	21.2
14	8798	Labourers: other cons.	54.2	74.9	20.7
15	3131	Nurses, grad., nonsuper.	185.5	206.1	20.6
16	8335	Welders	79.8	99.8	20.0
17	8584	Industrial farm mechanics	88.2	108.0	19.8
18	8581	Auto mechanics	140.7	160.0	19.3
19	8563	Sewing machine occs.	88.1	106.6	18.5
20	9171	Bus drivers	49.0	67.4	18.4
21	6121	Chefs & cooks	162.5	180.8	18.3
22	8780	Superv: other constr.	66.5	84.3	17.9
23	1130	Gen. managers	79.2	96.8	17.6
24	7195	Nursery workers	58.8	75.9	17.1
25	4143	E.D.P. equip. operators	71.3	88.1	16.8
26	6112	Police officers: govt.	53.8	69.3	15.5
27	4155	Stock clerks	91.5	106.6	15.1
28	2183	Systems analysts	56.8	71.9	15.1
29	4153	Shipping clerks	84.2	98.5	14.3
30	5133	Commercial traveller	95.9	109.6	13.7

*According to the *Standard Occupational Classification,* Statistics Canada, 1980.

TABLE 4.1 Occupations contributing most to employment growth: Canada, 1983-1992. (Source: *Canada, 1984, Annex 1, Figure 9.*)

in every three cases of reported technological innovation have occurred in offices and involve low-cost technologies such as word processing, personal computers, and office networks (Betcherman & McMullen, 1986). Most establishments introducing new technology (that is, "innovators") say these changes have created new jobs or substantially modified existing ones. But, in fact, non-innovators appear to create slightly more jobs than innovators.

Nor is it clear that technological change has had a major, positive effect on the nature of work, as the post-industrial thesis predicts. In general, most changes prove slight: many new jobs seem to require no more skill than the ones they replace. Nearly all establishments respond to new skill requirements by retraining the affected employees—often through brief, on-the-job programs. But skills that workers learn quickly on the job are unlikely to increase the work's complexity and challenge very substantially. About half of all retraining is to prepare women for clerical work—mainly data processing and word processing.

Do many jobs disappear when new technology is introduced? Some argue that job losses resulting from the greater efficiency of new technology must be balanced against the jobs created by additional sales (Betcherman & McMullen, 1986, p. 15). Others admit that technological change will drive some workers out of their jobs, especially in industries suffering slow economic growth; but they maintain that economic and market forces, not technology, ultimately determine employment levels (Ontario, 1985, p. 15).

Many disagree with these views. Critics of new technology point out that between 1980 and 1986, a period when microtechnology was widely introduced, Canadian banks cut 9000 employees (Rinehart, 1987, p. 85). While each older-generation robot eliminates 2.5 manufacturing jobs in West Germany, newer ones eliminate 5 to 10 jobs (Words Associated, 1986, p. 20). The Japanese Ministry of Labour found that 40 percent of companies introducing microelectronics later reduced their numbers of employees, and French job losses in banking and insurance due to information technology have been estimated at 30 percent (Schneider, 1984, p. 164).

Futures research, including the post-industrial thesis, certainly helps us to understand changes in work and careers. Yet the evidence supporting these models is contradictory. What should we conclude from the forecasts we have examined?

What Does the Future (Appear To) Hold? Different forecasting techniques yield somewhat different forecasts. But if the two most different approaches—linear extrapolation and futures research—point in a similar direction, we should consider taking that direction.

As already noted, linear extrapolation confines its attention to likely changes occurring in the next 5 or 10 years. It assumes that the near future will be a lot like the recent past. Much of our everyday experience shows that this is a reasonable assumption. Unfortunately, it is less helpful when we are planning a career that we hope will last 40 years, not 5 or 10.

Job Futures: An Occupational Outlook to 1995, which is based on COPS (Employment & Immigration Canada, 1988), predicts that the following 10 occupations will need the most new recruits between now and 1995 (numbers in parentheses are the numbers to be hired): waiters (89 000); retail salespeople (64 000); secretaries and stenographers (52 000); bookkeepers (51 000); chefs and cooks (51 000); tellers (38 000); janitors (38 000); truck drivers (26 000); accountants (23 000); and elementary school teachers (22 000).

All of these top-growth jobs are in the service sector, not manufacturing. This certainly agrees with Bell's post-industrial thesis. However, most of the top-growth jobs are not highly creative and do not require a lot of postsecondary education.

More worrisome is the fact that this set of predictions does not agree very closely with an earlier version of itself. Compare these recent predictions with those COPS made only four years earlier, as presented in Table 4.1 above. The predicted need for waiters has suddenly grown from 28 700 to 89 000; for chefs, from 18 000 to 51 000; and elementary school teachers are now in the top 10, whereas four years ago they did not appear in the top 30 occupations.

On the other hand, the predicted need for secretaries and stenographers has dropped from 87 500 to 52 000; for bookkeepers, from 80 300 to 51 000; for truck drivers, from 72 000 to 26 000. Carpenters, security guards, and office clerks have dropped out of the top ten occupations in this latest set of predictions.

These changes may reflect real changes in labour supply and demand, not problems with the prediction method. Moreover, people planning to enter occupations that require little educational preparation—waiter, teller, office clerk—may be able to adjust to a changing labour demand fairly painlessly. But people basing their higher education on COPS predictions will find adjustment more difficult.

Do we get a better result by consulting futures researchers? An example is given by Cetron (1984), who predicts the 500 best jobs of the future, "where they'll be and how to get them." Cetron's forecast and the COPS forecast agree that large numbers of additional waiters and waitresses, retail sales clerks, secretaries and stenographers, bookkeepers, chefs and cooks, truck drivers, accountants, and elementary school teachers will be needed in the near future.

In terms of their present numbers, Cetron expects rapid future growth in opportunities for secretaries and stenographers, chefs and cooks, and accountants; but only average or slow growth for the other top ten occupations COPS identified. Cetron also distinguishes between what he calls "new" jobs and old jobs that he believes are becoming obsolete. Among the slow-growing or obsolete jobs, he includes factory assembler (that is, assembly-line worker), bank cashier, farm worker, and farm manager. Although some of these jobs are likely to hire many people in the foreseeable future, they offer a declining prospect for future employment, and hence a poor bet for a career.

On the other hand, some occupations will allegedly hire millions of new workers in the near future and grow very rapidly. Some of these jobs already exist, others scarcely do. They include computer software writer, administrative assistant, energy conservation technician, hazardous-waste disposal technician, and housing rehabilitation technician. Each will need over a million new (American) workers by the turn of the century. Other relatively unheard-of jobs that Cetron estimates will need more than half a million new workers in the next 20 years include CAD (computeraided design) product engineer, computer terminal operator, computer operator, industrial laser process technician, engineering and science technician, geriatric-service worker, laser technician, and energy technician.

The picture futurists present, then, is of an industrial economy that is rapidly becoming post-industrial. Agriculture and manufacturing will offer people jobs of very different kinds from the past. Food will be increasingly produced on the ocean floor, in space, or in factories and laboratories. People in manufacturing will build, program, repair, and "supervise" robots. The use and

recycling of Earth's limited resources, whether for food or manu-
factured goods, will require more scientific know-how than ever.
Clerical workers in banks and offices will be replaced by com-
puterized equipment.

New technical specialties and new services—in sales and
information supply (education, guidance, consulting, and lobbying)—will rapidly establish themselves as major sources of work.
Some futures researchers predict that "five of the ten fastest-
growing jobs over the next few years will be computer-related,
with programmers and systems analysts growing by 70 percent
in the next ten years"; "services will account for 92 percent of
the jobs and 85 percent of the gross national product by the year
2000, compared with 70 percent of U.S. jobs and 60 percent of
GNP today"; and "25 to 35 percent of all paid work in the United
States will be done from people's homes by the turn of the century"
(*Outlook '87*, 1986, p. 5).

This rapidly and profoundly changing world of work demands
more and better education, whether you are training for a particular
vocation or not. To avoid being replaced by a machine, you have
to be more complex and more flexible than a machine. The "basics"
of education for a post-industrial work world include learning to
read and write effectively, communicate simply, manage information, and operate a computer. Moreover, Cetron advises you to
"learn your history and relate it to your future . . . learn to
learn . . . learn to think . . . and learn how to do it for the rest
of your life" (Cetron, 1984, p. 129).

Futurists believe that technical and service jobs now virtually
unknown will develop very rapidly; but this may be truer of the
American economy than of the Canadian one. The American
economy Cetron discusses is really much closer to post-
industrialism than the Canadian economy addressed by COPS.
Compare national expenditures on research and development. By
the early 1980s, Canadian research and development consumed
only one-third as much wealth per person as it did in Sweden,
and less than half what it did in the United States and Japan
(Harvey, 1988, Tables 6 & 7). As a percentage of the labour force,
scientists and researchers were less than half as likely to be
engaged in research and development in Canada as they were in
Japan or West Germany; Canada came well behind Holland, Swit-
zerland, and France in this respect.

Canada's relative backwardness in research and development
may account for its more traditional, industrial economy. Both,

in turn, result from the foreign control of Canada's industrial base. Multinational corporations operating in Canada carry out most of their (post-industrial) research and development activities at their head office (typically, in the United States).

This being so, post-industrial jobs for Canadians will only become more plentiful when research and development work is relocated by the multinational corporations, or when Canadians leave the country for post-industrial work elsewhere. (A third option, significant public investment in research and development, has yet to materialize despite much discussion of the possibility.) The likely impact of free trade on government research spending, the behaviour of multinationals, and the emigration of highly trained Canadians is hard to foresee.

What career should you enter? Whatever forecast we use, the estimates of employment opportunity for a variety of traditional *jobs* seem pretty stable. There is much less agreement about the opportunities in non-traditional *careers*. Indeed, COPS offers us job forecasts, not career forecasts: its time-perspective is very short. In the face of such uncertainty, get a good general education and examine your own heart. That is what Cetron means by "learn your history and relate it to your future." Pay a lot of attention to what you like doing and what you are good at. If you love, and are good at, a lot of things, use forecasts to choose a career from among your "loves."

Job Satisfaction

Job satisfaction is important. Most Canadians consider job satisfaction somewhat less important than marital, familial, and romantic satisfaction. And people learn to compensate for a dissatisfaction in one life domain with satisfaction in another, as we saw in Chapter 1. But satisfaction with your job remains an important part of life satisfaction. For a satisfying life, you will need to know more about job satisfaction: what it is, how you get it, and who has it.

Most people are "fairly satisfied" or "very satisfied" with their job (Atkinson, 1983a, Table 1; Environics, 1987). However, only half of all working Canadians would keep their current job if they were free to go into any type of job they wanted (Burstein, Tienhaara, Hewson, & Warrender, 1975; Environics, 1987). A great many had never planned to enter that job. In 1981, only 44 percent reported working in the field they had originally planned on—

half of these (in turn) because they could not find a job in their preferred field (Quality of Life survey, 1981). Less than one worker in four ended up doing a job he or she had really wanted.

At least 3350 articles or doctoral dissertations have been written on the topic of job satisfaction (Locke, 1976). Researchers have looked in three main directions to explain what causes people to be satisfied and dissatisfied with their jobs: *objective job characteristics*, such as working conditions, salary schemes, work schedule, union membership, and supervision patterns; *biographic characteristics*, such as age, gender, marital status, education, and religion; and *personality characteristics*, such as self-esteem, feelings of trust toward others, sense of mastery, and control over one's life (Burstein *et al.*, 1975, p. 26).

The bulk of research into causes of job satisfaction has focused on objective job characteristics.

> Previous research indicates that work satisfaction is engendered by work which is varied, allows autonomy, is not physically fatiguing, . . . is mentally challenging and yet allows the individual to experience success, and . . . is personally interesting. Satisfaction with rewards such as pay, promotions, and recognition depends on the fairness or equity with which they are administered and the degree to which they are congruent with the individual's personal aspirations. . . . The employee will be satisfied with agents in the work situation (supervisors, subordinates, co-workers, management) to the degree that they are seen as facilitating the attainment of his work goals and work rewards, and to the degree that these agents are perceived as having important values in common with him. (Locke, 1976, p. 1342)

Less is known about the contributions of personality and biographic characteristics to job satisfaction. For example, only one personality variable regularly appears to influence job satisfaction. Locke reports that "high self-esteem individuals will experience more pleasure in their work, other things being equal, than individuals with low self-esteem" (1976, p. 1344).

Moreover, studies have rarely compared the relative influence of objective job characteristics, biographic characteristics, and personality characteristics on job satisfaction. Two recent studies of job satisfaction—one a study of Canadians by King, Murray, and Atkinson (1982), and another a study of Americans by Rice, Near, and Hunt (1979)—try to do this, sorting through the three groups of characteristics to find out which matters most and by how much.

The two studies reach quite different conclusions about the importance of biographic characteristics in predicting job satisfaction. However, the study by King *et al.* —more believable because it collects more detailed data—finds that biographic characteristics add little to our understanding of job satisfaction once job and personality characteristics are taken into account.

One biographic characteristic that does predict job satisfaction quite reliably is age—that is, stage in the life cycle. As we have noted, people generally become more satisfied with life as they age. As well, older people are often less highly educated than younger people; and the less-educated are usually more satisfied with life (and work) than average Canadians. The data in Figure 4.1 show that, for both men and women, job satisfaction increases steadily with age.

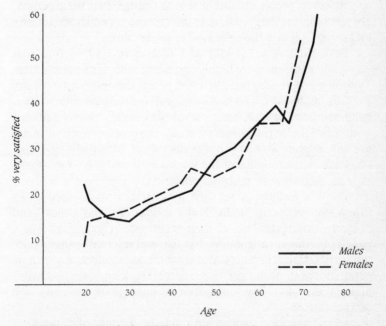

FIGURE 4.1   Percentage very satisfied with their job, by age and gender: Canada, 1981. *Includes people scoring 10 and 11 on an 11-point scale. A 10-year rolling average is used.* (Source: *Quality of Life survey, 1981.*)

King *et al.* find the following objective job characteristics particularly important influences on job satisfaction: occupational category, occupational prestige rating, yearly salary, years on the job, self-employment, union membership, shift-work require-ments, regularity of hours, control over the pace of work and overtime, degree of supervision, seriousness of danger, problems with working hours, and job-related mental or physical exhaustion at the end of the work day (1982, p. 125).

The Role of Personality   Whatever their job, people are able to change their behaviours, attitudes, expectations, desires, and even their values. Many sociological studies have shown the process by which people commit to, and identify with, particular jobs and careers (for examples, see Haas & Shaffir, 1978). So, for example, the factory worker promoted to supervisor gradually learns (and tries to adopt) the viewpoint of management; the young academic learns the viewpoint of grader, not graded; the physician or social worker learns to deal with suffering in a more practical, less idealistic way.

However, people are rarely able to change their basic person-ality. For this reason, you have to understand your own personality and try to fit it into the right kind of job or career.

Both King *et al.* (1982) and Rice *et al.* (1979) find that personality variables are highly correlated with work satisfaction. Typically, people who feel alienated or feel they have little control over life, and people who harbour negative sentiments about their neighbourhood, health, and general life course, are less satisfied with their jobs. In the King *et al.* study, these personality variables are only slightly *less* powerful predictors of job satisfaction than objective characteristics of the job itself; in the Rice *et al.* study, they are slightly *more* powerful predictors.

People's feelings about their jobs are best understood as an interaction between "individual expectations and traits" and "objective characteristics of their experience" (King *et al.*, 1982, p. 129). Feelings of alienation, distrust, and external control reduce job satisfaction. They may also combine with objective job char-acteristics such as danger, unpredictability, long hours, excessive supervision, and low occupational prestige to magnify job dissatisfaction.

Job/personality mismatching may be a cause of "burnout," the ultimate sign of job dissatisfaction and an apparently common malaise of professional and managerial workers (Freudenberger & Richelson, 1981). The internally motivated person who works in a setting that imposes strong external controls and/or random rewards for performance is a prime candidate for "burnout."

People need to know enough about their own personalities and the jobs they are thinking of entering to anticipate whether they will find a given job satisfying. You should not become a police officer if you hate rules and routines, or a novelist if you crave imposed order, or a door-to-door sales representative if you need continuous approval. Of course, less-satisfying jobs should be reorganized to eliminate their dissatisfying characteristics. All in all, universal job improvement and a better allocation of personalities to positions will increase everyone's satisfaction. But for the time being, career-choosers need to be particularly alert to the worst features of the job they are thinking of entering.

Unfortunately, social class significantly influences what people get out of their work life, just as it affects the rest of their life. People in the working class and lower middle class are particularly likely to hold jobs with objectively dissatisfying features: low pay, high risk of unemployment, shift work, dangerous or unpleasant working conditions, and so on.

Moreover, their jobs typically combine low prestige and a high degree of external control. Consider the data on job control provided by the Quality of Life (1981) survey: 45 percent of manual workers report being supervised frequently on their job, 34 percent are required to produce a quota at work, and only 30 percent are able to leave work to do an errand at any time. Further, 31 percent have experienced some unemployment in the past two years and 25 percent have experienced a layoff during the same period (Ornstein, 1988, Table 5). All these conditions and experiences create feelings of alienation, external control, and even distrust.

By contrast, only 8 percent of managers and technocrats report being supervised frequently and only 15 percent are required to produce a quota; on the other hand, 83 percent say they are able to leave work to do an errand at any time. Only 15 percent of the managers and technocrats experienced some unemployment in the preceding two years, and a mere 4 percent experienced a layoff in the same period. Managers' objective job conditions are very much better—more satisfying—than manual workers', and also much less likely to excite feelings of alienation, external control, and distrust.

The combination of personality and job characteristics may be particularly problematic for working-class people. If working-class life "incapacitates" by giving people low self-esteem, people in highly alienating and unprestigious work will suffer particularly great job dissatisfaction. They will also substitute "extrinsic" for "intrinsic" job goals: that is, shift away from looking for pleasure in work to looking for decent pay and working conditions.

In jobs where intrinsic satisfaction is generally high, workers are less influenced by the level of extrinsic satisfactions (for example, pay, working hours, working conditions) than in jobs where intrinsic satisfaction is low. "Among unskilled/semiskilled and clerical workers, pay, job conditions, and the social environment of the job are more important than among skilled workers or professional/technical workers. Extrinsic rewards become an important determinant of overall job satisfaction only among workers for whom intrinsic rewards are relatively unavailable" (Gruenberg, 1980, p. 268).

Managers and workers value extrinsic and intrinsic job facets differently. "Future research must be careful to distinguish between the categories of employees when discussing the contribution of various job factors to employee job satisfaction" (Ronen & Sadan, 1984, pp. 92, 94). People's job satisfaction will reflect the degree to which expectations are being met: lower-status workers will expect satisfactory extrinsic rewards, higher-status workers intrinsic ones. The disappointment of such expectations will diminish job satisfaction.

The key to job satisfaction, like the key to life satisfaction generally, is matching expectations to real possibilities. Given enough time, people can change their expectations; and they can take satisfaction from "substitute" rewards, once they expect them. As we saw in Chapter 1, in order to achieve satisfaction, people commonly learn to want what they can get. Trends in job satisfaction will reflect changes in the match-up between what people are getting and what they have learned to expect. What, then, are these trends?

Trends in Job Satisfaction   In a large review of the research on changing job satisfaction, Mortimer (1979) reports that

> workers in all occupations are expressing greater discontent with their jobs. This represents a reversal of

the previous stability in job satisfaction from the late fifties to the early seventies. Not surprisingly, the younger and college-educated workers are spearheading this new trend. Although there is little evidence that change has occurred in work values, the rising educational attainment of the labor force would suggest that aspirations have risen. What is certain is that workers of today, in all occupational categories, seek both intrinsic and extrinsic satisfaction from their jobs. (p. 16)

Mortimer finds American evidence of "declines in satisfaction in virtually all segments of the working population . . . [despite] a continuing high involvement with work as a central focus of life." Likewise, between 1977 and 1981, the percentage of Canadian workers saying they were "very satisfied" with their jobs dropped substantially. In fact, this was the largest drop in any of the numerous indicators used to measure the quality of life (Atkinson, 1983b, p. 48).

In the Quality of Life (1981) survey, workers aged 30 to 44 showed the biggest declines in job satisfaction, followed by workers aged 18 to 29. In addition, workers in "better" jobs showed greater declines than workers in "worse" jobs. Atkinson divided the seven occupational groups into two categories—professional and supervisory, and operational employee—with the higher-status (or "better") jobs within each category listed first. Drops in job satisfaction between 1977 and 1981 were greatest among the higher-status workers in both categories. Although workers in the higher-status occupations were still more satisfied than the rest, differences between the high- and low-status groups had narrowed.

Interestingly, workers' pay had little to do with the fall in satisfaction, even though the economy had worsened. Nonmonetary factors mattered more: job attributes apparently worsening between 1977 and 1981 were "influence on supervisor" and "opportunities for advancement." The relative drop in these attributes was so striking that Atkinson judged they played the biggest role in reducing general job satisfaction by 1981. All categories of workers reported less influence on decision-making in 1981, except for young workers aged 18 to 29, who had rated their influence low in 1977 as well. Declines in influence were also greater among females and among older, more experienced employees.

The even greater drop in employees' perceptions of their opportunities for promotion shows that this was the area of work reducing satisfaction most between 1977 and 1981. Women, workers aged 30 to 44, professionals, managers, and skilled labourers felt the greatest losses of opportunity. In explaining the drop in opportunities for advancement, Atkinson focuses on the economic recession of the early 1980s, and changes in Canada's demography. As Staines (1979) suggested, job satisfaction must be understood in the context of larger, society-wide transformations.

Faced with the recession, employers tried to cut down the number and cost of their employees. This effort was particularly directed at employees with high salaries—managers, professionals, and skilled labourers—often through programs encouraging early retirement. Senior employees were, and are still being, removed but not replaced by others in line for promotion. Recall that the highest-status employees in each of Atkinson's two categories reported the greatest losses in job satisfaction. A major cause was shrinking opportunities for promotion due to employers' cost-cutting strategies.

Meanwhile, between 1971 and 1981, the number of Canadian workers aged 30 to 44 jumped to 32 percent. More and more employees in this age range were competing for a fixed and sometimes diminishing number of middle- and upper-level jobs. As a result, this age group perceived fewer opportunities for advancement between 1977 and 1981. Because the number of workers aged 30 to 44 will grow by another 25 to 30 percent between 1981 and 1991, Atkinson predicts intensified competition. Unless newcomers into the labour force scale down their expectations, perceptions of little opportunity for advancement will continue to pull down Canadians' feelings of job satisfaction.

Canadian women experienced even sharper drops than men in satisfaction with their jobs, influence on superiors' decisions, and perceived opportunities for advancement. In 1977 women generally expressed more job satisfaction than men, but by 1981 they were slightly less satisfied. Male–female differences in job satisfaction are partly caused by women's continued underrepresentation in higher-status occupations. Women in the skilled and semiskilled occupations—including most office and sales jobs—experienced major drops in job satisfaction between 1977 and 1981 because of reduced opportunities for advancement and, much more than for males, less influence on superiors' decisions.

The most recent research on job satisfaction shows these trends continuing. Job satisfaction continues to decline generally, but most particularly among the young and more highly educated workers. Workers today are particularly dissatisfied with opportunities for advancement or promotion, benefits, and chances to participate in decision-making. And, of professional workers, women are more dissatisfied with their opportunities for advancement than are men (Environics, 1987).

Responses to the current frustration with limited opportunity take various forms. Some people are working longer hours than ever before. On the other hand, increasing numbers say they expect to make major changes: 43 percent expect to change careers, 50 percent to change employers, 32 percent to take early retirement (that is, before age 60), and 59 percent to take retraining or further education (Environics, 1987).

People's orientations to "the job" are changing, too, suggesting a substitution of family and leisure activities for job and career concerns. In a recent national poll (Environics, 1987), 42 percent of respondents indicate that they are unwilling to give up leisure time, and 51 percent are unwilling to accept a transfer, even if it would advance their career. Women are particularly unwilling to give up leisure and family time for the sake of their careers.

Can You Find Satisfaction?   Some people believe that *no* forecasts are of any use. For example, Selleck (1982, pp. 41–42) argues that occupational forecasts often produce unreliable projections because current methods are not sufficiently developed, data are often incomplete or obsolete, and the labour market changes unpredictably. However, others (for example, Stager, 1983) view occupational forecasts as essential to any effective career strategy; this book shares their view.

The recent past is not a perfect guide to the near future, much less the distant future. But linear extrapolation has some value. Similarly, demographic patterns are very important in identifying good opportunities. Take them into account if your intended career is geared to a particular age group, or is now heavily loaded with young or old workers.

Our economy is increasingly a service economy, and service work depends on flexibility and on cognitive and interpersonal skills (Hunter, forthcoming), not just a single job skill and credential. Get as much education and as many appropriate credentials as you can: but most of all, learn how to learn, think, and communicate. The bachelor's degree—whether in arts, commerce, or engineering—continues to be a good credential for many career purposes. Increasing numbers are finding that degrees in administration, management, or law offer additional skills and flexibility in a great many service industries.

Occupations that serve capitalism most directly—such as bookkeeping, accounting, financial counselling, and corporate law—are doing well today. Occupations that do not turn a profit—such as jobs in education, social services, and the fine arts—go through better and worse periods. The self-employing, self-regulating professions—medicine and dentistry in particular—continue to be safe, well-paid services, while other professions such as architecture, certain kinds of engineering, and law are much more tied to the business cycle.

Because of the unpredictability of many careers you might choose, you should pay a great deal of attention to your own feelings, interests, and aptitudes. If you can, avoid a career that does not interest you, because it is not likely to satisfy you. Can everyone get job satisfaction? Some jobs are downright dissatisfying. At the same time, some people are harder to please than others; they would not be happy even with a job they had invented for themselves. One way to minimize your own frustration is by being clear on where the problem lies. Know yourself well enough to know whether the problem is you or your job. Know yourself—your interests, aptitudes, and weaknesses—well enough to choose a job that shows off your best features, not your worst.

Futures researchers expect major changes in the objective job conditions that influence satisfaction. For example, technology will likely blur the boundaries between work and play, freeing creativity; "horizontal" (that is, less hierarchical and more egalitarian) organizations will become the new global standard; workers will have legal rights to jobs and affirmative action will expand; job-seekers and managers alike will create (and use) new career categories; part-time work will increase, bringing change to social mores and standards of comparison; training and retraining workers will be an important challenge for unions; and retirement may become obsolete (ASPA, 1984).

The rapidly changing world of work needs people and organizations that can change. Organizational change is a lot easier when employees exercise self-control and have internalized the goals of the employer. Economist Richard Edwards (1979) has called this kind of structure "bureaucratic control."

Bureaucratic control promises career rewards for conformity and effective performance; it is most common in large, complex offices that manage production, provide services, or manipulate information. Employees see that by getting good evaluations and pleasing their supervisors, they can advance up the hierarchy to ever better, more responsible, and higher-paying jobs. This leads employees to think about the future consequences of their actions. This form of control generates a strong sense of loyalty to the organization, because the fates of the organization and the worker are so closely tied. Such motivations are crucially important in work that cannot be closely or continuously supervised, a characteristic of professional and semiprofessional work.

This kind of control seems most likely to provide highly educated workers with job satisfaction in large organizations. Moreover, it is compatible with technological and organizational change, as long as the organization continues to make good on promises of job security and career advancement. It seems to satisfy a great many of the criteria Locke (1976) has identified as objective job characteristics that lead to job satisfaction. This kind of control certainly seems to have worked well in Japan!

Concluding Remarks

Choosing the job that is right for you—the job that will satisfy you—is not simply a matter of knowing which fields will be hiring a great many people in the foreseeable future.

An important job characteristic, as we have seen, is the locus of control. You will probably want to find out whether the job (and career) you are intending offers sufficient opportunity for autonomy and responsibility, combined with a secure career ladder. Some jobs and organizations will offer more of these than others. Before starting out on a particular career, be sure to speak to people who are in it and find out their experiences.

Do people get what they want out of their work and careers, or learn to want what they can get? On the one hand, what people get may result from earlier choices, especially educational ones. For women, marital and childbearing choices also influence work and career, as we shall see in the chapters that follow. Yet most people are just as unaware of the long-term consequences of their educational, marital, and childbearing choices as they are of long-term trends in the job market. They need better information about the likely consequences of their decisions.

Moreover, people often choose careers without considering their own aptitudes, passions, or interests. So they often fail to get what they wanted because they did not know all the things they were choosing when they exercised their choice. As well, people are likely to change their minds about what they want as they get older. What they want at one age or stage in the life cycle is not necessarily what they will want at a later stage.

Do people learn to want what they get? To a large degree they do. As people age, they become more satisfied with their work and career. And people who grow up in difficult economic conditions, as have the post-baby boomers, tend to have more moderate, practical goals, so they will always be more satisfied than people with too-high goals.

Although this book is aimed at helping you make better choices, many problems you face will require collective, not individual action. Job reform is certainly one area where collective action will be needed. Reforms are unlikely to take place unless the affected workers bring enough collective pressure to bear on management. Unions play this role in many workplaces. Technology will not solve these problems. To solve them completely requires collective action; in the long run, many such problems may get solved.

But we live in the short run. Take collective action but take individual action as well: know yourself, prepare yourself, change. These principles will prove as important in Chapter 5, which is about another—quite different—domain: the family.

References

ASPA (AMERICAN SOCIETY FOR PERSONNEL ADMINISTRATION). (1984). *Work in the 21st century: An anthology of writings on the changing world of work*. Alexandria, VA: ASPA.

ATKINSON, T. (1983a).   Changing attitudes toward work in Canada. *Canadian Business Review, 10*(1), 39–44.

_____. (1983b).   Differences between male and female attitudes toward work. *Canadian Business Review, 10*(2), 47–51.

BELL, D. (1973).   *The coming of post-industrial society.* New York: Basic Books.

BETCHERMAN, G., & MCMULLEN, K. (1986). *Working with technology: A survey of automation in Canada* (Catalogue No. EC 22-133/1986E). Ottawa: Economic Council of Canada.

BLAU, P.M., & DUNCAN, O.D. (1967). *The American occupational structure.* New York: Wiley.

BOYD, M., GOYDER, J., JONES, F.E., MCROBERTS, H.A., PINEO, P.C., & PORTER, J. (Eds.). (1985). *Ascription and achievement: Studies in mobility and status attainment in Canada.* Ottawa: Carleton University Press.

BURSTEIN, M., TIENHAARA, N., HEWSON, P., & WARRENDER, B. (1975). *Canadian work values: Findings of a work ethic survey and a job satisfaction survey* (Catalogue No. MP 33-6/1975). Ottawa: Department of Manpower & Immigration.

CANADA. (1984). *Consultation Paper: Training* (Catalogue No. MP 43-159/1984). Ottawa: Supply & Services.

CASALE, A., & LERMAN, P. (1986). *USA Today: Tracking tomorrow's trends.* Kansas City: Andrews, McNeel & Parker.

CETRON, M.J. (1984). *Jobs of the future.* New York: McGraw-Hill Ryerson.

EASTERLIN, R.A. (1980). *Birth and fortune: The impact of numbers on personal welfare.* New York: Basic Books.

EDWARDS, R. (1979). *Contested terrain: The transformation of the workplace in the twentieth century.* New York: Basic Books.

EMPLOYMENT & IMMIGRATION CANADA. (1986). *Job futures: An occupational outlook to 1992* (Catalogue No. MP 43-181/1986E). Ottawa: Supply & Services.

_____. (1988). *Job futures: An occupational outlook to 1995* (Catalogue No. MP 43-181). Ottawa: Supply & Services.

ENVIRONICS RESEARCH GROUP. (1987, November). How do you like your job? *Report on Business Magazine*, pp. 112-125.

FOOT, D.K. (1982). *Canada's population outlook: Demographic futures and economic challenges.* The Canadian Institute for Economic Policy Series. Toronto: Lorimer.

FREUDENBERGER, H.J., & RICHELSON, G. (1981). *Burn-out: The high cost of achievement.* Toronto: Bantam Books.

GRUENBERG, B. (1980). The happy worker: An analysis of educational and occupational differences in determinants of job satisfaction. *American Journal of Sociology, 86*(2), 247-271.

HAAS, J., & SHAFFIR, W. (Eds.). (1978). *Shaping identity in Canadian society.* Scarborough: Prentice-Hall.

HARVEY, E.B. (1988). Science and technology. In J. Curtis & L. Tepperman (Eds.), *Understanding Canadian society.* Toronto: McGraw-Hill Ryerson.

HUNTER, A.A. (forthcoming). Formal education and initial employment. *American Sociological Review.*

KETTLE, J. (1980). *The big generation*. Toronto: McClelland & Stewart.

KING, M., MURRAY, M.A., & ATKINSON, T. (1982). Background personality, job characteristics, and satisfaction with work in a national sample. *Human Relations, 35*(2), 119–133.

LOCKE, E.A. (1976). The nature and causes of job satisfaction. In M.D. Dunnette (Ed.), *Handbook of Industrial and Organization Psychology* (pp. 1297–1349). Chicago: Rand McNally.

MARSHALL, K. (1987, Winter). Women in male-dominated professions. *Canadian Social Trends*, pp. 7–11.

MORTIMER, J.T. (1979). *Changing attitudes towards work*. Studies in Productivity Series. Scarsdale, NY: Work in America Institute.

ONTARIO. (1985). Task Force on Employment and New Technology. *Final Report: Employment and New Technology*. Toronto.

ORNSTEIN, M. (1988). Social class and economic inequality. In J. Curtis & L. Tepperman (Eds.), *Understanding Canadian Society*. Toronto: McGraw-Hill Ryerson.

OUTLOOK '87 AND BEYOND. (1986). Bethesda, MD: World Future Society.

PICOT, W.G. (1987, Spring). The changing industrial mix of employment, 1951–1985. *Canadian Social Trends* (Statistics Canada, Catalogue No. 11-008E, pp. 8–11). Ottawa: Supply & Services.

QUALITY OF LIFE SURVEY. (1981). Unpublished raw data from large survey of life satisfaction conducted at the Institute for Behavioural Research, York University, Toronto.

RICE, R.W., NEAR, J.P., & HUNT, R.G. (1979). Unique variance in job and life satisfaction associated with work-related and extra-workplace variables. *Human Relations, 32*(7), 605–623.

RINEHART, J.W. (1987). *The tyranny of work: Alienation and the labour process* (2nd ed.). Toronto: Harcourt Brace Jovanovich.

RONEN, S., & SADAN, S. (1984). Job attitudes among different occupational status groups: An economic analysis. *Work and Occupations, 11*(1), 77–97.

SCHNEIDER, R. (1984). Technological development and its aftermath. In P. Ayrton, T. Engelhardt, & V. Ware (Eds.), *World View 1985*. London: Pluto Press.

SELLECK, L. (1982). *Manpower planning and higher education policy*. Toronto: Council of Ontario Universities.

STAGER, D. (1983). Dynamic information for entrants to the highly qualified labour market. *Canadian Journal of Higher Education, 13*(1), 65–74.

STAINES, G.L. (1979, May–June). Is worker dissatisfaction rising? *Challenge*, pp. 38–45.

TEPPERMAN, L. (1985). Musical chairs: the occupational experience of migrants to Alberta, 1976-80. *Social Indicators Research, 16*, 51–67.

WOODS GORDON. (1986). *Tomorrow's customers* (19th ed.). Toronto.

WORDS ASSOCIATED. (1986). *Workable futures: Notes on emerging technologies* (Catalogue No. EC 22-132/1986E). Ottawa: Economic Council of Canada.

Chapter Five

Single or Married: *what you want and what you get*

Introduction

Chapter 1 showed that Canadians put a high value on romance and family life. It follows that average Canadians should attach great importance to getting married, being married, and staying married. If so, married Canadians should be more satisfied with their lives than unmarried Canadians.

On the other hand, evidence of dramatic change in family life surrounds us. That is not to say family life in the past was static or uniform. Change is the rule in social life, not the exception. Furthermore, diversity always exists within continuity. Yet change today may be more rapid and diversity more marked than in the past. It may be impossible today to talk about the *typical* family or the *typical* marriage. Major trends include smaller families, more single-parent families, more families created by remarriage, more dual-earner families, and more people living alone. The old-style "monolithic" family model (Eichler, 1981) no longer applies, a fact with far-reaching consequences for the ways we prepare ourselves to live, marry, and make social policy (Eichler, 1988).

Three questions bearing on this topic appear to interest students: (1) Should I marry or remain single? (2) Should I have (many) serious relationships outside marriage? and (3) What should I look for in a partner? Let us restate these questions so they can be addressed with data:

1. *How does marital status (married versus single, separated, divorced, or otherwise) affect people's life satisfaction?* Answering this question forces us to examine evidence that marriage brings the outcomes or benefits people hope it will.
2. *Do non-marital romantic relationships provide as much satisfaction as marital relationships do?* and *Does "experience"*

make people more aware of what is needed for marital satis-
faction, or better able to choose the right partner? To answer
these, we will need to know something about what Canadians
actually do—about the prevalence of, duration of, and satisfaction with various kinds of romantic relationship—and
what Canadians think about these relationships.

3. *What qualities in a mate produce the maximum marital*
   satisfaction and stability? and *Do similarities or differences*
   between mates do more to increase the likelihood of satis-
   faction and marital stability?

Readers who are already married may find this chapter interesting if it helps them understand the choices they have already
made: when and why they got married, and to whom. Moreover,
they may find that the discussion of marital satisfaction helps
them understand and evaluate the experiences they are currently
having in marriage. As before, this chapter will close by considering
whether, in the domain of marriage and family, people get what
they want or learn to want what they get.

To Marry or Not to Marry

Is marriage really satisfying? Surveys show that marriage runs
from the heights to the depths of satisfaction. Marriage is an
extremely variable state, but most Canadians report being very
satisfied with marriage. Moreover, married Canadians—both male
and female—are twice as likely to be very satisfied with life than
separated Canadians, and 60 percent more likely to say they are
very satisfied than divorced Canadians (Quality of Life survey,
1981). The proportion of never-married people expressing great
satisfaction lies midway between that of the married and that of
the separated or divorced. They are less satisfied than the married—
not surprising in view of the importance Canadians attach to being
married—but more satisfied than the divorced and separated, for
whom marriage (or a particular mate) has proven unsuccessful
and dissatisfying.

Given the satisfaction marriage appears to bring, one is
surprised to discover that by 1985 rates of first marriage had fallen
to an all-time low in Canada. This declining national marriage
rate has been led by large declines in Quebec, which "has not
only the lowest rate of all the provinces but one of the lowest

rates in the world" (Statistics Canada, 1987, p. 19). The trend of people, particularly young people, opting for common-law unions over marriage partly explains this decline in marriages.

As well, there is evidence that people are merely delaying, not rejecting marriage, so that the average age at first marriage is increasing. In 1984 the average age of females at first marriage was 24.3 years, close to the highest since registration began in 1921 (namely, 24.9 years, recorded in 1942 during World War II). Grooms, averaging age 26.6 at first marriage in 1984, are still quite far from their all-time high (28.3 years, recorded in 1938 during the worst part of the Great Depression).

Historically, late marriage has been associated with high proportions never marrying (Hajnal, 1965). Both are a response to unfavourable economic conditions that make marrying and childbearing too risky. People who delay marriage beyond a certain age often lose interest in ever marrying; they become accustomed to the single life and, for women, childbearing becomes riskier or impossible. So both increased common-law cohabitation and delayed marriage reflect a flight from marriage and will likely lead to lower percentages of people ever marrying.

Data in Table 5.1 show that the probability of marrying for the first time drops steadily from age 20 onward, and increasingly quickly after age 25. After age 35, the likelihood of marrying is well below 50 percent, especially for women. What is particularly remarkable is the declining probability since 1971, of marriage

	Men			Women		
	1971	1976	1981	1971	1976	1981
At age			%			
15	95.3	92.7	89.1	95.1	92.8	89.7
20	94.9	92.3	88.2	93.3	90.8	88.1
25	88.1	85.2	81.7	79.6	77.8	75.0
30	70.6	68.7	63.8	58.3	57.3	52.2
35	51.0	50.4	44.1	37.2	39.4	33.4
40	36.3	35.5	29.1	27.0	25.8	21.5
45	25.4	24.9	20.0	17.6	17.2	13.9

TABLE 5.1 Probability of marrying for never-married people, by gender and age: Canada, 1971, 1976, and 1981. (Source: *Nagnur and Adams, 1987, p. 5.*)

at any given age. For example, a 30-year-old male is only 90 percent as likely to marry in future as the same-aged male ten years earlier, in 1971. Thirty-year-old women show a similar 10 percent decline in marriage chances by 1981. Project these trends forward to 1991 and the result is intriguing for people who have never married.

On the other hand, one type of marriage has grown much more common: remarriage. The number of marriages in which at least one of the spouses was previously married has more than doubled since 1968, when divorces became easier to obtain. And, given fewer first marriages, remarriages came to represent over twice as high a proportion of all marriages in 1985 as they did in 1968 (Statistics Canada, 1987, Table 5; Ambert, 1988). Recently, three marriages in ten were remarriages for one or both partners.

This tendency of the divorced to remarry is one main source of evidence that marriage remains a desired state. Canadians who divorce are not rejecting marriage *per se*, but only a particular partner. The search for an ideal mate continues. According to Ambert (1988), lower-SES women need remarriage for sheer economic survival. In general, remarriage rates may reflect economic as well as cultural and psychological forces in society. The recent decline in remarriage rates may reflect an easing of these economic pressures.

Marriage appears to give most Canadians life satisfaction, but it also creates the risk of separation and divorce, two very dissatisfying conditions. In fact, divorced and separated people are about twice as likely as married people to feel a low level of satisfaction with their lives. So for many, marriage raises life satisfaction above what they would get by never marrying. But, for many others who remain in bad marriages—for example, the 10 percent of wives who are battered—or end up divorcing, marriage lowers life satisfaction. Leaving aside the unhappily married who remain together, how likely is the event of divorce or separation? Marriage is not quite so attractive if the chance of marital breakdown is high.

Rates of divorce remained fairly steady—at about 200 divorces per 100 000 married women aged 15 and over each year—from 1952 through 1968 (Statistics Canada, 1982, p. 4). With law reforms that made divorcing a spouse easier after 1968, the rates shot up fivefold—to 1000 divorces per year per 100 000 married women—by 1978. Rates levelled off in the 1980s, then started to fall (Statistics Canada, 1987, p. 22).

This decline in marriage breakdowns may be more apparent than real. Some couples may have been waiting for recent amendments to the Divorce Act before starting proceedings. Other couples may be breaking up and forming new (common-law) unions without going through the formalities of divorce.

By 1984, when Statistics Canada conducted a national Family History Survey (Burch, 1985), one man in ten and one woman in eight who had ever been married had divorced at least once. Among ever-married men and women who were aged 40 to 49 in 1984—people who had been exposed to 16 years of easy access to divorce in their prime marrying years—nearly one man in seven and one woman in six reports a divorce (Burch, 1985, Table 3A). Another 4 to 5 percent of ever-married people report having separated but not divorced at some point in their marriage (Burch, 1985, Table 3C).

Your risk of divorce upon marrying is at least 30 percent if current rates continue to prevail (Burch & Madan, 1986). Some (for example, McKie, Prentice, & Reed, 1983; Eichler, 1988) believe that the divorce risks facing young people today are closer to 40 percent.

However, people from different regions of the country and different educational levels vary widely in rates of divorce. The rates are much lower than average in the East—Atlantic provinces and Quebec—and much higher than average in the west—British Columbia (Burch, 1985, Table 19). Likewise, people who complete a postsecondary education are about half as likely to ever divorce as people with no more than a secondary school education (Burch, 1985, Table 20). Age is also an important factor: your risk of divorce is higher the younger you are when you marry, and higher too if this is your own (or your spouse's) second or later marriage (Ambert, 1988, Chapter 6).

Determinants of Marital Satisfaction   The recently married will have enjoyed greater freedom to experiment sexually, and to marry whom and when they wanted, than earlier generations were able to do. For this reason, we might think they are more likely to have made the "right" choice for the right reasons. They *should* be more satisfied with marriage. Yet the data do not confirm our expectations. Except for young people in their very earliest years of marriage, older people are slightly more satisfied with marriage, and with life generally, than younger people of the same marital status (Quality of Life survey, 1981).

So greater choice does not necessarily produce greater satisfaction. Alternatively, the growth in choice through sexual freedom has been offset by a reduction in economic choice. Two incomes are almost a necessity, for reasons Ehrenreich (1983) has spelled out in a history of the demise of the "breadwinner ethic."

The factor influencing marriage's effect on life satisfaction most significantly is gender. On average, married women are more satisfied with life than never-married women, who are, in turn, more satisfied with life than divorced and separated women. But as we shall see, the sentiments of married women are extremely diverse.

Divorced and separated women are much less likely to be highly satisfied with life than divorced and separated men. Although divorced and separated men have much higher rates of emotional problems than divorced and separated women, divorced and separated women tend to suffer many more severe financial and social hardships than divorced and separated men (Gove, 1970; Ambert, 1980, 1988). They have greater difficulty finding satisfactory work, getting a living wage, and meeting eligible people of the opposite sex. Further, women suffer more difficulties in aging than men do.

In addition, divorced and separated women more often have the major responsibility for raising the children of a broken marriage. After divorce, about one father in three pays for child support regularly and about one in two sees his children regularly. At all ages, divorced men have higher remarriage rates than women, and remarry more quickly. Their involvement in new families lessens their commitment (financial and emotional) to previous ones. As a consequence, in Canada today, a majority of female-headed, single-parent families live below the poverty line. After a marriage breaks down, men usually continue in the same line of work, more easily meet single (typically younger) women, and are free of most child-raising duties. Women can depend on none of these opportunities.

Marriage remains a greater risk for women than for men. Though women appear to gain more life satisfaction from a marriage's success, they also lose far more if the marriage fails. Overall, husbands are more satisfied with their marriages than wives (Rhyne, 1984). But wives are both more likely than husbands to be very satisfied with their marriage *and* more likely to be somewhat dissatisfied. That is, marital satisfaction is more variable and less predictable for women. Generally, married and remarried women are less happy maritally than married and remarried men (Ambert, 1988).

The psychic costs of a failing marriage fall more heavily on female than male shoulders. Further, "women have higher expectations of marriage than men and thus tend to evaluate their current situations more critically" (Rhyne, 1984, p. 8). In any event, the correlation between marital satisfaction and overall life satisfaction is much stronger for wives than it is for husbands. Because of structured inequality, marriage is more necessary for women than for men. The most satisfied couples are in egalitarian marriages where the husband and wife share responsibilities equally; the least satisfied are in traditional marriages where the husband is head of the household and the wife is subservient.

Men, not women, benefit more from marriage. Men need and like marriage more than women and are much more likely to remarry. Research shows that men's best friends are their wives, while wives almost never list their husbands as best friends. Moreover, marriage increases men's life expectancy far more than women's. Keyfitz (1988) shows that Canadian men increase their life expectancy five years by marrying, while women increase it only one-and-a-half years. By this measure, marriage is over three times as beneficial to men as to women. Moreover, other measures of physical and emotional well-being (for example, see those cited in Bernard, 1973) point in the same direction.

When you review the responsibilities women have in families—ably documented in Meg Luxton's *More Than a Labour of Love* (1980)—the finding that men are more satisfied with marriage is understandable. It is not just that women have higher expectations about marriage than men: men actually benefit more from marriage.

Marriage has no significant effect on a man's occupational attainment. But it has a definite *negative* influence on a woman's occupational attainment. Women in the full-time labour force who do *not* bear children are unaffected by marriage. But "the birth and presence of children . . . depress the achievements of younger women in the full-time labour force" (Boyd, 1985, pp. 271, 273).

The Changing Qualities of a Relationship   Like gender, age influences marital satisfaction. Married people under age 65 are more likely to feel moderately satisfied than extremely satisfied with marriage (Quality of Life survey, 1981). After age 65, a majority are extremely satisfied. Between ages 31 and 45—the period of child-raising—people are nearly *twice* as likely to feel moderate satisfaction as they are to feel highly positive satisfaction with their marriage.

This U-shaped relationship between marital satisfaction and age is found for both men and women (see Figure 5.1). A similar U-shaped relationship between marital satisfaction and duration of marriage is also found in the Quality of Life (1981) data. Moreover, the same relationship is found if we analyse separately people married only once and people married before.

Asked about their marital satisfaction, nearly three in four newlyweds (people married less than a year) who are without children will express the very highest level of satisfaction—a score of 11 on an 11-point scale. Let us call that state of mind "enchantment"; it is a state of mind that Dorothy Tennov (1979), who called something similar "limerence," says lasts for about two years on average, among those who experience it at all.

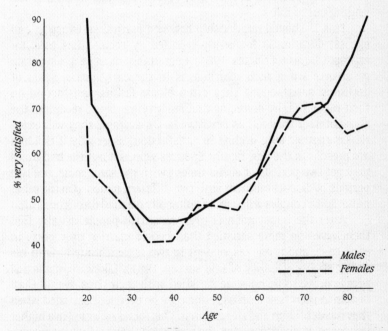

FIGURE 5.1 Percentage very satisfied with marriage, by age and gender: Canada, 1981. *Includes people scoring 10 and 11 on an 11-point scale. A 10-year rolling average is used.* (Source: *Quality of Life survey, 1981.*)

Among people married from one to five years, the percentage still "enchanted" has dropped to just over one person in two. Part of the decline in marital satisfaction is due to childbearing, an effect we shall discuss at length in Chapter 6. After that, around 45 percent remain enchanted until a marriage has gone on for 31 years or more, when the percentage edges back up to roughly two people in three. People married more than 50 years are nearly as likely to be enchanted with marriage as when they were newlyweds!

Some of this return to satisfaction with marriage is more apparent than real. People in our society are supposed to be happy with marriage, and are embarrassed to say otherwise. Unhappy people tend to drop out of surveys, are difficult to locate, and are generally less likely to answer questions. Moreover, these findings are based on cross-sectional, not longitudinal, data—which is to say we are comparing different people at different ages, not the same people as they age. Yet the same findings have been obtained in so many different studies that one is reluctant to dismiss the finding out of hand.

This U-shaped relationship between marital satisfaction and marital duration is frequently reported by sociologists (see, for example, Lupri & Frideres, 1981). Regrettably, most people separate or divorce when their marriage is in the early years, years of declining satisfaction. They often blame falling satisfaction on their mate and, by divorcing and remarrying, try to recapture the enchantment they felt as newlyweds. On average, they will experience another long decline in satisfaction, especially if children are present in the new family. Spouses who last out the bad times may get two periods of enchantment with the same mate, not two periods of disenchantment with two different mates. (On the other hand, some couples will remain unhappily married throughout life.)

After the honeymoon is over, remarried people usually find themselves no more satisfied than people married only once. In each case, about one respondent in two is "enchanted" with his or her spouse (Quality of Life survey, 1981). Likewise, remarried people prove to be no more satisfied with their lives overall than people in their first marriage, and may be even less satisfied when they have children and stepchildren. This fact is reflected in a higher incidence of divorce among the remarried than in first marriages. The failure of remarriage to yield higher average satisfaction does not prove that people should always stay with their first mate.

But it does suggest that people's ignorance of the ways marital satisfaction rises and falls over time may lead to faulty decision-making.

Social class has a significant effect on marital satisfaction (see, for example, Ambert, 1988). Generally, lower-SES people (especially women) report the lowest levels of past and current marital happiness. Further, social class affects the degree to which marital satisfaction influences overall life satisfaction. Marital satisfaction is likeliest to affect the life satisfaction of upper-middle-class people, whether positively or negatively. Prosperous people can afford to be more concerned with self-fulfilment and other intangible (that is, non-material) life goals, including marital satisfaction.

However, the best predictor of marital satisfaction is a marriage's ongoing quality. The day-to-day activities and concerns of spouses affect marital satisfaction far more profoundly than the social and economic characteristics of spouses. "Overall marital satisfaction is lower among those with frequent disagreements and infrequent shows of affection" (Rhyne, 1984, p. 21); this is not surprising. But does marital satisfaction produce kissing and reduce fighting (that is, disagreement), or do kissing and shared understanding produce marital satisfaction?

An experiment is needed to answer this question conclusively, so here is some homework. If you have a steady romantic relationship with someone, try kissing your friend more often and fighting less; then measure the changes in your "marital" satisfaction. If you can only kiss more and fight less by suppressing your real feelings, or if your changed behaviour fails to improve your relationship, you will have learned something valuable, both personally and theoretically.

"Kissing and fighting" may sound like trivial concerns or a trivialization of important ones until you remember that marriage is a supercharged way of living. Domestic violence—wife abuse, elder abuse, child abuse, and even husband abuse—is a problem we read about in the newspaper every single day. People who never thought they were capable of such acts may find themselves committing them. We know relatively little about rates of domestic violence in the past, so measuring the trend is difficult if not impossible. What we do know, according to reliable statistics, is that more people (especially women) have been murdered by their spouse than by a stranger.

Should you get married or remain single? To sum up thus far, marriage has riskier, less predictable outcomes for women than for men. Both spouses have the chance of gaining more life satisfaction (as well as less satisfaction) through marriage than the average never-married person can expect to attain. Marriage will also generally increase your income, standard of living, and longevity. Yet men apparently gain most from a marriage that succeeds, and the costs are higher for women—especially for mothers and poorer women—if it fails. So the key to deciding about marriage, especially if you are female, is a realistic assessment of the marriage's chance for survival and your chances of supporting yourself and your children if the marriage fails.

Though never foolproof, gathering evidence during courtship is very important. If you think there is too much fighting and not enough kissing in your non-marital relationship, marriage will not solve the problem. Remember that the "enchanted newlywed" period is typically followed by many years of declining satisfaction, especially if children are present. The U-shaped data on marital satisfaction tell us that the situation will worsen long before it improves.

Remember, too, that kissing and fighting remain important throughout marriage: in fact, they help to shape marital satisfaction. Moreover, they indicate the ongoing quality of the relationship. The costs of a wrong guess are enormous, especially (though not exclusively) if you are female. Learn as much as you can about your relationship before taking the plunge into marriage, get ready to support yourself, and do *not* have children until you are fairly certain that the marriage will not fail. Most important, perhaps, flee a relationship in which physical violence occurs. It is likely to recur.

Trying a Relationship Before Marriage

Non-marital relations today are more varied and sexually active than ever before. Data on high school students (Bibby & Posterski, 1985) show a very high exposure to non-marital sex, including sexual intercourse. And new housing patterns make living with someone to whom you are not married easier than ever.

By 1984, about one respondent in six had been in a common-law partnership at one time or another (Burch, 1985, Table 4A). Among young people aged 18 to 29, the proportion was much higher: about one man in five and one woman in four had ever been in such a relationship. In fact, "on Census Day in 1981 approximately 6% of the couples enumerated were not legally married, and half of the 704 000 or so persons involved were between 20 and 30 years of age" (Statistics Canada, 1987, p. 25).

What do people experience in serious romantic involvements outside marriage? Compared to marriage, how satisfying are these relationships? Are they satisfying enough to make marriage obsolete? Or are they very much like marriage—no better or worse, but without the legalities?

These are questions you might ask yourself if you are considering a serious romantic relationship. If personal ethics rule it out, a marriage-like involvement outside marriage would probably prove dissatisfying and even distressing. Do not change your ethics or values to test a potential partner. Rather, try to fit the information provided here into your world view. Doing so may help you understand your own goals and opportunities better.

Before discussing the effects of a serious involvement outside marriage, we should take note of a methodological problem. The kinds of people who enter such relationships are probably the kinds of people who value them, want them, and can handle them. So if we discovered, for example, that people in serious non-marital relationships were twice as satisfied as people in marital relationships, this finding would *not* prove that marriage is obsolete or that *everyone* would be twice as likely to get satisfaction out of a non-marital relationship. Remember, different kinds of people have—for a variety of reasons—selected either marital or non-marital relationships. What satisfies one kind of person will not necessarily satisfy another.

General conclusions on this issue are only possible if we experiment with people—randomly putting some into one kind of relationship and similar people into another—or control statistically for all the relevant variables: people's values, personality types, social backgrounds, parental influences, and so on. But we cannot experiment with people in this way, and the complexity of the problem, combined with a shortage of data, makes the second solution almost impossible too.

So our goals will be simpler: we will compare people's experiences in different kinds of relationships, recognizing that the participants are also, conceivably, different kinds of people. Let us look at the results and speculate on what they might mean.

The Quality of Life (1981) survey asked married respondents and respondents involved in a serious relationship with a "friend" identical questions about their satisfaction with the marital or marriage-like relationship. The data reveal a surprising similarity in responses.

Both groups prove to be equally satisfied (or dissatisfied) with the amount of love shown (31 percent are extremely satisfied) and the way their spouse/friend deals with the respondent's children (32 percent are extremely satisfied). Both are equally likely to disagree many times about money (6 to 7 percent) and how to spend the evening (5 percent) and are almost identically satisfied with the interest their spouse/friend shows in their work (25 to 26 percent are extremely satisfied), the amount of time they spend together (24 to 27 percent), and their spouse/friend's understanding of the respondent's feelings (26 percent of married respondents and 32 percent of unmarried respondents are extremely satisfied).

Overall, married respondents are only slightly more likely to give their relationship the very highest rating—an 11 on the 11-point scale; 25 percent do so, compared to 21 percent of respondents in a non-marital relationship. On most points, then, married and unmarried respondents are about equally satisfied (or dissatisfied) with their romantic involvement.

However, the two groups differ in other ways. Of the two, married respondents are much more satisfied with the assistance they get working around the house (33 percent are extremely satisfied, as compared with 21 percent of the unmarried respondents). Although the unmarried respondents are more likely to report having been kissed many times in the preceding month, married respondents are more likely to report that all their sexual needs are being met.

Most important of all, perhaps, people in a non-marital relationship are nearly twice as likely as married people to feel that their freedom is limited by the relationship: 12 percent of the unmarried respondents frequently feel this, compared with 7 percent of the married group. Finally, the unmarried respondents are over five times as likely to report having thought about ending the relationship during the past year: one in three had thought about it, compared with only one in sixteen married respondents.

What happens to these serious, non-marital relationships in which so many partners think yearly about breaking up? The 1984 Family History Survey (Burch, 1985) reveals that just under half the people in common-law unions end up marrying their common-

law partner. The percentages are even higher for younger respondents: for example, of people aged 30 to 39 in 1984 who had ever
been in a common-law relationship, 52 percent of males and 50
percent of females married their common-law partner. The high
likelihood of marrying a common-law partner suggests that
common-law unions are perceived as trial marriages or as the
prelude to a marriage (Burch, 1985, Table 5). This "trial marriage"
interpretation is supported by evidence (Burch, 1985, Table 4A)
that the vast majority of people ever in a common-law partnership
have been in only one. (On the other hand, this form of behaviour
only became common after 1970, so there has not been much time
for multiple unions.)

According to these data, a serious non-marital involvement
is almost indistinguishable from marriage in most important
respects. Male cohabitors are as violent toward their partners as
are their married counterparts. But there is one important difference
between the two groups: one relationship is based on a firm
commitment and the other is not. People who are married are more
likely to have mentally, as well as legally, committed themselves
to the relationship and followed up with actions that rest on such
a commitment: most especially, having children and incurring
major joint expenses (for example, buying a home).

On the other hand, one child in six today is born outside
marriage. Childbearing is no proof of marital commitment, any
more than childlessness is proof that such a commitment is missing.
Marriage and non-marriage are becoming similar to one another,
so one can see a time ahead when the decision of whether or not
to marry will be less important than it is today. Like so many
other things, the importance of the marital decision corresponds
to a transient historical phase.

Evidence from nineteenth-century England indicates that
common-law marriage was once widespread in the working class.
Legal marriage was of greater concern to the middle and other
property-owning classes, since rights to support and property were
at stake. Now, most provinces in Canada ensure payment of support
to needy spouses, whether a stable (three-year or more) relationship
was legalized or not; and only for a minority are significant
property rights an issue. Stable romantic relationships are similar,
whether formalized by a marriage licence or not.

What, then, is the typical history or life cycle of a serious
romantic relationship, whether marital or not?

The Life Cycle of a Relationship   Love tends to follow a self-maintaining course (Collins, 1982). It begins with enchantment—commitment based on very strong, non-rational feelings—and consolidates itself with hard-to-escape commitments: for example, lifestyle, children and debts. As the non-rational enchantment starts to decline, mounting rational considerations about these commitments assume greater importance in keeping couples together until later on in marriage—with the decline of debts and child-raising burdens—enchantment starts to grow again. Middle age is a time of marital rediscovery for many.

This pattern makes the life cycle of a love relationship very much like the life cycle of a religious or political movement (Max Weber, 1958). Each begins with "charismatic" attachment (to a lover or leader). This powerful, irrational attachment moves people to make extraordinary efforts and commitments. A "routinization" of charisma follows: institutions are created that capitalize on people's faith in the original inspiration. These institutions—increasingly rational and rationalized—are better able than their charismatic, non-routinized, non-rationalized counterparts to withstand the tests of faith that people experience in everyday life and even the periodic, quite dramatic trials of faith—the major disappointments—they encounter.

From time to time, people renew their faith by fundamentally reassessing it and the lives they have built on it. A major family crisis may be the catalyst for such a renewal of faith; equally, it may destroy the family. And the elimination of long-term family pressures, such as the end of child-rearing and a paid-off mortgage, may also be the catalyst.

In comparing the family to other self-renewing institutions, Collins (1982) is not arguing that married people, having "routinized the charisma" of a relationship, love each other less than people still at the "charismatic," "enchanted," or "limerent" stage. In fact, the Quality of Life (1981) data would not support such a conclusion. At marriage, people simply enter a qualitatively different phase of the relationship: a phase that is, in most respects, neither more nor less satisfying than the premarital relationship. Later stages of marriage are also qualitatively different. Though routinized, a marriage may be both satisfying and capable of charismatic self-renewal, like any other social arrangement. (Of course, it may also be stable but unsatisfactory and non-renewing.)

The one area in which marriage excels is in reducing concerns with freedom and new relationships. Commitment to a marriage is simply more serious than commitment to a non-marital relationship. Therefore, to judge from these data alone, the answer to the question "Should I have (many) serious relationships before marrying?" is "Yes, if you have doubts about your prospective mate or your willingness to make a commitment; but otherwise, no." Marriage is no better or worse than non-marriage, but it is different.

Trial Marriage versus Early Marriage   Young people often find themselves in a state of love, enchantment, or limerence; in that state, they may have trouble imagining how they can continue living without the object of their affection. What should a person in that situation do? Three solutions suggest themselves: marry your beloved, cohabit but do not marry, or delay making a decision until you have a great deal more evidence about yourself, your mate, and the relationship between you. What choice makes the most sense?

Sociological evidence argues forcefully against early marriage as a solution. "The divorce rate among [those who marry young] is estimated at from two to four times that among persons who marry after 20 years of age. The divorce rate is related to low educational levels, low economic levels, premarital pregnancies, and possibly to personality difficulties" (Leslie & Korman, 1985, p. 396; see also Scanzoni, 1972, pp. 6–28).

As always, the cost of failure falls most heavily on the woman. By far, the most numerous single parents are separated and divorced women. Single-parent families have become much more numerous lately, and a large proportion live below the poverty line. Single mothers are more likely than other women to have married (and had children) too soon, before getting enough education and job skills for economic independence. "In the longer run, this lack of job-related resources may have limited their power within a marriage or union and, thus, may have predisposed its termination" (Pool & Moore 1986, p. 49).

The message is clear: you should not marry before you are ready. Even more important, you should not enter parenthood too soon, or for the wrong reasons. (We will discuss this further in Chapter 6.) Getting married does not ensure the stability of a relationship, and having children does not keep a couple together, much less improve a shaky relationship.

Does this argue that the smitten couple should live together unmarried? Evidence suggests higher-than-average divorce rates for people who live together before marriage. This may be a temporary fact, subject to change as people become more accustomed to cohabitation and the wise use of their freedom. Or it may reflect differences in romantic stability between people who are inclined to cohabit before marriage and those who are disinclined. So it may not be cohabitation *per se* that leads to higher risks of divorce. But of two risky choices, early marriage remains the riskier, for obvious reasons.

When is marriage "too early?" Our culture has long promoted the ideal that men should finish their education, get established in a career, and *then* marry; Hogan (1981) calls this the "normative pattern." But many factors conspire against this normative pattern. Wars tend to interrupt young men's formal education and take them away from their loved ones; this separation exerts a powerful pressure to marry before their education is complete and before career-building has gotten under way. In fact, World War II and its aftermath helped destroy the notion that marriage and university attendance were incompatible.

Economic recessions, on the other hand, throw traditional patterns into doubt because they make it harder for young people to find work and achieve economic security. Education and career-building become harder to plan for and control. Such uncertainty breaks the traditional link between economic security and the establishment of a family. Under these conditions, getting married appears no more foolish than not getting married.

Beneath these and other temporary factors, Hogan detects a growing trend toward non-normative sequencing, even in peaceful and prosperous times: a trend toward marriage before the completion of education and career-building. Some reasons may include the progressive lengthening of formal education, the growing availability of student loans and married-student housing, the rising availability of full- and part-time work for students and/ or their spouses, the growth of part-time education, and, of course, the increased protection from unwanted pregnancy modern birth control provides.

What happens to the increasing numbers of young men who marry before their education is complete and their career has been set in motion? "Initially, married men who seek employment tend to find better-paying and somewhat higher-status jobs than single men. . . . But the man who is single has greater freedom to seek a better job. Unrestricted by family responsibilities, single men tend to enjoy quicker career advancement" (Hogan, 1981, pp. 200–201).

Additionally, men who (for reasons of marriage) have left school and entered the labour force relatively early tend to rely more on family connections to secure a first job. This tends to situate them in jobs with relatively poorer prospects for career advancement. (Remember Granovetter's findings, discussed in Chapter 2, which show that the "best" jobs travel through networks of acquaintanceship.) Men who marry early and rely on family connections for work are more likely to start out in organizations that are small and limiting. Because they are married, their geographic mobility is restricted and they are less able than the single man to risk moves, changes, and transfers that would increase their acquaintanceships and overall marketability.

How does non-normative, early marriage affect marital stability—specifically, the chance of divorce? Like other commentators on early marriage, Hogan finds that early marriers

> have rates of marital instability more than 50% higher than men marrying on time or relatively late. . . . It seems likely that men who marry early are relatively immature at the time of marriage. Their choice of a marriage partner might be ill-considered because of this immaturity, or problems associated with the sudden entry of an immature man into a marital union may produce strains that result in marital discord. (1981, pp. 204–206)

These risks appear to have lessened somewhat in recent decades. But despite improved chances, the data still argue against early marriage, which continues to increase the risk of career limitation and divorce as compared to the "normative pattern." By implication, the data argue in favour of non-marital relationships that do not result in pregnancy or limit career mobility, as marital relationships might.

The answer to our second question, then, is in many ways less ambiguous than our answer to the first. Yes, people who feel comfortable with the idea of a serious non-marital involvement, and feel they cannot delay some kind of living together, should go through with it. Cohabitation gives the participants greater knowledge about each other and the quality of their relationship; half the time, it ends in marriage. By leaving open the door for a decision *not* to marry, it allows for further maturation and thus reduces the risks of becoming parents too early and of hindering careers. But, as we have seen, it does not at present reduce the risks of a divorce later.

There is no reason to fear that non-marital relationships will prove so satisfying that they will replace the conventional attractions of legal marriage. On average, cohabitation is no more or less enchanting than marriage, other factors (such as childbearing) being equal.

To repeat an earlier point, people who are morally opposed to serious non-marital relationships such as cohabitation should feel no obligation to change their minds. They will simply have to work harder to get the information they need *before* marriage, and adapt to unforeseen disappointments *after* marriage.

Choosing a Mate

No mate selection process, however sound, will guarantee the survival of your marriage. This is because, throughout life, you are constantly changing, your mate is changing, and the socially structured pressures (constraints and opportunities) surrounding you are changing. But some selections may produce more marital satisfaction than others, and some are riskier than others. For example, people who divorce many times tend to be less careful in their mate selection than people who divorce only once (Ambert, 1988). Bad mate-choosers are probably to be avoided as mates. It is worth our while examining what social science knows about mate selection and the results of better and worse choices.

I will soon argue that the very idea of "mate selection" is misguided, in the same way that "job selection" wrongly describes how people find work. But for the time being, let us proceed with the metaphor of mate selection, since most people think of mating and marriage as a selection process—which, in a limited sense, it is.

The strongest theory in this area, exchange theory (see, for example, Homans, 1974; Blau, 1964), holds that all social behaviour, even apparently non-rational emotional behaviour like mating and marriage, can be usefully viewed as an interpersonal exchange that must balance. People are self-interested and wish to maximize their well-being in everything they do. When they give up something, they want to get something as good or better in return. Failure to make an equitable or balanced exchange produces disappointment and resentment. Whoever has the greater "resources" in the marriage has the greater power (Blood & Wolfe, 1960; Scanzoni, 1972).

If so, we should expect to find that people mate with and marry others of similar social value, since each stands to gain as much from the relationship. Most mating takes place between people of approximately equal physical attractiveness (Hatfield & Sprecher, 1986). When mates are not equally attractive, the less attractive person usually brings another valued attribute—wealth, power, social position—to the relationship. If balance is not achieved, satisfaction soon declines and the relationship will deteriorate (Hatfield & Sprecher, 1986).

This may explain the so-called "mating gradient"; the mating of attractive young women with more-prosperous, usually divorced, older men. When people of different occupational levels, educational levels, or other status characteristics do marry, men generally marry downward. This fact holds several implications. First, marriage is a more common means of upward social mobility for women than it is for men. Second, cross-class marriage—which, like interracial and other mixed marriages, appears to be increasing—may serve to reduce class conflict in a highly unequal society.

Across societies, the average groom is slightly older than his bride, although this difference is narrowing for first marriages. Sometimes the age differences are very great. In our own society, the age gap between brides and grooms is particularly wide—nearly ten years, on average—when grooms are marrying for the second time. To such a union, the younger woman brings youthful good looks and childbearing capability; the older man brings social position. The opposite match (bride much older than groom) is less often observed, presumably because older women are less often able than older men to bring high social position to the relationship (see Ambert, 1988, for a discussion on age differences in remarriage). Moreover, men may not find high social position alluring in a woman, given our culture's preference for male domination of females.

So in one sense, however unconsciously, mating is a bargain struck between approximate equals. Homogamy, the tendency for like people to marry, "has been verified for age, marital status, social status, race, religion, and ethnic background. . . . [However,] there is some evidence that people seek marital partners who complement themselves in personality" (Leslie & Korman, 1985, pp. 396–397). Thus, psychological complementarity and social likeness may be the norm.

Even so, the question of whether to marry someone like or unlike you is not all that simple. For the mating "bargain" to satisfy, your mate must be as valuable as you in the "marriage market." In practice, balancing a mate's "market value" against your own is a subtle process involving many factors: for example, age, appearance, race, class, and personality. As in many other market transactions, we learn most about a thing's market value by seeing who is bidding what for the "good" in question.

Rephrasing the question somewhat gives a slightly different answer. If a market imbalance does exist, it will show itself through instability in the relationship: kissing will decline, fighting will increase, compromises will be few and far between, or one spouse will do all the compromising. In that sense, you will know the viability of an exchange from its ongoing quality, not from some abstract evaluation of your mate's marketability relative to your own.

Evidence about the stability of "mixed marriages" is scanty and somewhat contradictory. As mixed marriages become more common, their acceptance will increase; with acceptance, their viability will increase. If we judge by comparative divorce rates, the difficulties supposed to beset mixed-race or mixed-class marriages are rarely found to be as great as expected. It also appears that age and status differences are more problematic than religious differences between mates (Leslie & Korman, 1985, p. 397). For example, younger women in marriages with older (usually divorced) men are relatively unhappy maritally, and such marriages display a higher-than-average divorce rate (Ambert, 1988). It is not easy to determine whether the problems are due to age-mixing, bad choosing, or other factors (for example, child support obligations from a first marriage).

Why People Do Not Optimize   The metaphor of a mating or marriage "market" is largely fictional. We learned in Chapter 2 that people find the best jobs through personal contacts, not through impersonal shopping. Similarly, people rarely find mates by shopping for them, as one might shop for a television set. In part, we do not shop for a mate because we do not really know what we want, and will not know until we find it. More important, we could never live long enough to marry if we approached mating as a shopping problem.

Like most rational people, we do *not* seek the ideal or "optimal" solution to our mating problem: that is, we do *not* try to optimize. Rather, we "satisfice": we seek a "good enough" solution, within the constraints life has handed us (March & Simon, 1958). The reasonable person draws no useful distinction between the satisfactory and the ideal: for most purposes, whatever satisfies *is* ideal, under the circumstances.

According to March and Simon, most human decision-making aims at discovering and selecting *satisfactory* alternatives. "Only in exceptional cases is it concerned with the discovery of optimal alternatives. To optimize requires processes several orders of magnitude more complex than those required to satisfice" (1958, p. 141). This is the difference between searching a haystack for the *sharpest* needle and merely searching for a needle that is sharp enough to sew with.

Choice is certainly a burden and people are not happier for having it. But once they have tried it, they would be very unhappy to go back to a condition in which they had no choice. So the practice, and illusion, of choice remains. But the human race could not reproduce itself and survive if people were "optimizers."

Consider the arithmetic of the problem. Suppose that, as an idealistic adolescent, you listed ten qualities you felt you absolutely must have in a mate. Your mate must be attractive—at least in the top fifth of all possible mates. Your mate must be fun—again, at least in the top fifth of all possible mates. He or she must be interesting to talk to—again, at least in the top fifth of all possible mates. Imagine making up a "shopping list" in this way. Now, what is the probability that your ideal mate actually exists?

If the various qualities you are looking for are uncorrelated, only one person in five to the tenth power—one in 9.8 million—will meet all your requirements. Equally, there is only one chance in 9.8 million that your "perfect" mate will consider *you* the perfect mate. So by this scenario, the chances in favour of meeting and mating with the "perfect mate" are nearly zero: one in 9.8 million squared.

Even more-modest goals will not find you a mate if you seek to optimize. Suppose that, instead of requiring your ideal mate to be among the top fifth in attractiveness, you only require him or her to be in the top half. You similarly lower your standards for each of the other requirements you had listed. This helps to solve your mating problem: now, you only need to look for that one person in a thousand (that is, two to the tenth power). The probability of meeting and mating with an ideal mate who is making similar calculations has improved: it is now one in a thousand squared, or one in a million.

But at most, you only know a few thousand people by their first name. The chance of meeting and mating this way is extremely unlikely. Some people may think they have teamed up with the "perfect partner," and one time in a million they may have. But more likely than not, they have not sought or found their mate by shopping for "the right characteristics," and they have merely decided after the fact that their mate is perfect.

The arithmetic shows that even lowering your original standards will fail to solve your mating problem, if you attempt to optimize. Other solutions are just as fruitless. Some people try meeting more potential partners: if you knew six thousand people instead of two thousand, this would triple your chances. But getting on a first-name basis with six thousand people is very difficult and time-consuming, and the odds are still enormously stacked against you.

Expanding your acquaintanceship network selectively seems to be a way around this. By joining certain kinds of groups, placing or answering personal advertisements, or using matchmaking services, you will more quickly meet new people with the qualities you require. These mating techniques have become much more popular lately, especially among the middle-aged, whose opportunity to meet a large number of new people is seriously restricted. *Take note: postsecondary school will expose you to more potential mates than you will ever pass among again.*

Many people hesitate to shop for mates in this way, finding it demeaning or fearing the unpleasantness of blind dates that do not work out. Most people try to solve *this* problem by reducing the number of qualities they require in a mate. Now the potential mate must excel in one or two respects and merely satisfy in half a dozen more. Imagine that you and your "perfect mate" are now looking for someone who excels (is in the top 20 percent) in one quality and is better than average (that is, in the top 50 percent) on just four other particular qualities. The probability of finding a person with the qualities you seek is one in 1250; the probability that you will satisfy his or her requirements is now one in 1250. Even so, the chance of meeting and mating is still less than one in a million (that is, one in 1250 squared).

However you revise the shopping list and extend your range or number of contacts, the chance of mating this way is nearly zero. That tells us that people cannot and do not find a mate in this way. Rather, people fall in love with others who are close-at-hand. As in so many other areas of life, we come to value what we know best and have available: people like ourselves. That is why social homogamy is so common. We become satisfied with the possible, not the ideal.

Even if arithmetic did not rule out shopping for a perfect mate, our other social relationships probably would. For even in an economically rational, "market-based" society like our own, people tend to avoid behaviours that violate customs associated with their household, kin group, religious or ethnic group, and community. This tends to eliminate from consideration—often automatically and unconsciously—potential mates who are quite unlike our friends and family in important ways. We are freer to choose than people who lived in small homogeneous communities in earlier times, because we can more readily bear the costs of social exclusion if our mate is deemed inappropriate. But this factor has by no means disappeared as a limitation on those we consider potential marriage partners.

Findings on intermarriage show that some of this communal pressure is particularly intense in small ethnic and religious communities. Attitudinal barriers to marriage outside one's ethnic, racial, or religious group have lessened in the last two decades (Lambert & Curtis, 1985). But hostility to marriage between whites and non-whites, Jews and non-Jews, and Protestants and Catholics remains great among many ethnic minorities; Anglo-Saxon and Francophone groups are apparently more tolerant of such inter-marriages. Tolerance appears to increase with group size and decrease with ethnic institutional completeness: it is greatest in groups that allow their members the most contact with members of other groups and are least threatened with group disappearance through outmarriage.

Such attitude change may follow behaviour change, not the reverse. A study of Canada's major language groups concludes that "endogamy [that is, within-group marriage] varies positively with the number of available potential mates belonging to the same group; negatively with the average distance to them; negatively with the number of available potential mates belonging to different groups; and positively with the average distance to the latter" (de Vries & Vallee, 1980, p. 168).

This model of marriage choices, a "residential propinquity" model, is almost identical to a widely used model of migration. Just as people decide to stay where they are even if slightly better opportunities are very far away, so too people often decide to marry people who are socially and geographically near-at-hand even if slightly better mating opportunities are much farther away.

This process of satisficing, of marrying the close-at-hand, may sound very cold-blooded and disheartening; but in the actual event, feelings of love are quite genuine. People in love *feel* like they have discovered the one perfect mate, and in a sense they have. But they do not do it, could not have done it, by following a shopping list. Moreover, a person rich and leisured enough to actually shop the world for the "perfect" mate might never be any more satisfied than the "satisficer." The romantic wanderer's exposure to great variety and unlimited expectation might prove profoundly *dis*satisfying.

Concluding Remarks

The family is changing rapidly. Family life in general is not "dead," as critics of modern life have claimed. But the "traditional" family—two opposite-sex married people living together with their dependent children, neither having cohabited (or been a parent) before, and only one of them (that is, the husband) earning an income—is now experienced by a minority of Canadian adults. It has passed into history; we have no reason to think it will return.

Within the new context, many people still find marriage satisfying: they say so when asked, and remarry after divorce. Although large numbers are entering common-law unions, such unions are largely trial runs for legal marriage: witness the high proportion that end in marriage.

The problems of marriage appear, increasingly, to be problems of doubled career strain—witness the growth of dual-career families—and parenting. In large part, the potential problem a couple faces can be resolved through less, and more carefully timed, childbearing. Evidence suggests that voluntary childlessness may increase further, a matter Chapter 6 will discuss at greater length.

Spousal sharing of duties is even more important, and norms on this score seem to be changing, though behaviours change more slowly.

The most interesting changes so far have involved women. Women have already changed their conception of and relationship to marriage in significant ways. More women than ever have equipped themselves for independence. Even working women who have married are placing less importance on that relationship in the overall scheme of their lives (Baruch, Barnett, & Rivers, 1983, p. 294). In future, the most interesting and far-reaching changes will involve men. They have yet to catch up to the gender revolution at work and at home.

Across modern societies, divorce remains one of the most significant life events, affecting large numbers of adults in traumatic ways. Worse, it is an event for which we scarcely prepare ourselves. The North American mythology of romantic love and mating—one true love 'til death do us part—ill prepares young people for the everyday realities of married life, within which divorce looms as an ominous, ever-present risk. Few are prepared for the strains and difficulties of married life, much less the hardships of divorce.

Like marriage rates, divorce rates reflect a preoccupation with personal fulfilment. If our culture continues to value personal freedom and continuous gratification as much as it has in the last few decades, people will continue to change their marital status as often as they can afford to. The motivations to end a marriage will remain just as high: only the costs of doing so will vary. A healthy economy makes all status-changing—marriage, divorce, career-shifting, geographic relocation—easier and safer. Therefore, the key to predicting the future may lie in the economy's health and vigour. High divorce rates may be a more-or-less permanent feature of our marriage system.

Do people get what they want from marriage, or learn to want what they can get? On the one hand, people are increasingly free to marry or not to marry; to have the kinds of marital and non-marital relationships they want to; to choose the kind of mate they wish. On the other hand, what we want is certainly patterned. Canadians learn to want marriage as the preferred form of adult life. We mate with people who are nearby and socially like ourselves (because they are nearby), not with "ideal" mates. Some divorces may occur because mating is constrained by proximity. More occur because most of us have also learned to expect things out of life that marriage can scarcely provide: especially, the freedom to develop as individuals.

Do we learn to want what we get? Largely, we do. We fall in love with the close-at-hand, believing that we have discovered the "perfect" mate. On the other hand, people rarely get what they expect from divorce. Women, who rarely choose divorce, are particularly hurt by it; but even males who divorce and remarry find the same marital satisfactions and dissatisfactions as males who had never divorced and remarried. People are slow to learn new wants.

The only solution social science can offer at present is more information about reality. And this solution is best where free choice is involved. Chapter 6 examines problems of parenthood: what you want and what you get.

References

AMBERT, A.-M. (1980). *Divorce in Canada*. Toronto: Academic Press.

_____. (1988). *Ex-Spouses and new spouses*. Greenwich, CT: JAI Press.

BARUCH, G., BARNETT, R., & RIVERS, C. (1983). *Lifeprints: New patterns of love and work for today's women*. New York: Signet Books.

BERNARD, J. (1973). *The future of marriage*. New York: Bantam Books.

BIBBY, R.W., & POSTERSKI, D.C. (1985). *The emerging generation: An inside look at Canada's teenagers*. Toronto: Irwin.

BLAU, P.M. (1964). *Exchange and power in social life*. New York: John Wiley.

BLOOD, R.O., & WOLFE, D.M. (1960). *Husbands and wives: The dynamics of married living*. New York: Free Press.

BOYD, M. (1985). Educational and occupational attainments of native-born Canadian men and women. In M. Boyd, J. Goyder, F.E. Jones, H.A. McRoberts, P.C. Pineo, & J. Porter (Eds.), *Ascription and achievement: Studies in mobility and status attainment in Canada* (pp. 229–295). Ottawa: Carleton University Press.

BURCH, T.K. (1985). *Family history survey: Preliminary findings* (Statistics Canada, Catalogue No. 99–955). Ottawa: Supply & Services.

BURCH, T.K., & MADAN, A.K. (1986). *Union formation and dissolution in Canada: Results from the 1984 Family History Survey* (Statistics Canada, Catalogue No. 99–963). Ottawa: Supply & Services.

COLLINS, R. (1982). *Sociological insight: An introduction to non-obvious sociology.* New York: Oxford University Press.

DE VRIES, J., & VALLEE, F.G. (1980). *Language use in Canada* (Statistics Canada, Catalogue No. 99-762E). Census Analytical Study. Ottawa: Supply & Services.

EHRENREICH, B. (1983). *The hearts of men: American dreams and the flight from commitment.* Garden City, NJ: Anchor Books.

EICHLER, M. (1981). The inadequacy of the monolithic model of the family. *Canadian Journal of Sociology, 6*(3), 367-388.

———. (1988). *Families in Canada today* (2nd ed.). Toronto: Gage.

GOVE, W.R. (1970). Sex, marital status, and psychiatric treatment: A research note. *Social Forces, 58*, 89-93.

HAJNAL, J. (1965). European marriage patterns in perspective. In D.V. Glass and D.E.C. Eversley (Eds.), *Population in History* (pp. 101-143). London: Edward Arnold.

HATFIELD, E., & SPRECHER, S. (1986). *Mirror, mirror: The importance of looks in everyday life.* Albany: State University of New York Press.

HOGAN, D.P. (1981). *Transitions and social change: The early lives of American men.* Studies in Population Series. New York: Academic Press.

HOMANS, G.C. (1974). *Social behavior: Its elementary forms* (rev. ed.). New York: Harcourt Brace Jovanovich.

KEYFITZ, N. (1988). On the wholesomeness of marriage. In L. Tepperman and J. Curtis (Eds.), *Reader in sociology: An introduction.* Toronto: McGraw-Hill Ryerson.

LAMBERT, R.D., & CURTIS, J. (1985, February). The racial attitudes of Canadians. *Past and Present*, pp. 2-4.

LESLIE, G.R., & KORMAN, S.K. (1985). *The family in social context* (6th ed.). New York: Oxford University Press.

LUPRI, E., & FRIDERES, J. (1981). The quality of marriage and the passage of time: Marital satisfaction over the family life cycle. *Canadian Journal of Sociology, 6*(3), 283-305.

LUXTON, M. (1980). *More than a labour of love: Three generations of women's work in the home.* Toronto: Women's Educational Press.

MARCH, J.G., & SIMON, H.A. (1958). *Organizations.* New York: John Wiley.

MCKIE, D.C., PRENTICE, B., & REED, P. (1983). *Divorce: Law and the family in Canada* (Statistics Canada, Catalogue No. 89-502E). Ottawa: Supply & Services.

NAGNUR, D., & ADAMS, O. (1987, August). Tying the knot: An overview of marriage rates in Canada. *Canadian Social Trends*, pp. 2-6.

POOL, I., & MOORE, M. (1986). *Lone parenthood: Characteristics and determinants (Results from the 1984 Family History Survey)* (Statistics Canada, Catalogue No. 99-961). Ottawa: Supply & Services.

QUALITY OF LIFE SURVEY. (1981).   Unpublished raw data from large survey of life satisfaction conducted at the Institute for Behavioural Research, York University, Toronto.

RHYNE, D. (1984).   *Marital satisfaction in Canada: A descriptive overview.* Toronto: York University, Institute for Behavioural Research.

SCANZONI, J.H. (1972).   *Sexual bargaining: Power politics in the American marriage.* Englewood Cliffs, NJ: Prentice-Hall.

STATISTICS CANADA. (1982).   *Vital statistics, Volume II: Marriages and divorces* (Catalogue No. 84–205). Ottawa: Supply & Services.

_____. (1987).   *Current demographic analysis: Report on the demographic situation in Canada, 1986* (Catalogue No. 91–209E). Ottawa: Supply & Services.

TENNOV, D. (1979).   *Love and Limerence.* New York: Stein and Day.

WEBER, M. (1958).   *From Max Weber: Essays in sociology.* H. Gerth & C.W. Mills (Eds. and Trans.). New York: Oxford University Press.

Chapter Six

Childless or Parent: *what you want and what you get*

Introduction

Raising a child is a unique experience. It is time-consuming and often expensive. It can be frustrating, grueling, and disappointing; also, thrilling, surprising, and delightful. In all of these respects, raising a child is like falling in love, running a business, learning a trade, writing a book, tending a farm, and mastering a musical instrument or sport. So even though the decision to raise a child is unique, other decisions you have already made are similar; you can bring your own experiences to bear on the parenting decision.

Moreover, many of the decisions you have already made *should* influence your decision to raise children. After all, you have only so much time, money, and energy to spend in living; you must decide how to spend these scarce resources in the most satisfying way. For you, raising children may *not* be among the most satisfying ways.

This chapter will limit itself to two very important questions about parenthood, out of many that might be discussed: (1) Should I have children, and if so, how many? (or, Should I have any children at all, and if so, why?) and (2) Are people with children able to find a satisfactory balance between home and career responsibilities, and if so, how? (or, How does the presence of children affect people's—and particularly women's—abilities to enjoy other important domains of their lives, especially work and marriage?)

Answering the first question will force us to consider what people say about parenthood and what they do; national and international trends in childbearing; and the results of decisions people are currently making. People throughout the modern world have been addressing similar questions about parenthood for over a century. Thus these questions, and the solutions people have considered, are far from new or uniquely Canadian. You will not be the first (or last) person to ask them.

Answering the second question will return us to concerns we addressed in earlier chapters on education, work, and marriage: concerns about gender inequality and the particular problems modern women face in meeting their obligations. Again, people—especially women—throughout the world have been grappling with these issues for much of this century. Gender-based parenting problems are far from solved, but knowing that they are widely shared may put your own thoughts about the matter into clearer perspective.

As in previous chapters, we conclude by considering whether, in the domain of parenthood, people get what they want or learn to want what they get. But we must note from the outset that many people who become parents do not freely choose parenthood at all. For some, parenthood results from an unwanted pregnancy and a sensed responsibility to bear the child, rather than abort it. For others, parenthood results from marriage to a person who already has children.

Likewise, many people do not choose the conditions under which they end up raising their children, particularly mothers whose spouses desert them, abuse them, abuse their children, fail to take part in child-rearing, or maintain heavy commitments to children of an earlier marriage: in short, a great many mothers.

So people do not always choose what they get, or get what they choose. They are not necessarily to blame when parenthood goes wrong. The following analyses are intended to help when people *do* have a choice in the matter, in the hopes they will choose wisely.

Should I Have Children?

The survival of humanity has historically depended on a continuing "Yes!" in answer to this question. But parenthood is not as widely desired or needed today as it was in the past.

Four centuries ago, when mortality rates were very high, many births were needed for a family, community, or society to stay at its original or desired size. A large proportion of all children died in infancy; many others failed to reach adulthood, marry, or reproduce. As a result, about as many people entered parenthood in one generation as had entered it in the previous generation, and the total population stayed at a fixed size. With this, the ratio of people to land, and to the food supply, remained the same for long periods of time, allowing traditional social relations to continue.

But around the seventeenth century, mortality rates in Western Europe began to drop. Despite fluctuations due to famines, epidemics, and wars, they have continued to drop ever since. Today, a larger-than-ever proportion of children survive to childbearing age, and a larger proportion of their children survive infancy; as a result, the people-to-land ratio has changed dramatically.

What some theorists (for instance, Malthus, 1798/1959) considered poverty due to overpopulation first became a social and political problem around the beginning of the nineteenth century. Since then, debates between Malthusians and Marxists have raged over whether the "population problem"—a problem of scarcity— could best be solved by limiting childbearing or by sharing wealth more equitably, thereby increasing the world's productive capabilities. To some degree, the "Green Revolution" (Boulding, 1981, p. 328) has already solved some of these problems by improving food production methods.

Yet these debates continue today, particularly in respect to the rapid population growth of less-developed countries. Though some believe that the world's current population can be adequately fed and housed by redistributing the world's wealth and technology, few would hold that current population growth rates can continue indefinitely. Even within countries like Canada, where overpopulation and rapid growth are not a problem, most people have an awareness of population (and related environmental) issues their parents lacked thirty years ago.

Childbearing is not always the result of a conscious decision. But when carried out by design, childbearing is one of several decisions people will make that has an enormous impact on their extended family, community, nation, and world. As these impacts become more obvious and pressing, do not be surprised if governments come to play a part in this decision by offering very strong incentives or disincentives to childbearing. Quebec has recently offered tax incentives for bearing three or more children. Such policies have also been put into effect in other countries: for example, in Nazi Germany, to encourage (Aryan) childbearing, and in the Republic of China, to discourage it. Public policies affecting access to abortion already influence childbearing decisions in Canada.

So while the survival of the human race once depended on an almost universal "Yes" answer to the question "Should I have children?", today it increasingly depends on the answers "No," "Maybe," or "Not many." People have to choose parenthood more carefully today, with a greater awareness of the reasons for their choice, and its consequences for their lives.

What People Think about Childbearing   To the extent that childbearing *is* a decision, and a purely personal one, what people think about parenthood will remain very important. What do children—the next generation of parents—think about parenthood? Of more than 600 000 American schoolchildren who participated in a "future survey" (Johnson, 1987), "The great majority, over 80%, expect to marry, although boys were slightly less likely than girls to indicate that. Most children expected to have two, one, or three children, in that order of preference; again, boys were considerably more likely to choose 'none' " (Johnson, 1987, p. 37).

Children from Grade 4 and up were asked who will care for their children and who will hold another (that is, non-child-raising) job when they grow up and marry. Like the rest, most Grade 4 children are likely to answer that "both" parents will care for the child; but over 40 percent expect the mother to be solely responsible for child care, and only one in three Grade 4 pupils thinks that mothers will hold another job in addition to parenthood. After Grade 6, two pupils in three think that both parents will be responsible for child care, and half say that mothers will hold another job as well.

Schoolchildren soon become aware that modern marriage requires shared parental responsibility and two incomes. But even the young children who seem to know that spouses will need to co-operate in raising children and earning a family income fail to recognize how these facts will affect married life. Surveyed schoolchildren and adolescents routinely reveal that girls expect to get married and have children, and few expect a career even if they do work (see, for example, Baker, 1985).

The attitudes of older adolescents are closer to current childbearing practices. Two surveys of unmarried postsecondary students reveal a decline between 1968 and 1977 in both expected and desired fertility among males and females, whether Francophone or Anglophone. Hobart (1984) finds "three indirect influences [on desired family size]—religiosity of the respondent, religiosity of his/her parents and size of the parental family. . . . A final possible parental family influence on respondents' parenthood interest was the degree of commitment to the parental family" (p. 130).

Some previously significant influences on desired family size—notably rural or urban residence, nativity, education, and income—seem to be losing their importance (Hobart, 1984). However, research shows that fathers, older people, and people raised in traditional (often large) families to which they remain strongly attached are least changed in their thinking about parenthood.

The most extreme non-changers may be characterized as "pronatalist." One group combines a strong sentiment favouring the traditional family and gender roles with an opposition to abortion. Surveyed anti-abortionists are very frequent churchgoers (63 percent go once or more a week) who fear that homosexuals, feminists, and the media are destroying the family. "What has galvanized them," says sociologist Lorna Erwin, "is their perception that the family is under attack, and they see [the danger] everywhere" (*Globe and Mail*, April 2, 1987). This sense of a danger to tradition and belief in absolute right and wrong—moral absolutism—keep attitudes static in the face of universal changes in family life and parenthood.

Sociologist Jean Veevers (1980) finds an "emerging counter-culture" she calls *antinatalism* at the other end of the attitude spectrum. Couples choosing to remain childless are put under intense social pressure to make the opposite decision. Far from starting out as women's liberationists, many voluntarily childless women become more sympathetic to the goals of women's liberation after experiencing this pressure. Sentiments about parenthood have been polarizing in the last few decades, then. But sentiments aside, what do people actually do, and with what consequences?

What People Do: World Trends in Fertility   The story of modern parenthood really begins when the worldwide decline in childbearing got its start. Around 1871, marital childbearing in Europe and North America began a significant and never-to-be-reversed fall. Starting dates varied somewhat, with France in the lead. No one knows precisely why the massive change centres on 1871, or how the onset of change in one region connected with change in another region. (For a review of the historical findings, see Coale & Watkins (Eds.), 1986.)

Yet the fact remains that since 1871, marital childbearing has almost steadily decreased to a current level that, in Canada and many other developed countries, is well below the number needed to replace the parental generation. In Canada, this trend has been interrupted only twice: by the Great Depression of the 1930s, which produced far fewer births than one might have expected; and by the baby boom of the 1950s and 1960s, which produced far more births than expected.

"Demographic transition theory" (Coale, 1969; Tepperman, 1986) argues that nineteenth- and twentieth-century fertility declines really began with eighteenth- and nineteenth-century mortality declines due to improved sanitation, public health, nutrition, and medical care. As mortality fell and childbearing continued at its earlier level, total populations grew very rapidly, putting enormous pressures on each nation's economy. With more infants surviving, each family's economy also came under greater pressure. One result of this growing population pressure was migration to the New World. Another was international warfare to capture neighbouring countries and colonies for resources, markets, and room to live.

Reduced infant mortality and industrialization made large families unnecessary, even a liability. To merely maintain a family over generations, parents needed only two children, not the four or more that were needed when many children died before reaching adulthood. Increasingly, urban middle-class parents decided that their children would do better in life if fewer, so that each received more of the family's care, encouragement, and financial support (Banks, 1954).

The particulars of change have been quite different in the Third World. There, mortality has fallen far more quickly than it did in the West, thanks to modern medicine. In these countries too, parenthood today is a mainly motivational issue. Modern technology allows people to prevent all but the pregnancies they want, though this technology is still imperfectly distributed or utilized (especially among the young), even in our own society. In developing societies, the distribution of birth control devices (pills, IUDs, condoms) is progressing rapidly, due to pressures to promote family planning. For example, the World Bank requires a national commitment to birth control before giving out funds to enable industrialization in Third World countries. (On the other hand, recent pressure from American fundamentalists has simultaneously led to the withdrawal of funds from family planning organizations distributing contraceptive devices.)

Presumably, Third World parents will see the advantages in limiting their childbearing—just as parents in the West have done since 1871—and they will freely limit their childbearing. Yet change is slow in coming, with the result that world population is rising rapidly. The 5 billionth person was added to the world's population around July 11, 1987; United Nations demographers predict the 6 billionth in 1998, the 7 billionth in 2010, and the 8 billionth in 2023. This is amazing growth, given the history of the human population up to this century.

Futurist Ralph Hamil (1987, p. 36) tells us that the newborn 5 billionth human may be called Mohammed Wang, "using the world's most popular given and family names." He will be male, since slightly more males are born than females; and Asian, for most of the human species—over half—lives in Asia today. The balance of world population is shifting dramatically and, according to some, so may the balance of world power (Wattenberg, 1987).

What People Do: Canadian Trends in Fertility   Canada also began its own "secular decline of fertility" a century ago (Romaniuc, 1986). Since then, the total fertility rate has fallen from an average of 6 births per woman to 1.7 (in 1985), below the level required to replace the Canadian population. This fall to smaller family sizes has been punctuated by phases of faster and slower decline. Even the enormous baby boom was a mere deviation from the downward trend.

Understanding this historical trend is critical if we are to predict and/or influence the future of childbearing in Canada. But scholars disagree on whether a declining or stationary population is desirable, given its tendency to "age" the population. Some "view low fertility as a chronic condition of advanced society. They . . . reconcile themselves to the idea of no growth and aging, and . . . advocate the need for institutional and social adjustments to the prevailing demographic environment" (Romaniuc, 1986, p. 32). Others, who view population growth as a desirable or necessary condition for national prosperity, but also think low fertility an inevitable condition of industrial societies, advise more immigration. Others still look for ways of stimulating population growth within the society. For this last group, selecting and implementing the "right" pronatalist policy again depends on the outlook of the observer.

As noted, Canada's total fertility rate today is well below the level of 2.1 births needed to replace generations (Statistics Canada, 1987). A pattern of delayed childbearing is also emerging. More

women are having their first child after the age of 30. The youngest
birth cohorts—Canadian women born after 1952—may not bear
enough children to replace themselves, but some are merely delaying parenthood. Finally, Quebec's fertility rate, for a long time
Canada's highest, is now Canada's lowest, at 1.4 births per woman.
This accords with Quebec's lowest-in-Canada rate of marriage.

Because their understanding of the past is incomplete, demographers disagree about the likely future level of childbearing
in Canada. Statistics Canada (1985), for example, defends different
assumptions about the future. Depending which one we choose
to believe, Canada's population can be expected either to rise from
roughly 26 million in 1988 to 28 million in 2006 and fall back
to 26.8 million by 2031 (according to the declining-fertility/low-
immigration estimate), or rise to 30 million in 2006 and 32.7
million in 2031 (according to the constant-fertility/high-
immigration estimate). The difference in estimates is nearly six
million people by 2031, or nearly one-quarter of Canada's current
population.

However, "greater proportions single or cohabiting, later marriage and increased marital interruption may well produce (even)
more fertility decline" (Beaujot, 1987, p. 12). Most of the changes
taking place in the family today tend to work against childbearing.
The century-long downward slide in births may be accelerated by
these changes in marriage, leading to a twenty-first century
Canadian population that is very much smaller than today's, unless
immigration increases dramatically or strong pronatalist policies
are undertaken.

Canada's most likely future seems to include increased immigration, a population growing very slowly for the rest of your life
(Foot, 1982, p. 91), and the prospect of an enormous baby-boom
generation moving into old age and economic dependency as you
work your way through adulthood.

How will individual Canadians experience these societal
trends? In general, we will all be surrounded by more old people
and problems of aging. Deaths will occur more frequently than
births. Concerns with aging parents and friends will outweigh our
concerns with growing children. Especially for females, loneliness
and isolation in old age may become widespread problems. Fulfilling our duties as good children will become more onerous than
fulfilling our duties as good parents.

You will spend a larger portion of your life being a spouse but not a parent. Instead of bearing children for 10 to 15 years, as in earlier generations, women today already bear children over a mere 5 years or less. The period when one or more children are present in the home has dropped from 30 to 20 years. And perhaps most important, instead of spending almost no time alone with a spouse in the "empty nest," married people can expect to average 20 to 30 years in that state (Gee, 1986, p. 277).

This means spending more years alone with your spouse than in the company of children, the opposite of what most married people have experienced in the past century and a half and, perhaps, for most of human history. To fully appreciate the significance of this reversal, we need to consider how the presence of children affects people's lives.

Consequences of Parenthood   At first glance, satisfaction appears to increase with the number of children a parent has produced: the more, the merrier. For example, fathers of three or more children appear more satisfied with life and marriage than fathers with only one or two children—who are in turn more satisfied than married men without any children (Quality of Life survey, 1981). Mothers with varying numbers of children express no statistically significant differences in satisfaction.

But further analyses show that the relationship between satisfaction and number of children has to be interpreted in the opposite direction. It is not that having children makes people (especially fathers) satisfied, but rather that satisfied people are more likely to have children. Couples who are very satisfied with their marriage are more likely than other couples to bear children and also more likely to feel satisfied with life. Couples dissatisfied with their marriage who bear many children are no more satisfied with life than equally dissatisfied people who bear fewer children. And maritally satisfied people with *many* children are only slightly more satisfied with life than maritally satisfied people with fewer children.

So the parenting decision is largely an effect, not a cause, of marital and life satisfaction. Moreover, parenting will not make you more satisfied with life if you are dissatisfied with marriage, and it will contribute little to your marriage if you are already satisfied.

Not surprisingly, people who report that being a parent has "always" or "usually" been enjoyable are more likely to report high levels of life satisfaction than people for whom parenthood has less often been enjoyable. In turn, enjoyment of parenthood declines as the number of children increases (Quality of Life survey, 1981). Parents of only one child are more likely to report being "always" satisfied with parenthood, and less likely to report being "usually," "sometimes," or "hardly ever" satisfied, than parents of two or more children. Further, the enjoyment of parents with two children cannot be distinguished from that of parents with three, four, or more children. After the first two, adding more children does not increase the enjoyment of parenthood.

Even taking the "quality of the experience" into account, quantity of childbearing has no clear effect on life satisfaction. Parents who report "always" enjoying parenthood do *not* report increasing life satisfaction as their number of children increases. Among respondents reporting that parenthood has only "usually" been enjoyable, life satisfaction actually decreases with the addition of more children.

The mothers of many children are least likely of all mothers to report enjoying parenthood. The number of children at home has less effect on fathers' enjoyment of parenthood, suggesting that the unenjoyable burdens fall mainly on mothers.

As well, the reported enjoyment of parenthood is age-related: the people enjoying parenthood most are either under 30 or over 65 years of age. Likewise, the people feeling most satisfied with the way their children are growing up are under 30 or over 65 (see Figure 6.1). The younger group has scarcely experienced parenthood; the older group has left it far behind. Reporting the very least enjoyment of parenthood are women in their prime child-raising years, ages 31 to 45. Fathers' enjoyment of parenthood is less affected by age than mothers', for the reason given above: fathers typically have less to do with the process (Quality of Life survey, 1981).

Accordingly, younger women are more likely to advise against bearing many children than are older women (Quality of Life survey, 1981). This reflects a change in thinking about the ideal family size and more-immediate experience with raising children. Older women can readily advise bearing many children because they are farther removed from child-raising burdens (see also Campbell, 1980, p. 191).

Many factors—gender, age, and marital satisfaction among them—are mixed up together, so that drawing a simple conclusion is impossible. The best single bet, however, is that a happily married couple will find no children or one child nearly equally enjoyable. Their enjoyment of life, marriage, and parenthood may lead them to think that more children would be even better, but our data do not support such a conclusion. With more children, their satisfaction with life and marriage will remain unchanged or decline; it will not increase, in most cases.

Both husbands and wives are more likely to be "very satisfied" with their marriage if some or all of their children are living away from home (Rhyne, 1984, p. 19). Moreover, the marital satisfaction of husbands and wives is highest before parenthood begins and after the children have left home. This too argues that children diminish marital satisfaction in the average family. Bearing this

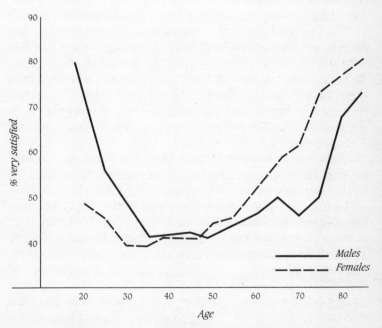

FIGURE 6.1 Percentage very satisfied with the way their children are growing up, by age and gender: Canada, 1981. *Includes people scoring 10 and 11 on an 11-point scale. A 10-year rolling average is used.* (Source: *Quality of Life survey, 1981.*)

out, four parents in ten would *not* like to see their "living-away" children more often than they already do. One in five parents say their children have upset them in the past month; of these, about half report that their children have upset them more than once or twice (Quality of Life survey, 1981).

How many children should you have? That's like asking how many businesses should you run, how many mates should you have, how many books should you write, how many musical instruments should you master. Just because one (of each) is wonderful does not mean that two will be twice as wonderful or three, three times as wonderful. In fact, each addition may bring less new satisfaction than the one before it; the novelty wears away and you have ever fewer resources to give each one.

From the children's own standpoint, fewer may be better. We are all familiar with arguments in favour of large families: most often cited are the "economies of scale"—that is, children come cheaper by the dozen. For example, older children can help take care of the younger ones and give each other companionship.

On the other hand, the rivalry between children for their parents' attention and love will be less in smaller families. Families with only one or two children—currently the most common sizes— do not contain "middle children," who often feel less loved than their first-born and last-born siblings. Proportionately more children are first-borns, who (psychologists have shown) tend to be competitive, sociable, and eager to win approval—traits you may find appealing.

Research consistently shows a small but significant negative effect of family size on adult status attainment. The smaller the family your child comes from, the more likely he or she is to attain high educational and occupational status (Pineo, 1985). The more care and encouragement a child receives, the more likely that child is to succeed, as we saw in Chapter 4 (Porter, Porter, & Blishen, 1982). This is another reason for having few rather than many children, if any at all.

Stages of Parental Satisfaction   The onset of parenthood is a particularly trying time. "Young parents . . . express more feeling of strain at this stage than at any other period of their married lives" (Campbell, 1980, p. 187). Campbell reports a particularly strong difference between the mothers of young children and young, married women still without a child. The young mothers are more likely to find life hard, feel tied down, express concern about financial matters, and worry about having a nervous breakdown (Campbell, 1980, pp. 187–188).

Raising small children also strains the marriage: disagreements become more common, both husband and wife feel they get less companionship from their mate than they once did, and both marital satisfaction and enjoyment of parenthood are declining or low. "Two out of five of these mothers of small children go so far as to admit they sometimes wish they could be free of the responsibilities of being a parent, a much larger proportion than is found among mothers of older children" (Campbell, 1980, p. 188).

In some ways, this period is the hardest parenthood will ever get. Once mother resumes paid employment, financial pressures begin to lighten. Balancing a job and child care is complex, but the parents of a school-age child feel less tied down, less strained or burdened by parenthood, and more likely to enjoy it. Once their children reach ages 6 through 17, spouses start to feel they understand each other better. "But they do not regain the strong sense of companionship . . . they had as young couples until they reach the next stage of life, when the children have grown up" (Campbell, 1980, p. 189).

Marital satisfaction generally declines with the passage of time, whether children are present or not. However, at all ages and marital durations, married women without children are more satisfied with their marriages than women with children (Lupri & Frideres, 1981, p. 300). Married men without children are also more satisfied than same-aged fathers except between the ages of 45 and 65, but the effects of parenthood on marital satisfaction are generally weaker for men than for women. American studies confirm that childless couples are more satisfied with their lives and marriages than couples with children (see, for example, Polonko, Scanzoni, & Teachman, 1982).

Thus it is primarily the couple with children whose marital satisfaction declines over time, then recovers sharply in middle age, around the time the children leave home. Marital satisfaction falls lower for women who work outside the home than for those who do not. Conversely, marital satisfaction falls lower for the husbands of the latter than for the husbands of the former (Lupri & Frideres, 1981). In all cases, marital satisfaction bottoms out when the children are adolescents. Feeding, clothing, and educating the children becomes increasingly burdensome. The greater need for money in middle age, at the very time when family income has started to level off, is often called the "life-cycle squeeze."

Two kinds of marital conflict arise out of parenthood as children reach adolescence. A woman who does *not* work outside the home may start to feel greater marital satisfaction at the very time her husband, smarting under a greater financial burden, is feeling the lowest satisfaction ever. A woman who *does* work outside the home may feel declining marital satisfaction, due to combined pressures at home and on the job, at the very time *her* husband is starting to feel greater marital and life satisfaction.

How long these conflicts last will be determined by the time it takes all the children to pass through adolescence and leave home. The fewer the children and the more closely they are spaced, the shorter the period of minimal satisfaction for one or both spouses and the briefer the marital conflict parenthood produces.

The "generally high level of satisfaction with life and with the various domains of life which we find associated with . . . [later] married life is probably more strongly influenced by the simple fact of growing older than it is by the departure of the children" (Campbell, 1980, p. 191). Yet freedom from responsibility to their children certainly contributes to this increased sense of well-being. Parenthood, then, is a story with a happy ending; the early and middle parts are a bit more difficult.

For this reason, parenthood should be chosen carefully and for good reasons. Avoid having any children, or too many children, for the wrong reasons: to make you satisfied with marriage or life, for example. Childlessness can be chosen and parenthood avoided if you put your mind to it. People are increasingly able to distinguish between marriage, sex, and childbearing as aspects of intimate life. Each activity can be carried on separately from the others, and each demands a separate choice based on good reasoning. No one will thank you for making the wrong choice, even if you make it with the best intentions.

Table 6.1 contains some questions you might ask yourself to determine whether you are "parent material." Whether you are currently contemplating parenthood or not, you may get something out of answering these questions.

TABLE 6.1 The NAOP (National Alliance for Optional Parenthood) "Am I Parent Material?" test. (Source: *Veevers, 1980, pp.162,164.*)

Raising a child? What's there to know?
1. Do I like children? When I'm around children for a while, what do I think or feel about having one around all of the time?
2. Do I enjoy teaching others?
3. Is it easy for me to tell other people what I want, or need, or what I expect of them?
4. Do I want to give a child the love (s)he needs? Is loving easy for me?
5. Am I patient enough to deal with the noise and the confusion of the 24-hour-a-day responsibility? What kind of time and space do I need for myself?
6. What do I do when I get angry or upset? Would I take things out on a child if I lost my temper?
7. What does discipline mean to me? What does freedom, or setting limits, or giving space mean? What is being too strict, or not strict enough? Would I want a perfect child?
8. How do I get along with my parents? What will I do to avoid the mistakes my parents made?
9. How would I take care of my child's health and safety? How do I take care of my own?
10. What if I have a child and find out I made a wrong decision?

Have my partner and I really talked about becoming parents?
1. Does my partner want to have a child? Have we talked about our reasons?
2. Could we give a child a good home? Is our relationship a happy and strong one?
3. Are we both ready to give our time and energy to raising a child?
4. Could we share our love with a child without jealousy?
5. What would happen if we separated after having a child, or if one of us should die?
6. Do my partner and I understand each other's feelings about religion, work, family, child-raising, future goals? Do we feel pretty much the same way? Will children fit into these feelings, hopes, and plans?
7. Suppose one of us wants a child and the other doesn't. Who decides?
8. Which of the questions in this test do we need to *really* discuss before making a decision?

What's in it for me?
1. Do I like doing things with children? Do I enjoy activities that children can do?
2. Would I want a child to be "like me"?
3. Would I try to pass on to my child my ideas and values? What if my child's ideas and values turn out to be different from mine?
4. Would I want my child to achieve things that I wish I had, but didn't?
5. Would I expect my child to keep me from being lonely in my old age? Do I do that for my parents? Do my parents do that for my grandparents?
6. Do I want a boy or a girl child? What if I don't get what I want?
7. Would having a child show others how mature I am?
8. Will I prove I am a man or a woman by having a child?
9. Do I expect my child to make my life happy?

TABLE 6.1 (*continued*)

Does having and raising a child fit the lifestyle I want?
1. What do I want out of life for myself? What do I think is important?
2. Could I handle a child and a job at the same time? Would I have time and energy for both?
3. Would I be ready to give up the freedom to do what I want to do, when I want to do it?
4. Would I be willing to cut back my social life and spend more time at home? Would I miss my free time and privacy?
5. Can I afford to support a child? Do I know how much it takes to raise a child?
6. Do I want to raise a child in the neighbourhood where I live now? Would I be willing and able to move?
7. How would a child interfere with my growth and development?
8. Would a child change my educational plans? Do I have the energy to go to school and raise a child at the same time?
9. Am I willing to give a great part of my life—AT LEAST 18 YEARS—to being responsible for a child? And spend a large portion of my life being concerned about my child's well-being?

Balancing Parenthood and Work

We have seen that parenthood intrudes on other domains of life: marriage and career in particular. Another question students commonly ask about parenthood is how they will be able to balance the demands of raising children and succeeding in a career.

This problem of balance is getting harder as more and more women enter the full-time paid labour force. Statistics from the 1986 census (*Globe and Mail*, March 2, 1988) reveal that male and female work patterns are converging: men are spending less time in the labour force and women more. Between 1981 and 1986, the percentage of Canadian working-age women holding a paid job or looking for one rose from 51.8 percent to 55.9 percent. (Equivalent male rates dropped from 78.2 percent to 77.5 percent in the same period.)

Most interesting of all, the participation rate of women with children under six years old rose from 49.5 percent to 62.1 percent in a mere five years. It is these women, with young children to care for, who are most likely to work for pay and will have the greatest difficulty balancing domestic and job demands.

The problem of balance first appeared with changes in family life three or four centuries ago. In the Middle Ages, the extended household was more common than any other kind and much more common than it is today. Even in Western Europe, households often included grown children, aunts and uncles, and servants, as well as fathers, mothers, and children. Child care and making a living were familial, even communal, activities. People took responsibility for other people's children, freeing adult men and women to work in the fields or, if in a town, at a trade.

Child care was not seen as requiring a lot of attention. It is only in recent centuries that people have regarded childhood as a special period requiring special care (Ariès, 1962). For these reasons, children could be cared for while women went about their normal daily work (producing subsistence). Children who could not be taken care of and could not be afforded were sent into "service." These arrangements made early marriage and unlimited childbearing feasible.

Around the sixteenth or seventeenth century, the "European marriage pattern" established itself (Hajnal, 1965). Characterized by a high age at marriage and a high proportion of people never marrying, the rise of this arrangement seems to coincide with the rise of nuclear families in Western Europe. The traditional "non-European pattern" continued for several centuries more in Eastern Europe, Africa, and Asia, but it has been disappearing even there during this century.

In the European pattern, marriage depends on economic independence: for farmers, on having a piece of land, and for craftsmen, on having a trade and shop. Marriage and childbearing are delayed until economic independence is assured. For many in the past, that meant a long delay in marrying and, for many women, delay beyond the age when childbearing was possible. In these cases, postponement might turn into a permanent state.

The precise sequence of changes from one family pattern to the other is unknown, but several key changes are interrelated. First, unlike the extended family, the nuclear family is relatively small and needs size limitation. Late marriage reduces the average size of a family that is not practising contraception (Henry, 1976, pp. 90-121); so it was useful for groups that could not (or would not) practice other forms of birth control (for a Canadian example, see Tepperman, 1974).

Second, even more than the extended family, the nuclear family demands a co-ordinated division of labour between domestic and other duties. Without grandparents, uncles and aunts, or sisters and brothers to help raise the children, one or both parents have to assume the domestic chores for their own family. Historically, the sexual division of labour may have become more marked in this kind of family than it had been in the extended family.

Finally, the nuclear family requires more understanding and

co-operation between spouses. Spouses rely on each other for more assistance, support, and care. Despite the sexual division of labour, marriage tends to evolve in a direction demanding more and better communication between spouses.

Elizabeth Bott (1957) illustrates the nature of this problem in a classic study of marriage, *Family and Social Network*. She compares two sets of families. One lives in a stable working-class London community full of childhood friends, parents, and other relatives—essentially, an extended family setting. The other set, from a similar background, lives in a new community full of socially and geographically uprooted people.

Spouses in the first—the "traditional"—community maintain their childhood ties and rely heavily on parents, relatives, and old friends for support, child care, and sociability. Husbands and wives have somewhat limited, stereotypical communication with each other, and rigidly define their roles and duties along gender lines. For example, husbands do not change diapers or cook; wives do not repair the car or go out much with friends. Spouses in the second community, cut off from old friends and family ties, form new networks of friends-in-common. They share activities and interests and even share domestic duties more. In general, their isolation from old relationships, sharing of new friends, and greater reliance on each other for support produces new kinds of communication and co-operation within the household.

In going from the old-style, quasi-extended family in the traditional community to the nuclear family in a new community of strangers, people gain privacy, independence, and more chance of upward social mobility. As a consequence, spousal communication and sharing have increased. Survey data indicate that more young married people today endorse the *idea* of communication and sharing—indeed, equality between spouses—than would have done so a generation ago. And, as the Bott study and others have since shown, spouses have started to *act* differently too. But Canadian families are a long way from spousal equality, as we shall see. This inequality becomes particularly noticeable and troublesome when wives take paid work.

As more women enter the paid labour force, this "new family" comes under even greater pressure to balance its various activities. The desire for privacy, independence, and upward mobility spreads to nearly everyone; male and female, child and parent all want more of each. So far, "democracy, individualism and meritocracy, the values most closely identified with two centuries of Western history, are conspicuous by their absence from the family" (Degler, 1980, p. 471). But all of this is changing.

To achieve a balance, families now purchase many domestic services from "outsiders"; but they still need to find better ways of integrating members' diverse interests and schedules. The problem of scheduling arises out of one simple fact: the day contains only 24 hours. Male and female time use differs markedly in two main respects: time spent in paid work and time spent housekeeping and parenting (Horna & Lupri, 1987; Lupri & Mills, 1987; Michelson, 1985).

Survey data reveal that, in the average American family, women are solely responsible for deciding what is for dinner and preparing it, managing the household budget, and raising the children. Women and their partners are jointly responsible for major expenditures: where to go on vacation, how much to spend on major purchases, how much to save, how much insurance to carry and where to buy it, and how to invest savings. Men are solely responsible for deciding what to watch on television (Casale & Lerman, 1986, p. 94). Canadian families are similar.

In a young dual-earner family, the presence of young children makes an enormous difference to the average number of hours wives work each weekday (counting both paid work and unpaid housework/child care): they vary from 10.6 hours (no children) to 14.3 hours (all children are aged six and over) to 16.2 hours per day (one or more children are under six). Husbands' average work hours only increase from 10.3 to 12.1 hours per weekday as young children are added to the family (Lupri & Mills, 1987, p. 41).

Husbands' home duties increase very little when their wives work full-time for pay, even when small children are present. Instead, wives work an average of three hours per day more, the standard of familial housekeeping and child care may drop, and more services may be purchased from outside sources: nannies, cleaning services, fast-food restaurants, and so on.

So mothers with full-time paying jobs work longer hours than husbands or any other kinds of wives. They have little free time during their waking hours. As a result, time pressures cause these women extreme tension. With more activities to complete within

24 hours, they are less able to tolerate unforeseen snags or hitches. But life with children is *full* of snags and hitches. Not surprisingly then, employed mothers report a lot of tension in activities that would be easy if time were plentiful: activities like waking the children, getting them ready for school or daycare, caring for the baby and for the older children, preparing food, cleaning the house and getting to work on time (Michelson, 1985).

People feel more tension than usual in activities they cannot control, or have not chosen. Not only are women involved in more activities than men; they generally have less choice about when and where to spend their time, and suffer more tension as a result. For their part, husbands suffer less tension than their wives and their tensions are more often work-related. Among a mere four activities that cause men greater-than-usual tension, two—commuting to and from work, and doing their job—are directly related to paid employment. Husbands can involve themselves more fully in their jobs because they suffer fewer competing pressures. Moreover, husbands typically contribute to housework at their convenience; their activities include house maintenance, repairs, and gardening, which they are inclined to view as leisure or semi-leisure (Horna & Lupri, 1987).

A prime tension-producer for both spouses is daily travel. Many family responsibilities disproportionately carried out by women—such as shopping for food or taking children to and from day-care—require travel, and "women often travel with less efficient resources and fewer choices" (Michelson, 1985). They less often have access to the family car or enough choice over where daycare, shopping, and work will be located. Toronto women, for example, are about three times as likely as their husbands to use public transportation, especially for trips to and from work. The divergence of daycare locations from an "optimal location," either near home or on a direct line between home and work, adds at least 28 percent more time to the mother's (and child's) trip to such centres (Michelson, 1985).

Somehow, working women get all their chores done. Contrary to expectations that working parents would feel guilty about giving their children too little time and attention, a majority of parents in dual-career families feel otherwise. About half feel their children are just as well off as children from homes in which only one parent works for pay, and about one-quarter feel their children are even better off (Casale & Lerman, 1986, p. 125).

The major problem modern parents face is not guilt, then. For single parents, it is typically the shortage of money. For married parents, it is the strain of too many duties, conflicts arising out of unequal parental arrangements, and financial concerns arising out of increased reliance on paid child-care and housekeeping services. Married parents most often fight about financial matters (53 percent), job demands (50 percent), disciplining children (50 percent), and the demands of their spouse's job (47 percent). Problems in the marital relationship are primarily caused by poor communication (22 percent), not seeing each other enough (12 percent), not doing enough together (12 percent), and money (12 percent) (Casale & Lerman, 1986, p. 97).

Too little time for marital interaction may sometimes be a blessing. Many couples report that their brief time together is pleasant precisely *because* they lack the time or energy to argue. Most want to make their time together as pleasant, or at least quiet, as possible (Casale and Lerman, 1986).

During an average adulthood starting in 1980, a married woman can expect to work 14 percent more hours than her husband, if present levels of childbearing and related work patterns continue (Meissner, 1982). So if you are an employed woman, you are likely to work harder and get less pay and recognition for each hour worked than your spouse. Many of your most stress-filled activities, especially parental ones, will yield no career advancement, pay, or public recognition. In fact, they will steal time and energy from your career.

When asked, most people report that they are satisfied with their lives, and since women are unable to alter the domestic inequity, they cope and regard it as inevitable. What will the effects on their children be? Most adolescents continue to hold traditional sex-role ideals (Baker, 1985). But there has never yet been a generation of Canadian adolescents raised in dual-earner families. What sense do they make of their parents' (or mother's) frustration, and how will they live as adults? We will learn the consequence of this in due course.

Individual and Collective Solutions   Women do a number of things about this problem of balance. Some career-oriented women choose to marry but not to bear children. Others bear one or two children in a very short time, to limit the interruption of their careers.

Many of these latter women return to full-time work almost immediately after bearing children. This pattern is most common among highly educated women with careers (not merely jobs) whose salaries are large enough to pay for high-quality child care. Less educated and less career-oriented women are more likely to leave the paid work force until their children begin attending school full-time. Accordingly, labour force participation is much higher for women with children over five years old than it is for mothers of younger children. However, at no age do average mothers ever attain as high a level of labour force participation as similarly educated women without children (Statistics Canada, 1984). This difference may be due to the parental obligations and tensions that continue even after children are in school full-time. But increasingly, women are returning to work immediately after childbearing: this appears to be the trend of the future.

Another—and apparently growing—solution to the problem of balance is part-time work, defined as less than 30 hours of paid work per week (Labour Canada, 1983, p. 17). Much part-time work results from an inability to get full-time work; since 1975, involuntary part-time work has become more than twice as common a portion of all part-time work (Akyeampong, 1987, p. 27). However, voluntary part-time work also continues to grow as a proportion of all paid work, especially among married women.

Labour unions generally oppose the expansion of part-time work because it may reduce the availability of full-time work, may not be fully voluntary, and currently allows employers to avoid paying the fringe benefits full-time workers normally receive. As part-time work becomes even more common, we will probably see the prorated payment of fringe benefits to part-time workers, and some of these objections will disappear. At present, part-time work guarantees women's continued subordination in poorly paid, low-status jobs by continuing to make them primarily responsible for child care.

Most female part-time workers aged 25 to 54 appear to want part-time, not full-time, work for a variety of reasons, among them the need to fulfil personal and family responsibilities (Labour Canada, 1983, p. 53). Few female part-time workers want more hours of paid work per month than they already have (Labour Canada, 1983, p. 69). Part-time work allows enormous flexibility and many varied patterns (Labour Canada, 1983, p. 67) and, under the best circumstances, can almost be tailored to a worker's timetable needs. Part-time work helps women to fulfil domestic obligations and meet income needs when virtually single-handed child-rearing makes full-time paid work extremely difficult.

Indeed, if part-time work continues to increase, gets unionized, and pays benefits prorated to time spent on the job, it will become an increasingly attractive option for both fathers and mothers. One can imagine future generations organizing their life cycles differently from today's, moving in and out of jobs and, within jobs, between full-time and part-time status, to accommodate changing domestic demands and personal well-being. Gender-based differences in work life may disappear, replaced by differences based on education or social class instead. Flexible job-sharing is one way this change may come about.

However, such flexibility does not suit current thinking about careers, much less existing institutional arrangements. Today highly educated professional and managerial women who seek part-time work are not likely to be considered serious about their work. Even if given the part-time work they want, women may significantly hinder their prospects for major responsibility by allowing that impression to stand. This means that employed mothers, the main voluntary part-time workers, must weigh carefully whether they want to have a career and, equally important, be *perceived* as having a career.

British women employed full-time are much more likely than their husbands to prefer more time off over more pay in their current job (Young & Willmott, 1975, p. 115). Moreover, employed women are more likely than their husbands to put thoughts of a career out of their minds. Compared with their husbands, female full-time employees are much less likely to say there is a "career ladder" in their work, report they have "a lot of say at work," feel "pressed" or "sometimes pressed" at work, report doing overtime work during the previous week, or travel more than 10 miles to their job. Such differences are even greater between female *part-time* employees and their husbands (Young & Willmott, 1975, p. 116).

By and large, wives are less likely than husbands to hold jobs that interfere with their domestic duties. Avoiding such interference is easier in some jobs—for example, clerical and manual jobs—than it is in professional and managerial work (Young and Willmott, 1975, p. 117), suggesting that highly educated mothers will be the most pressured women of all.

This agrees with the Canadian finding that women in male-dominated professions are least likely of all women to marry, stay married, or bear children (Marshall, 1987). Of all women, the highly educated will have most difficulty balancing parental and occupational duties.

For these reasons, the employers of educated women face increasing demands for company-sponsored or public child care, and more-flexible work schedules. As well, rising numbers of dual-income couples make joint decisions about domestic task-sharing, work time, job transfers, and relocation. Child-rearing needs demand employer accommodation through "flextime," part-time work, sabbaticals (for both women and men), and more working at home.

Partners in two-career families are increasingly resistant to job transfers requiring relocation, long regarded as central to career development. Companies will find it increasingly necessary to ease the burdens of relocation by providing job-search assistance for the accompanying spouse, child-care and real-estate arrangements, relocation counselling, and orientation to the new community.

Goods and services to make housekeeping easier are increasingly demanded. To take a well-known example, the fast-food industry is growing more rapidly than most. In the 1980s, North American restaurants have seen a dramatic increase in their breakfast business over previous years. The use of daycare for preschool children is also increasing and good daycare seems unlikely to result in serious emotional disturbance for the child (Rutter, 1981). But even so, good daycare is hard to find and, for many parents, impossible to afford.

Proposed Solutions   Without other institutional and societal changes to ease the burdens of motherhood, the flight from parenthood may continue and even accelerate. Some solutions are economic. One is to provide more goods and services directly to the families of women who work outside the home: for example, more, better, and cheaper daycare. Another is to pay women higher wages, enabling them to purchase the services they need. This, in turn, requires legislation to prevent and remedy income discrimination against women, and to ensure that payment for part-time work is prorated against full-time pay and benefits.

A more contentious proposal involves paying for housework. At present, women's housework and child care provide a substantial unpaid benefit to their husbands' employers. Married male workers show up for work regularly, in good health, and well turned-out *because* their wives do the unpaid work needed to ensure it. Employers can expect husbands to take work home and work until finished, travel as part of their job, and think more or less continuously about their work *because* wives keep up unpaid housekeeping and child care services regardless. Some observers believe that employers should pay their employees for wives' services by raising salaries, or governments should pay wives directly through taxes raised on corporate earnings.

Perhaps the ideology of parenting as mother's responsibility must change, as should society's definitions of the "clockwork of careers" (Hochschild, 1975), to accommodate child-raising and respect it as a collective, societal responsibility, not an individual's problem. More generally, people who care for dependants—whether children, the physically infirm, or the very old—should be paid by the state for their labours, whether performed at home or in an institution. It is not so obvious that wives should be paid for taking care of husbands who are perfectly able to take care of themselves.

Resistance to all these alternatives is strong. Most men still take for granted the services mothers and wives provide, and devalue them because they do not yield a cash income. Further, many oppose increasing services to employed women or paying wages for child care on the grounds that these actions would raise income taxes and/or the prices of goods and services. Yet what is at issue is the distribution of benefits between the genders.

More moderate proposals include improving public transportation to make employed women's travel easier and faster; loosening zoning restrictions so that shopping and child care will be closer to people's homes; allowing round-the-clock shopping for goods and services, to give employed women a greater opportunity to get their household chores (for example, food shopping) done when most convenient; and increasing flextime to allow paid work and work-related travel to mesh more easily with domestic duties (Michelson, 1985). Universal high-quality, low-cost daycare is much needed and is unlikely to harm children, even preschoolers (Rutter, 1981).

Many of these changes require public spending and/or impose new burdens on other workers. This means they will be resisted, at least in the short run. Whether they are implemented or not, duties will have to be redistributed within the household. Particularly, fathers will have to become more involved in child care and assume a greater share of the tensions associated with too little free time. This will force men to spend less of their time and mental energy on their work or leisure.

In the short run, men may view such changes as uneconomic or irrational. After all, why should a man sacrifice an hour of his time for household duties and child care to save his spouse an hour, even if she spends it on paid work? When both are employed full-time, the typical man is earning about 42 percent more per hour than the typical woman. To give up $1.42 of family income to get $1.00 back seems hardly sensible, some men might argue.

A larger, longer-run perspective answers this argument. First, to do otherwise exploits married women at home, and they are already exploited and discriminated against at work. Second, it gives employers a false message about the true cost of work and a false conception of what they can reasonably expect their workers, whether male or female, to do. Such misinformation delays the search for humane solutions to the problem of integrating parenthood and work. Third, the present arrangement perpetuates traditional stereotypes of marriage in the eyes of children, ensuring that daughters will suffer the same tensions as their mothers.

Women today are working more hours than their grandmothers did and the gap between male and female hours of labour is increasing each year (Meissner, 1982). That the workload is becoming more burdensome is reflected by a general decline in women's attitudes toward homemaking. Further, more women are worrying about having a nervous breakdown (Campbell, 1980, pp. 130, 133). Women are also much more likely than men to report feeling depressed, worried, or frightened (Campbell, 1980, p. 131).

Yet on the whole, "most women seem to be in the role they prefer, and those who have chosen homemaking are as satisfied with their lives as those who have made the other choice" (Campbell, 1980, p. 139). Further, given the injustices women face in our society, what is surprising is how close women's sense of well-being comes to men's.

Freer choice has allowed women who want to work outside the home to get the satisfactions paid employment can bring. Many women who remain in the home are just as satisfied, which leads to several major conclusions. The first is that, *given a choice*, people look for and sometimes find the life situation that will give them the most life satisfaction. Second, people largely accommodate themselves to what their life demands, especially if they have chosen it. Finally, adulthood is becoming more complicated and stressful for women, whichever adult role they choose to play.

Concluding Remarks

This chapter has presented a somewhat bleak picture of parenthood, in order to counterbalance the unrealistic picture of parenthood presented by the mass media.

In reality, parenthood can be extremely gratifying, exciting, and educational. One learns a lot about life, other people, and oneself in raising children to adulthood. Further, parents typically fall in love with their children, just as they did with their mate, not because of the child's ideal qualities, but because he or she is lovable, loving, needy, and close-at-hand. On the other hand, parenthood is extremely demanding of time, money, and emotional energy. It may require important sacrifices.

Some of the difficulties associated with parenthood can be remedied by a better sharing of household duties between spouses. Other difficulties can be remedied by the government provision of better daycare facilities, the assurance of paid maternity (or parental) leave, and other assistance. But ultimately the problem will rest in parents' own hands. People will have to choose more carefully between parenthood and other demanding, fulfilling activities: romance, leisure, career, education, and so on. No one can do everything well, or enjoy trying. People should make the parenting decision with that simple fact in mind.

Do people get what they want out of parenthood? Though some people are undoubtedly pressured into it, more and more people are freely deciding whether or not to become parents. As a consequence, more people are likely to be satisfied with the result: to feel they have gotten what they wanted. Moreover, a majority of people feel quite satisfied with their decision.

Yet this satisfaction varies. The people most responsible for parenting—mothers between the ages of 30 and 45—are least satisfied. Their satisfaction declines the more children they have: more is usually not better. Further, mothers with paid jobs are least satisfied. Balancing marriage, parenting, and paid work calls for tremendous energy and patience. Few people find such continuous demands satisfying. So working mothers are least likely to get what they wanted.

Chapter 7 will address questions having to do with residence: where people choose to live, and with what results.

References

AKYEAMPONG, E.B. (1987, Autumn).   Involuntary part-time employment in Canada, 1975-1986. *Canadian Social Trends*, pp. 26-29.

ARIÈS, P. (1962).   *Centuries of childhood: A social history of family life*. New York: Vintage.

BAKER, M. (1985).   *What will tomorrow bring? A study of the aspirations of adolescent women*. Ottawa: Canadian Advisory Council on the Status of Women.

BANKS, J.A. (1954).   *Prosperity and parenthood: A study of family planning among the Victorian middle classes*. London: Routledge & Kegan Paul.

BEAUJOT, R. (1986).   Dwindling families: making the case for policies to sustain or raise the birthrate in Canada. *Policy Options, 7*(7), 3-7.

_____. (1987).   *The family and demographic change: Economic and cultural interpretations*. London, ON: University of Western Ontario, Department of Sociology.

BOTT, E. (1957).   *Family and social network*. London: Tavistock Publications.

BOULDING, K.E. (1981).   *Ecodynamics: A new theory of societal evolution*. Beverly Hills, CA: Sage Publications.

CAMPBELL, A. (1980).   *The sense of well-being in America: Recent patterns and trends*. New York: McGraw-Hill.

CASALE, A.M., & LERMAN, P. (1986).   *USA today: Tracking tomorrow's trends*. Kansas City: Andrews, McMeel & Parker.

COALE, A.J. (1969).   The decline of fertility in Europe from the French Revolution to World War II. In S.J. Behrman, L. Corsa & R. Freedman (Eds.). *Fertility and family planning* (pp. 3-24). Ann Arbor: University of Michigan Press.

_____, & WATKINS, S.C. (Eds.) (1986).   *The decline of fertility in Europe*. Princeton, NJ: Princeton University Press.

DEGLER, C. (1980).   *At odds*. New York: Oxford University Press.

FOOT, D.K. (1982).   *Canada's population outlook: Demographic futures and economic challenges*. The Canadian Institute for Economic Policy Series. Toronto: Lorimer.

GEE, E.M. (1986).   The life course of Canadian women: An historical and demographic analysis. *Social Indicators Research, 18*, 263-283.

HAJNAL, J. (1965).   European marriage patterns in perspective. In D.V. Glass and D.E.C. Eversley (Eds.), *Population in history* (pp. 101-143). London: Edward Arnold.

HAMIL, R.E. (1987).   The arrival of the 5-billionth human. *The Futurist, #21*(4), 36-37.

HENRY, L. (1976).   *Population: Analysis and models*. London: Edward Arnold.

HOBART, C.W. (1984).   Interest in parenthood among young Anglophone and Francophone Canadians. *Canadian Studies in Population. 11*(2), 111-133.

HOCHSCHILD, A.R. (1975, October).   Disengagement theory: a critique and proposal. *American Sociological Review, 40*, pp. 553-569.

HORNA, J., & LUPRI, E. (1987).   Father's participation in work, family life and leisure: a Canadian experience. In C. Lewis & M. O'Brien (Eds.), *Reassessing fatherhood: New observations on fathers and the modern family (pp. 54-73)*. London: Sage Publications.

JOHNSON, L. (1987).   Children's visions of the future. *The Futurist, 21*(3), 36-40.

LABOUR CANADA. (1983).   *Part-time work in Canada*. Report of the Commission of Inquiry into Part-time Work. Ottawa: Supply & Services.

LUPRI, E., & FRIDERES, J. (1981).   The quality of marriage and the passage of time: Marital satisfaction over the family life cycle. *Canadian Journal of Sociology, 6*(3), 283-305.

LUPRI, E., & MILLS, D. (1987).   The household division of labour in young dual-earner couples: The case of Canada. *International Review of Sociology*, New Series, No. 2, 33-54.

MALTHUS, T.R. (1959).   *Population: The first essay*. Foreword by K.E. Boulding. Ann Arbor: University of Michigan Press. (Original work published 1798.)

MARSHALL, K. (1987, Winter).   Women in male-dominated professions. *Canadian Social Trends*, pp. 7-11.

MEISSNER, M. (1982).   The domestic economy: Now you see it, now you don't. In N. Hersom and D.E. Smith (Eds.), *Women and the Canadian labour force* (pp. 343-366). Proceedings of a workshop organized by the Social Sciences and Humanities Research Council of Canada at the University of British Columbia in January 1981. Ottawa: SSHRC.

MICHELSON, W. (1985).   *From sun to sun: Daily obligations and community structure in the lives of employed mothers and their families*. Totowa, NJ: Rowman & Allanheld.

PINEO, P.C. (1985).   Family size and status attainment. In M. Boyd, J. Goyder, F.E. Jones, H.A. McRoberts, P.C. Pineo, & J. Porter (Eds.), *Ascription and achievement: Studies in mobility and status attainment in Canada* (pp. 201-228). Ottawa: Carleton University Press.

POLONKO, K.A., SCANZONI, J., & TEACHMAN, J.D. (1982, December). Childlessness and marital satisfaction: a further reassessment. *Journal of Family Issues, 3*, pp. 545-573.

PORTER, J., PORTER, M., & BLISHEN, B.R. (1982).   *Stations and callings: Making it through the school system*. Toronto: Methuen.

QUALITY OF LIFE SURVEY. (1981).   Unpublished raw data from large survey of life satisfaction conducted at the Institute for Behavioural Research, York University, Toronto.

RHYNE, D. (1984). *Marital satisfaction in Canada: A descriptive overview.* Toronto: York University, Institute for Behavioural Research.

ROMANIUC, A. (1986, November). *Fertility in Canada: A long view.* Paper presented at The Family in Crisis: A population crisis?, a colloquium organized by the Federation of Canadian Demographers, University of Ottawa.

RUTTER, M. (1981). Social-emotional consequences of day care for preschool children. *American Journal of Orthopsychiatry, 51*(1), 4–28.

STATISTICS CANADA. (1984). *Women in the world of work* (Catalogue No. 99-940). Ottawa: Supply & Services.

_____. (1985). *Population projections for Canada, provinces and territories, 1984–2006* (Catalogue No. 91-520). Ottawa: Supply & Services.

_____. (1987). *Current demographic analysis: Report on the demographic situation in Canada, 1986* (Catalogue No. 91-209E). Ottawa: Supply & Services.

TEPPERMAN, L. (1974). Ethnic variations in marriage and fertility: Canada, 1871. *Canadian Review of Sociology and Anthropology, 11*(4), 324–343.

_____. (1986). Population processes. In L. Tepperman & R.J. Richardson (Eds.), *The social world: An introduction to sociology* (pp. 87–111). Toronto: McGraw-Hill Ryerson.

VEEVERS, J.E. (1980). *Childless by choice.* Toronto: Butterworth.

WATTENBERG, B.J. (1987). *The birth dearth.* New York: The American Enterprise Institute, Pharos Books.

YOUNG, M., & WILLMOTT, P. (1975). *The symmetrical family.* Harmondsworth: Penguin Books.

Chapter Seven

Locations and Lifestyles: *what you want and what you get*

Introduction

Many students are interested in questions related to where they might live: in what country or province; whether in a city or suburb; whether alone or with friends or family. This chapter will argue that where you live is how you live. It will discuss patterns of location in Canadian society—where people live and why—and the lifestyles associated with different locations. Finally, it will consider the satisfactions associated with each kind of location.

People are not completely free to choose where they live. For many, location is determined by the availability or cost of housing; for others, by the availability of an appropriate job; and for others still, by the location of family and friends. As in so many aspects of life, choice is also limited by social class: the rich have a wider variety of choices than the poor.

But within this context of unequal opportunity, both rich and poor try to locate themselves where they believe they will be most satisfied. Because they have some choice in this, their locations reflect their life goals and concerns. Typically, people who move from one location to another are seeking more satisfaction as their goals and opportunities change. To answer the question "Where should I live?" we must consider what kind of life you want to live and what opportunities you have for living that life. That is the reason this chapter treats questions of location and lifestyle together.

Like earlier chapters, this one will end by considering whether people usually get what they want or learn to want what they get.

Locations

Location as a State of Mind   Where you live both affects and reflects your state of mind. First, where you live is an *environment*, a stage on which you play your social roles for many hours each day. Location determines what you will see, hear, smell, and touch when you are at home. Where you live is not merely a physical environment, but also a social environment, determining *who* you will see and interact with regularly, what ideas you will be exposed to, and what behaviours will be observed, as well as what and who you will *not* be exposed to, see, and learn from. Such selective contacts will capacitate you in some ways and incapacitate you in others.

Beyond that, where you live is an *opportunity structure*. By bringing you into contact with some people and activities, it makes some futures more likely than others. Your acquaintanceships, friendships, and social networks are largely shaped by where you live. These networks are important in coupling you to or decoupling you from major institutions, as we learned in Chapter 2. Further, where you live will reflect your class (and ethnic) group and keep you part of it. Locked into your own community, you are also locked out of other communities.

Finally, where you live is a *state of mind*. Where you grow up shapes your ideas about how and where you want to live as an adult. Maturing ideas about *how* you want to live take material form in *where* you choose to live. The choices we make about where to live—on the coast or inland, in a small or large place, alone or with family or friends, and so on—express concretely the future we desire and the good life we intend to live. For example, "the upwardly mobile executive who moves from one residence into another, more elegant one is moving in psychological as well as physical space" (Campbell, 1980, p.159).

In all these respects, your location is like your social class: both shape and reflect choices, capacitate and incapacitate, close in and out, couple and decouple. But other factors besides social class will influence your idea of the good life and, with it, your location. They include age, stage in the life cycle (for example, marital and parental status), and the strength of your ethnic or regional identity.

Despite their similarities, social class and location are different enough to justify separate treatment. Asked "Where would you like to be 10 years from now?" a person might answer in social class terms (for example, the owner of a successful business) or locational terms (for example, living in a big old house just outside Vancouver). The two types of answer fit together, but they are not the same. Moreover, social class influences your choice of location; but within a given social class, different kinds of choice are possible.

The notional character of location—how location reflects life plans—first became apparent to me through a battle between two Canadian communities I shall call "Littletown" and "Metropolis."

Metropolis had grown very rapidly and needed more room to expand. It also needed a larger tax base. To gain land and tax revenues, Metropolis asked the province to let it annex several surrounding communities, including Littletown. Each of the threatened communities hired consultants to help them argue their case before a provincial board that would decide the matter. My job was to challenge the conclusions Metropolis' consultants had drawn from a survey of Metropolis and Littletown residents.

The Metropolis-sponsored survey established that about two-thirds of employed Littletowners commuted to work in Metropolis every day. In Metropolis' eyes, this made Littletown just a "bedroom suburb" of Metropolis. Littletowners also used Metropolis for shopping (especially large purchases) and certain kinds of recreation. But Littletowners felt their community was socially and culturally distinct from Metropolis. They claimed that Metropolis was poorly planned and governed, in comparison with their own community. They feared that annexation would destroy Littletown's unique cultural heritage. In rebuttal, the Metropolis consultants argued that unjustified anti-annexation attitudes were promoted by a few who stood to gain from continued Littletown independence.

Yet Littletown's lifestyle *was* different from Metropolis'. A large proportion of Littletowners had previously lived in Metropolis. They had left Metropolis to live in a style they believed was possible in Littletown and not in Metropolis. Less concerned with achieving the goals Metropolis' government had staked out— chiefly growth, business, and a "big-city air"—Littletown's government provided just what people had come to Littletown to get: a small community with satisfying schools, services, and recreation.

Littletowners had the best of both worlds: a large city and its work opportunities on their doorstep, and a small, close-knit, well-run community where they could sleep and relax. They feared losing control over local institutions and becoming just another neighbourhood among the many that made up Metropolis.

When you think about it, small communities often depend on larger, adjacent communities for jobs; their economy relies on selling goods and services to the neighbour. And people in small communities often prefer their own way of life to the one available next door. That is why most Maritimers stay in the Maritimes, despite high unemployment rates, and most Canadians stay in Canada, rather than move to the wealthier United States. People usually want the best of both worlds. So the Littletown *versus* Metropolis confrontation was a classic battle of lifestyles.

Littletown was the environment Littletowners preferred, and it represented an alternative to the Metropolis lifestyle and way of governing. In fact, most peoples' choices about location are choices against something as much as choices in favour of something else. What locations are average Canadians choosing for and against, then?

Where Canadians Live Today   A majority of Canadians live in Ontario (population 9.1 million in 1986), Quebec (6.5 million), British Columbia (2.9 million), and Alberta (2.4 million). Taken together, these four provinces comprise just under 80 percent of the Canadian population.

Further, most Canadians live in a metropolitan area. In 1986, 7.7 million people—30 percent of Canada's people—lived in metropolitan Toronto, Montreal, or Vancouver. About 12.5 million, or 50 percent, live in the 10 largest metropolitan areas; many remaining Canadians live in the next 15 largest metropolitan areas. Relatively few Canadians live in rural areas or small towns at any distance from large cities, but increasing numbers live in the suburbs of large cities (places like Littletown). Some, as distant as 40 miles or more from the downtown area, are still within daily commuting range.

People tend to live near other people. In fact, one person in seven lives five feet or less from his or her nearest neighbour. One in three lives ten feet or less from his or her neighbour, and six in ten people less than 30 feet away (Quality of Life survey, 1981). Not surprisingly, most people know at least some of their neighbours by name. One person in three knows at least ten families living closest to his or her dwelling, and over half know more than five of their neighbouring families by name.

Because of this proximity and acquaintanceship, seven in ten Canadian adults consider themselves "part of the neighbourhood" (Quality of Life survey, 1981). So much for the fear that modern life spells the end of "community!" What's more, people tend to live near others like themselves. Half say their neighbours belong to the same social and cultural group as they do; only one person in three feels out of place culturally and socially. Residential segregation by ethnic group and social class is as highly developed in Canadian cities as anywhere in North America (Balakrishnan, 1976, 1982).

Finally, about three people in four live in family households as the spouse or child of the household head. Next most common is living alone; about one household in five contains only one person. The percentage of Canadians living alone has been rising rapidly since 1940 (Thomas & Burch, 1985). As well, other living arrangements have become more common, especially in large cities. The type of household you live in is influenced by your age and stage in the life cycle. Nowhere is this demonstrated more dramatically than in the housing arrangements of people aged 18 to 29.

The vast majority of 18- and 19-year-old Canadians—85 percent of males and 73 percent of females—live in their parents' home (Statistics Canada, 1982). But less than ten years later (ages 25 to 29), the vast majority—64 percent of males and 78 percent of females—have become spouses and/or parents in their own household. Another 8 to 10 percent are living alone—four or five times as many as live alone at ages 18 and 19.

No equally large change of household arrangements occurs again until middle age—when, with children grown up, large numbers of widows and widowers, divorcés and divorcées, start to live alone, or with non-relatives, or in non-families. ("Family" is defined for these purposes as "one or two adults and one or more related child(ren)." Thus, if you live with an aunt or a brother, you live with relatives in a non-family.) In 1981 the bulk of Canadian live-alones—nearly half a million—were women aged 55 and over. Elderly women who are widowed or divorced are more likely to live alone if they have no adult daughters to live with (Wister & Burch, 1983).

Movement from One Location to Another   In Canada, people often relocate as their dreams and choices change. The migration of native-born male workers is particularly common (Pineo, 1985, p.486). One in three reports having lived permanently in another province at some point in his life. Further, two in three have lived permanently in cities other than the one in which they were born, and one male in two is *currently* living in another such city.

Every separation and divorce brings someone a change of location: at least a change of households, and sometimes even a change of cities or regions. Likewise, every marriage brings one or both spouses a change of location. Beyond these, increases in family size (through birth), decreases in family size (through death or children leaving home), changes in family income, and new job opportunities also lead to changes in location.

With so many economic and demographic events taking place, movement within cities is considerable. Over one-quarter of Canadian adults report having lived in their present dwelling only a year or less, and over half have lived there five years or less (Quality of Life survey, 1981). Further, more than a quarter doubt they will still be living in the same dwelling two years from today.

People often change neighbourhoods when they change dwellings. Nearly one adult Canadian in five reports having lived in his or her present neighbourhood a year or less, and 45 percent have been there only five years or less (Quality of Life survey, 1981). Change of dwellings is also associated, in many cases, with a change of cities or towns. Thus, 7 percent of survey respondents report having lived in their present city or town one year or less, and one in five has lived there five years or less. Asked where they expect to spend the rest of their lives, one in three say they expect to live elsewhere, implying they will change cities again.

The already-large cities and their surrounding suburbs gain most from this inter-city movement. Metropolitan Toronto, Vancouver, and Ottawa-Hull, three of Canada's four largest cities, all increased their population by 9 to 10 percent between 1981 and 1986. According to the most recent census, some smaller cities also posted large gains, among them Saskatoon (a 15 percent gain), and Kitchener, Oshawa, and Windsor (8 to 9 percent gains).

But the fastest-growing census subdivisions are Canada's "Littletowns": for example, bedroom suburbs of Toronto like Vaughan (which more than doubled in size between 1981 and 1986), and Markham and Ajax (which increased 40 to 50 percent). Suburbs of Ottawa and Halifax are also making large gains. Many businesses have recently moved to these rapidly growing communities, significantly increasing the white-collar and service jobs available there.

The amount of population movement is just as impressive if we shift our attention to provinces and even regions. Statistics Canada has devised what it calls a "churn rate" that measures the total amount of migration into and out of a given province or territory. The measure is useful for comparing provinces.

Several factors drive the churn rate up or down. One is the presence or absence of long-standing communities and what we earlier called "institutional completeness." Another is the presence or absence of strong regional cultures and, in the case of Quebec, a distinct language. Taken together, these factors largely account for the relatively low levels of churn in the Maritimes, Quebec, and Manitoba. But economic change—the development or collapse of "frontier," resource-based opportunities—works in the opposite direction, accounting for a high churn rate in Alberta and the Territories. Ontario has a very low churn rate because of stable economic opportunities, well-developed institutional completeness, and a large base population.

Interprovincial movements reflect changing economic conditions, then. The economic recession of the early 1980s caused a drop in interprovincial mobility, from the 16 per 1000 annual level recorded during most of the 1970s to 11 per 1000 in 1982–83 (Statistics Canada, 1987, p. 54). But more recent figures show a return to the higher levels of movement observed in the 1970s.

"Historically, the Canadian population has always been moving westward. The trend, though uneven, has been well established. . . . Consequently, [the westward migration] patterns of the 1970s are not new" (Foot, 1982, p. 74). Recent evidence bears out this conclusion, in large part. Though "population movements, both into and within Canada, have recently hit very low levels by historical standards . . . internal migration has returned to more traditional patterns following the slowdown in the oil boom in Western Canada" (Statistics Canada, 1987). Once again, migrants are strongly attracted to Ontario, in- and out-migration are nearly balanced in Quebec, and the Atlantic provinces are back to losing more migrants than they take in. The overall trend may be westward, but countervailing economic, social, and cultural forces also influence that movement dramatically.

Migration reflects a desire for both economic opportunity and a particular lifestyle. But what, exactly, do sociologists mean by "lifestyle," and why are they interested in the topic?

Lifestyles

Origins of Interest in Lifestyle   Sociological interest in lifestyle can be traced to at least two main sources in classical sociology. The first source is Max Weber and his writings on "commensalism" and "status group"; important followers include Karl Mannheim. The second source includes a stream of researchers on "community," beginning with the German sociologists Ferdinand Tonnies and Georg Simmel, then the "Chicago school" of sociology, including Louis Wirth and his disciples.

In contrast to Marx, who held that economic and class relations determined all other social relations, Weber was convinced that social organization is founded on a triad of principles: economic (or class), political (or party), and status group. People have economic and political allegiances, to be sure; but they also have status group affiliations that influence their view of life and their behaviour. These status groups do not simply organize people vertically—the way we now think of "social status"; they organize people horizontally as well.

A person's status group might be organized around language, ethnic, religious, or racial differences from the rest of society, or around other symbolic and non-economic principles. What defines a status group is its degree of *commensalism*: literally, the degree to which its members eat together, or more generally share activities and a common world view. A "status group" in Weber's terminology might today be called a "subculture." When we study the common behaviours of that group, we study a common "lifestyle."

Thus, what sociologists consider lifestyle today is nothing more nor less than subculturally shared patterns of behaviour that flow from a common, underlying world view. Such common behaviours serve to signify the boundaries of the group. People who live the same way are considered part of the group, while people who live differently are outsiders.

Thorstein Veblen's *Theory of the Leisure Class* (1934) shows how lifestyles come to define group boundaries. The very rich devise ways of consuming their wealth that are "conspicuously wasteful" in order to clearly define who is, or is not, within their group. By its nature, such consumption is exclusive to the very rich. Moreover, the people with the most established wealth continue to devise new forms of "conspicuous consumption" to delimit the boundaries of the "leisure class." To be a member, you must have enough time and money to keep up with this endless revision of fashions in conspicuous waste; you must also want to try.

Not all status groups test "candidates" so rigorously to determine who is in the group and who is out; but lifestyle behaviours, including consumption patterns, always distinguish insiders from outsiders. For this reason, sociologists have long claimed that you can tell a person's social position from his or her living room. Living-room furnishings display both the "taste" (hence, status group background) and the pretensions (or desired status group affiliation) of the householder. (For a humourous update of living-room assessment, see Fussell 1983).

Most members of a culture can "read" the status signals a person emits. This fact is demonstrated by community studies conducted by Chicago sociologist Lloyd Warner and his students since the 1940s (Davis, Gardner, & Gardner, 1941; Warner, Meeker, & Eells, 1960). In one community after another, researchers found community members could easily sort local townspeople into groups based on "reputation." In doing so, they regularly identified the same numbers of distinct status groups and sorted people into groups in similar ways.

Moreover, they told researchers similar things about the characteristics of each grouping: for example, how "upper-upper-class" people differed from "lower-upper-class" people. Thus, status groups, their membership, and behaviours appropriate to members, were well-known to people living in small, stable communities.

In large, new, or transient communities the boundaries of such groups are harder to specify and their membership, constantly turning over, is harder to agree on (Jaher, 1982). That is why people in large, mobile communities must rely more on visible behaviours to convey their actual or intended status. Such behaviours not only signal who they think they are or want to be taken for, but also what kinds of people they want to interact with, and in what ways.

For this reason, people—especially young people—wear clothing with the designer labels prominently displayed or easily inferred: for example, Polo, Roots, Club Monaco. Or they wear clothing and hair styles that convey a point of view: for example, punk versus preppy. Increasingly, people spend their time and money to convey an impression of who they are and who they want to be.

Sociologists studying lifestyle often focus on how people spend their time and their money. Each kind of spending indicates commitment, since few people have unlimited time and money. So spending behaviour is clearly the making of important choices under constraints. We shall now consider the two kinds of spending behaviour in turn.

Lifestyle and Money-Spending Behaviour   Researchers in marketing spend an enormous amount of energy figuring out how to influence people to buy particular goods or services. In this respect, market researchers and advertisers are "captains of consciousness" (Ewen, 1976). For example, in order to promote household products more effectively, one particularly gruesome piece of market research helped a publisher of romance magazines find out the secret fears and desires of working-class wives (Rainwater, Coleman, & Handel, 1962).

Marketing research has become more sophisticated with the development of VALS (Values and Life Style) surveying. Mitchell (1983) conceives of nine American lifestyle groups. Based loosely on Maslow's theory of a need hierarchy, Mitchell's typology relates buying behaviour to the social, economic, and demographic characteristics of each group.

Consider the group Mitchell calls "experientials." Comprising roughly 7 million Americans, or 11 percent of the adult population, the "experientials" are an important chunk of the baby-boom generation. A majority occupy the middle or upper class and over two-thirds have some postsecondary education, compared to 43 percent of the adult population. Experientials tend to live alone or cohabit, and they are city people, not suburbanites or rural residents. What lifestyle goes with their class and geographic location?

Compared to average American adults, experientials are liberal and independent (that is, party-free). They are very *un*likely to think that unmarried sex is wrong, or too much money is spent protecting the environment. They get a great deal of satisfaction from non-work activities, especially friends; but TV-watching is not their main entertainment.

Their financial status is also distinctive. Experientials' incomes are well above the national average. They are unlikely to have a credit card balance (owing) under $100, and are more likely than others to owe $1500 or more. The experientials are less likely than others to own their home or have a home mortgage, but more likely than any other group to owe over $50 000 in loans. This highly varied group contains some very wealthy and very upwardly mobile people. Experientials are a good credit risk and they borrow regularly against their credit. Much of their income (and credit) is consumed by higher-than-average rates of leisure activity.

In its activities, "this group is in many ways a more mature, less extreme version of the I-Am-Mes" (Mitchell, 1983, p. 130). Experientials swim, play racquet sports, and ski. "They engage more in yoga and home meditation than any other group and are distinctly concerned with the health aspects of food. They are more likely than any other group to work at a second job or free-lance" (Mitchell, 1983, p. 132).

How do "experientials" like to spend their money? Mitchell (1983, p. 132) remarks that "key characteristics of the Experientials—such as the search for direct and pleasurable experiences, their try-anything-once attitude, preference for process over product, and active outdoor orientation—are evidenced in their pattern of product ownership and use." Experiential households are much more likely than average to own compact, subcompact, and small speciality cars. More than any other group, they buy quality European cars, especially used ones. They are also above-average purchasers of motorcycles and racing bikes.

At home, experientials commonly purchase dishwashers, garbage disposals, recreational equipment, video games, stereos, and blank recording tapes. Wine and beer are their preferred alcoholic drinks, with tequila as an alternative. Experientials avoid coffee, (with or without caffeine) sugared foods, and drinks; they make above-average use of frozen Chinese and Mexican foods. You can sell experientials a lot of eye makeup and shampoo, but forget about aerosol underarm deodorants, feminine-hygiene sprays, after-shave lotions, or room air-fresheners. Experientials use veterinarians a lot, but rarely buy canned dog foods. And if you invite an experiential home for dinner, hide the margarine, Jello, and Planter's peanuts (Mitchell, 1983, Table 16).

If you have not guessed yet, Mitchell's "experientials" are young urban professionals—"yuppies"—finished with being "I-Am-Mes" and on their way to becoming "Societally Conscious."

The VALS approach to analysing lifestyle captures a wide range of attitudes and spending patterns, and relates them to social and demographic identifiers. Such research tells businesspeople what prospective clients "look like," where they can be found, and what psychic buttons to push to make a sale. But what about the non-monetary aspects of daily life? We learn more about these by studying the ways people spend their time.

Lifestyle and Time Use   "Time budget research" asks ordinary people to keep a detailed, running record of each day's events: what they did, for how long, and in whose company. The resulting data offer sociologists a rich insight into the variety of everyday lifestyles.

The first thing they discover is that the same kinds of people (for example, employed mothers) lead similar lives throughout the modern world (Robinson, Converse, & Szalai, 1972). Industrialization tends to erase national differences, causing lifestyles around the world to converge. Accordingly, international differences in time usage mainly reflect differences in the degree of industrialization and related processes: urbanization, media availability, education, family planning, and female labour force participation, among others. For example, in industrial societies, mass media are widely available, and the more mass media are available, the more time people will spend consuming them. A case in point is the time spent watching television.

However, we also find interesting, sometimes unexplained variations among industrial nations: for example, despite widely available programming, average West Germans watch a lot less television than average Americans (Robinson & Converse, 1972).

Domestic relations also seem to vary among industrial nations. People differ markedly in the amount of time they spend at home with their spouse, and the amount that is spent in the spouse's company alone, without children, relatives, or friends present (Varga, 1972). In countries where married couples spend more time alone together, divorce rates are lower. This suggests that divorce is caused, at least partly, by spouses spending too little time in intimate, "courtship" behaviour.

Time budget data also show cross-national variations in the amounts of sociability at work and at home. North Americans are more likely than most people to retreat from an intensely interactive work life into solitude or relatively passive family activity. But in many European cultures, leisure is as intensely interactive as work.

Finally, mothers who work outside the home enjoy more leisure and more control over their domestic duties in countries with good public daycare, where friends and relatives are readily available, or spouses co-operate more than in North America (Michelson, 1985; Szalai, 1972).

Lifestyles vary most between industrial and pre-industrial societies, but they also vary *within* industrial nations. Time budget data show that even neighbourhoods vary in lifestyle.

In choosing a place to live people are influenced by such characteristics as education, occupation, and income, but also by values and stage in the life cycle: whether married or single, childless or parent, older or younger. These characteristics lead them to move into some neighbourhoods and types of dwellings rather than others. Though often unanticipated, such moves may produce major lifestyle changes.

Consider the lifestyles of homeowners, whether suburban or downtown. "They have above average interests in gardening, go to church on Sundays, and spend time with their neighbours, who are similar to themselves. . . . Husbands (especially in suburban homes) exchange several kinds of mutual aid with their neighbours, and expect the same in return. The husband knows a number of people in his neighbourhood well. He participates actively in organizations" (Michelson, 1977, pp. 307–308).

Lifestyles consist of activity *dimensions*. For example, they may be person-centred (and if so, either family-centred or centred on other people) or centred on ideas or objects; passive or active, public or private, formal (organized) or informal, productive or consumptive; and in motion or at rest, at home or away from home, and indoors or out-of-doors (Reed, 1976).

People living in each type of residential environment— downtown apartment, suburban single-family dwelling, and so on—end up living in different activity dimensions. So, for example, a married woman who moves to a new house in the suburbs takes on a new package of activities. She is much more likely to spend her weekday hours preparing food, cleaning house, repairing the home, doing laundry, and caring for children than a married woman who lives in an apartment downtown. Conversely, the apartment-dwelling woman is more likely to spend her time travelling to work, working for pay, reading books, and attending to personal hygiene.

"Relatively typical of wives moving to downtown apartments is a very weak emphasis on domestic tasks. . . . The same holds for child care activity" (Reed, 1976, p. 202).

The married suburban woman is more likely to spend *Sunday* preparing food, cleaning house, attending church, and visiting friends and relatives than her counterpart who lives in a downtown apartment. Conversely, the apartment-dwelling woman is more likely to spend Sunday catching up on weekday duties (laundry, infant care, home repairs), preparing meals at home, attending to personal hygiene, and relaxing. Stated otherwise, the married apartment-dwelling woman's Sunday is more solitary, recuperative, and family-centred; the suburban housewife's Sunday more broadly sociable.

The activities of married men are much less "patterned" than those of their wives. Mens' activities also differ from their wives' in content. Still, their lifestyles also vary by location. On weekdays, married suburban men are busy working, travelling to work, and repairing the home—"a relatively active life style in common with their wives," but with less emphasis on social, home-centred, or passive activities. By contrast, downtown apartment-dwelling husbands are more likely to shop and visit friends during the week and to spend less time than other married men on "work, personal hygiene, at-home meals, and newspaper reading" (Reed, 1976, p. 207).

In choosing a place to live, people usually display different kinds of concerns. But interestingly, lifestyle "appears to operate more as a latent than as a strongly explicit consideration in residential choice-making" (Reed, 1976, Abstract). When people choose a place to live, they choose it with particular features in mind: house price and size, convenience to work, schools, and shopping, and so on. According to Reed, when choosing a place to live people do not take the likely lifestyle changes into account, perhaps because they are unaware of them.

Regional Variations in Lifestyle   Lifestyles vary most between industrial and pre-industrial societies, and also vary within industrial societies, as we have just seen. Moreover, they vary regionally within continents. Consider Garreau's (1981) evidence that North America contains nine "nations," not two. Many straddle the national border dividing Canada from the United States. Garreau's

"New England" includes the Maritime provinces; the "Foundry," much of Ontario; the "Breadbasket," much of the Prairie provinces; "The Empty Quarter," Northern Ontario, the rest of the Prairie provinces, inland British Columbia, and the Territories; and "Ecotopia," coastal British Columbia.

Garreau argues that political boundaries are no longer very useful in defining the regions of North America. Increasingly, distinct regional lifestyles derive from two main factors: economic forces and regional traditions. Both of these are, in turn, rooted in different land surface conditions and environmental concerns. In each region or "nation," wealth is generated differently, leading to different—even opposing—political and environmental concerns.

This suggests that provincial, state, and national borders are highly artificial and, today, have little basis in either economic or cultural life. Garreau claims that people are more attached to their regions and regional ways than they are to the nation as a whole (and this view is supported, for Canada, in Bell & Tepperman, 1979). But is the Canadian/American border as culturally blurred as Garreau makes out? And do North America's regions really differ from one another in lifestyle? To answer these questions, we must compare Garreau's findings—based on impressionistic evidence—with recent survey data.

Let us travel the continent from east to west, as Garreau did, seeking patterns as we go. First comes the "nation" Garreau calls "New England." For Garreau, the essential thinking of New Englanders (including Canadian Maritimers) is captured in words written by nineteenth-century Massachusetts philosopher and recluse Henry David Thoreau. Thoreau wrote: "The town's poor seem to me often to live the most independent lives of any. . . . Cultivate poverty like a garden herb, like sage. Do not trouble yourself much to get new things, whether clothes or friends. Turn the old; return to them. Sell your clothes and keep your thoughts. God will see that you do not want society" (cited in Garreau, 1981, p. 47).

The Quality of Life data seem to agree. Maritime Canadian concerns differ from central-Canadian Anglophone concerns. For example, Maritimers place a greater importance on family ties and religious values. Further, "in a region of Canada which for generations has been plagued with depressed economic conditions, when compared to the other provinces, there is no significant emphasis on prosperity and economic stability" (Blishen & Atkinson, 1982, p. 13).

Finally, data from the 1984 Canadian Election Survey (Curtis, 1987) point in the same direction. People were asked "What in your opinion was the income you deserved in 1983, all things considered?" Only 0.7 percent of employed Maritime respondents answered $100 000 or more, compared with 4.7 percent of Westerners, 2.9 percent of Ontarians and 1.9 percent of Quebeckers. Maritimers are also least likely of all Canadians to believe that they will be materially better off in four years, or their financial situation in five years will be near to the best they can imagine. However, Maritime respondents are nearly as likely as the more prosperous Ontarians to say that they are very satisfied with the "material side" of their life, and 30 percent more likely to say this than the more prosperous Quebeckers and Westerners.

The next region encountered on a westward route is Quebec. Garreau characterizes Quebec as intensely nationalistic, independent, and proud of its heritage. It is also romantic and sensual, as evidenced by the care taken with food and the appreciation of beautiful women. "Displays of sensuality happen in ways that give clues to national character," says Garreau (1981, p. 387).

Again, the Quality of Life data seem to agree. Quebeckers, both Francophone and Anglophone, depart strongly from the central-Canadian norm. Of Quebeckers, the Francophones in particular are more romantic and humanitarian than other Canadians. They value self-development and excitement significantly more highly than average. Finally, they are slightly more concerned with economic stability (on this, see also Baer & Curtis, 1984).

> The members of the French-speaking population of Quebec, more so than the population of any other region, see of utmost importance having a steady, secure income to provide for their basic needs and those of their families; having the affection and romantic love of a man or woman; being able to improve their skills and abilities, to keep improving themselves; serving other people who need help; having close friends and companions; and lastly, having a stimulating and active life (Blishen & Atkinson, 1982, p. 12).

Continuing west, Garreau arrives at the region or "nation" he calls the Foundry, which includes Southern Ontario's industrial heartland. "Enormous quantities of time, sweat and money have been invested in making this region what it is, and the Foundry's future will be determined by the extent to which North Americans decide they should, or will, walk away from that" (Garreau, 1981, p. 74). Since, according to Garreau (1981, p. 75), "the whole point of living in the Foundry is work," what determines people's state of mind and willingness to stay here is precisely whether they can find employment.

The data support Garreau less conclusively here. On the one hand, people do seem to come to Ontario to find jobs, and also leave Ontario to find jobs elsewhere (especially in the West). On the other hand, the Quality of Life data do *not* demonstrate a stronger desire for accomplishment or financial rewards in Ontario (or, more generally, in central Canada) than elsewhere. Indeed, central-Canadian concerns are the typical Canadian concerns we noted in Chapter 1: concerns for family security, love, and economic stability. This suggests a breakdown in Garreau's theory, and a distinction between the Canadian "Foundry" and the American "Foundry."

West of the Foundry, Garreau groups parts of Saskatchewan and Manitoba, along with Northern Ontario, Alberta, and the Territories, into the "Empty Quarter." Here, energy interests form a powerful lobby and fuel a strong, ongoing conflict with the federal government and Eastern financiers. According to Garreau, people in the Empty Quarter are enthusiastic, optimistic, and committed to material progress. Resources were made to be exploited, in their view.

The Breadbasket—North America's grain-farming and ranching region—includes parts of Manitoba, Saskatchewan, and Alberta. "As people stumble toward an explanation of what they value in their friends and neighbours around here, the words are *always* 'open,' 'friendly,' 'hardworking,' 'there when you need them,' 'down to earth.' . . . [There are] pressures not to flaunt wealth, or to ascribe success to 'luck'" (Garreau, 1981, p. 350).

However, none of this supposed difference from average Canadian values shows up in the Quality of Life data. Blishen and Atkinson (1982) find no marked value differences among people surveyed in Ontario, Manitoba, Saskatchewan, and Alberta.

Finally, Garreau comes to Ecotopia, which includes coastal British Columbia. This region is an "ecological utopia," full of majestic mountains, rivers, and forests; here, the quality of daily life is a central concern. People focus on how the natural environment should be used to give everyone the greatest pleasure now and in the future. This concern about life quality also produces extremes and smugness, Garreau says. "Even [Ecotopia's] search for new futures is burdened with some moralistic self-righteousness. It's not hard to find people in the Northwest who get as rigid with distress over the idea of a person eating an additive- and sugar-laden Twinkie as a devout Empty Quarter Mormon does about someone imbibing strong drink" (Garreau, 1981, p. 272).

Once again, the Quality of Life data seem to agree. Residents of British Columbia put a lower value than other Canadians on helping others, economic stability, prosperity, self-development, excitement, spiritual understanding, and romantic love. Indeed, British Columbians respond to all the values presented in the survey with less enthusiasm than other Canadians do, suggesting that "either British Columbians may be characterized as more relaxed and laid back about these life goals or the options presented in this survey did not include those things which are valued west of the Rockies" (Blishen & Atkinson, 1982, p. 14).

On balance, Garreau's claim that the Canadian–American difference is unimportant is falsified as often as it is supported by the Quality of Life data. Garreau's theory may simply be wrong; the Quality of Life data may be irrelevant to his theory; or Garreau's theory may apply better to the United States than to Canada. But both analyses agree that people in the Maritimes, Francophone Quebec, central Canada, and British Columbia differ from one another in their values and lifestyles. At a regional level, where you live is how you live.

Are different locations and lifestyles equally satisfying? And do people become more satisfied with their location and lifestyle over the course of their lives?

Location and Satisfaction

People who are free to choose a location and lifestyle as they wish should be generally satisfied with where and how they live. In this section we briefly examine people's satisfaction with various aspects of their location, including macrostructures (province and city) and microstructures (neighbourhood, dwelling, and household).

Satisfaction with Province and City   Just as Garreau would predict, most people report considerable satisfaction with their province of residence. Nearly two-thirds believe that their province is better than any other, or at least, better than most (Quality of Life survey, 1981). Over half believe that Ottawa treats their province fairly only some of the time or none of the time.

Asked in 1981 if any provinces had too much power, two-thirds said some provinces did. Named most often among the top "too-powerful" provinces were Alberta (named by 97 percent), and Ontario and Quebec (each named by 72 percent). Nearly half said they thought Ottawa paid too much attention to Quebec. When asked if any provinces had too little power, half the respondents said "yes"; they named each of the Maritime provinces with great regularity. Among the top "too-powerless" provinces were New Brunswick (named by 76 percent), Prince Edward Island (71 percent), Newfoundland (60 percent), and Nova Scotia (50 percent).

Researchers also find significant variations in people's satisfaction with city, town, or rural life. American quality of life research finds that city-dwellers are more likely to report "disagreeable experiences" and less likely to say that where they live is "a good place to live" than people living in suburbs, small towns, or rural areas (Campbell, 1980, p. 150). The difference becomes more marked the larger the city a respondent lives in.

Downtown city-dwellers in the United States are somewhat less satisfied with life overall, with the various life domains, and with their neighbourhood, than people who live in smaller places. Moreover, city people are more likely than others to report feeling "restless, lonely, depressed, bored and upset." They are twice as likely than people in small towns and rural places to express a willingness to leave the United States and settle in another country (Campbell, 1980, p. 151).

Yet "in light of these comparisons, it is rather surprising to find how little people in these communities of varying size differ in their expressions of positive affect. With regard to geographic location, there is virtually no difference in the proportions of white people who say they are very happy or who report having positive experiences in the recent past" (Campbell, 1980, p. 150). This ambivalence may be less marked—and the positive feelings much greater than negative ones—in Canada, where downtown areas of major cities are less rundown, racially segregated, and dangerous than comparable parts of American cities.

Two Canadian respondents in three think that all or most people in their city are friendly; over half think that the shopping and services are excellent or very good; and nearly 50 percent feel that recreation and sports opportunities are excellent or very good (Quality of Life survey, 1981).

Misgivings attach to other aspects of city life. For example, Canadians are nearly as likely to say the quality of air in their city is merely fair or poor as they are to say it is excellent or very good. And, while four in ten think their city's cultural and entertainment facilities are excellent or very good, over one-quarter think they are only fair or poor. Most seriously of all, nearly one respondent in two feels the city's job opportunities are fair or poor; only one in five feels the economic climate is excellent or very good. (Bear in mind, however, that this survey was conducted in 1981, during a serious economic recession.)

Satisfaction with Neighbourhood, Household, and Dwelling   Canadians are even more satisfied with their neighbourhood than with their city as a whole. More than half feel their neighbourhood is better than the last one they lived in and only one in five thinks it is worse (Quality of Life survey, 1981). Sixty percent report their neighbours are excellent or very good: only one in five reports having been upset or irritated by neighbours lately. Just under 50 percent say the shopping facilities are excellent or very good. Finally, more than 40 percent say the same about other homes and buildings in the neighbourhood, and neighbouring schools. In each case, only a small percentage report dissatisfaction with these amenities.

People mainly complain about the physical environment. Nearly as many report problems with noise from trains and traffic, air pollution, and faulty streets and roads as report these conditions are excellent or very good. Other frequently reported problems are inadequate parks and playgrounds, and insufficient safety from crime.

Of all neighbourhood characteristics, the things that people feel most satisfied about—their neighbours and other homes and buildings in the neighbourhood—are the most highly and significantly correlated with neighbourhood satisfaction. This finding is very similar to Campbell's in the United States, which shows that "satisfaction with neighbourhood is most strongly determined by the individual's perception of the condition of the neighbourhood housing, of the friendliness of its residents, of its security from criminals, and of the convenience to work and shopping" (Campbell, 1980, p. 156-157).

Neighbourliness is important to neighbourhood satisfaction. Neighbourhood satisfaction is lowest in large cities, because people move in and out too quickly to become neighbourly.

If you want to be satisfied with your neighbourhood, you should choose a place where you are likely to be satisfied with your neighbours. Choose neighbours who are socially and culturally like you and a neighbourhood that is relatively stable, where you can get to know them. Not only are people who live near others like themselves more satisfied with their neighbourhood, they are more satisfied with life overall.

People are slightly less satisfied with their house or apartment than they are with their neighbourhood as a whole. While two in three respondents report their present dwelling is better than the last place they lived, one in six reports it is worse. Nearly half report that something about their present dwelling bothers them.

Homeowners are generally more satisfied with their dwelling than home-renters. And *young* homeowners are especially satisfied with their dwelling. Owning rather than renting your home is especially gratifying when you are young. "Whether it is pride of ownership, sense of security, feeling of status, or some other psychological need that is fulfilled by the fact of owning one's home, there is no doubt that owners are more satisfied than renters, both in this country and elsewhere" (Campbell, 1980, p. 158).

All these location satisfactions—city, neighbourhood, and dwelling—are significantly correlated with overall life satisfaction. But neighbourhood satisfaction affects life satisfaction twice as strongly as dwelling satisfaction and city satisfaction do. The advice these data suggest? Buy a modest house in a neighbourhood you love, rather than renting (or buying) a fancier place in a neighbourhood or city you hate; and do it when you are young enough to enjoy it.

Why are people so satisfied with their locations and accompanying lifestyles? Few people want to live in high-rise apartments.

Yet even apartment-dwelling families are satisfied because they expect to move eventually. Their difficulties are only temporary and, therefore, can be tolerated; people know they will make changes in the future (Michelson, 1977). Locational expectations *are* eventually fulfilled, and most people end up getting more or less what they expected. People accommodate to temporary difficulties, while waiting for a future that is likely to arrive. Many life satisfactions are like that, which explains why so many people are satisfied with life.

Satisfaction with Time, Money, and Friends   Earlier, we connected lifestyle with the ways people spend their time and money. We now turn briefly to considering a dominant pattern in people's satisfaction with their lifestyle: namely, the connection with age.

Older people are more satisfied than younger people with the amount of free time they have available. Not only do older people have lower aspirations and expectations, they also have fewer work and family obligations to fulfil. In fact, they have more free time. Satisfaction with the amount of free time available rises continuously from about age 20 to 50, in similar ways for men and women. But after age 55, women tend to be more satisfied with their free time than men (see Figure 7.1).

Several reasons for this widening gender difference suggest themselves. Around age 55, mothers significantly reduce their parenting duties and may feel relieved to do so. Men reduce their work obligations slightly later, around 65, and may find the free time weighing heavily on their hands. Slightly later, women are likely to become widowed—a woman is much more likely to lose her spouse than a man is—and this further reduces their household duties. Though depriving them of companionship, widowhood does give women even more free time. Satisfaction with this free time will largely depend on the availability of friends and children. Gender differences aside, satisfaction with the amount of free time increases steadily with age.

Satisfaction with one's standard of living—how much money is available for spending and how it is spent—also increases with age, but in a different way (see Figure 7.2). Here, the relationship between satisfaction and age is far more markedly U-shaped, like the relationship between age and marital or parental satisfaction. Perhaps these relationships are similar in shape for similar reasons: namely, the effect of children's presence in the household.

Before children are present, a small income seems to suffice. The introduction of children places rapidly growing strains on a (possibly) less rapidly growing income and also influences the way in which available income will be spent. Relatively less income will be available for purely discretionary or leisure-related activities, just as less time will be available. Around age 50, when children start to leave the parental home, people's satisfaction with their standard of living begins to increase very rapidly. (In many cases, this also coincides with the elimination of major debts, like the mortgage.) The aging parents are freer to use their time, their household space, and their income as they wish.

Males' and females' satisfaction with standard of living differ less than their satisfaction with amount of spare time. This suggests that husbands and wives are more likely to agree on how family income is to be spent than they are on how time is to be spent.

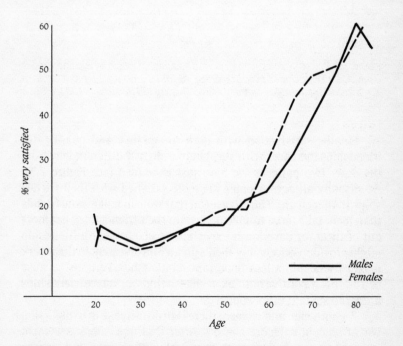

FIGURE 7.1 Percentage very satisfied with amount of spare time, by age and gender: Canada, 1981. *Includes people scoring 10 and 11 on an 11-point scale. A 10-year rolling average is used.* (Source: *Quality of Life survey, 1981.*)

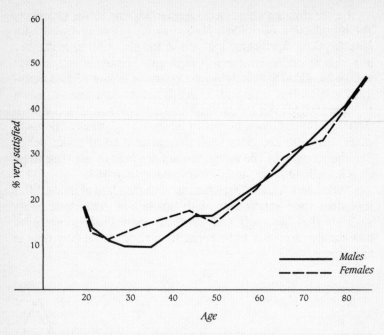

FIGURE 7.2 Percentage very satisfied with standard of living, by age and gender: Canada, 1981. *Includes people scoring 10 and 11 on an 11-point scale. A 10-year rolling average is used.* (Source: *Quality of Life survey, 1981.*)

Finally, satisfaction with both the quality and quantity of friendships increases with age, but in a slightly different way from the other two patterns we have just examined (see Figure 7.3). At virtually all ages, women are more satisfied with their friendships than men are. This may mean that women make more friends than men, take more trouble to sustain their friendships, get more out of them, or have lower expectations about what a friendship might provide. Conceivably, men's greater involvement in their work makes friendship a less important relationship. Perhaps because of a more competitive outlook, men also find workplace friendships harder to sustain than women do.

For both men and women, there is little increase in satisfaction with friendships before age 60. After that age, there is a rapid increase in satisfaction with friendships. Both men and women are now more able to invest time in their friendships than they were when children were living at home, or when holding a paid

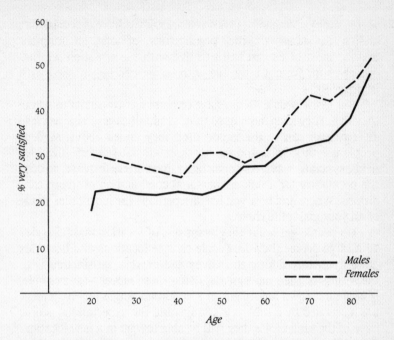

FIGURE 7.3 Percentage very satisfied with friendships, by age and gender: Canada, 1981. *Includes people scoring 10 and 11 on an 11-point scale. A 10-year rolling average is used.* (Source: *Quality of Life survey, 1981.*)

job. Their friends are also more able to invest time in the friendships, for similar reasons.

In short, lifestyle satisfactions with time, money, and friendship all increase with age.

Concluding Remarks

In choosing where to live, people probably come a lot closer to getting what they wanted than in many other areas of life. It is easier to continue changing locations over the life course than to continue changing educations, careers, marriages, or parental statuses.

Of course, many factors influence where you choose to live. They include where your work is located, where your spouse wants to live, what you can afford, and a variety of social and cultural barriers (for example, incomplete information and involuntary segregation). Campbell (1980) remarks, "We have a remarkable ability to adapt to the peculiarities of our environment and . . . most of us can learn to live with the situation we find ourselves in. We not only live with it, we can be satisfied with it" (p. 159).

But many people do not have to permanently adjust to where they live. They keep moving so that, gradually, they come as close as they ever can to the "good life" they dream about. Modern people use their time and money to create satisfactory lifestyles in idiosyncratic ways. As opportunity and variety increase, so does the possibility for a unique, personal combination of living conditions. Where and how you live are perhaps the most tailor-made of all your major life choices.

Do people get what they want out of location and lifestyle? To a large degree they do. People change locations and lifestyles quite frequently during their lives and express satisfaction with the results of their movements. Often these moves—for example, from a downtown apartment to a suburban single-family home— are motivated by a life-cycle change and the expectations people have of the kind of life they will be able to lead in a new location. But "What satisfies families in high-rise apartments in the short run is not what would satisfy them in the long run, nor in the short run either if they could not move elsewhere in the long run" (Michelson, 1977, p. 365). People are pulled forward by dreams.

Yet people's dreams and desires are also shaped by their experiences. So, for example, people who have stayed in or drifted back to high-rise apartments, after expressing an earlier desire for a suburban move, have now come to desire remaining downtown (Michelson, 1977, p. 335). People's actions are strongly influenced by factors only partly within their control (for example, aging and life-cycle changes) or well beyond their control (for example, social class, the availability of work and housing, and spouse's and children's desires). The consistently best predictors of residential mobility are macroeconomic changes in society: changes in the availability of jobs and housing. This explains Canadians' continuing shift westward and toward Ontario or, more generally, the churn rate for any given region.

But people learn to want what they get. Many who were driven or lured to a new location by economic opportunity develop a fierce loyalty to that region, province, city, or neighbourhood. People who have given up one thoroughly enjoyed lifestyle develop a strong liking for their new lifestyle. Lifestyles based in particular locations are often "subcultures," supplying people with a great deal of "meaning" as well as enjoyment.

The patterns of return migration by Newfoundlanders and other native-born Canadians, and by foreign-born migrants to their home country, suggest that economic opportunities and local lifestyles may not be enough to keep people where they have come to live. Others stay but hive themselves off from the local lifestyle through "institutional completeness." But these are the exceptions, not the rule. Most migrants do stay, and the longer they stay, the more they assimilate into the local lifestyle.

We now examine the problem of a gap between what you want and what you get, and draw some general conclusions from the findings presented in this book.

References

BAER, D.E., & CURTIS, J.E. (1984). French Canadian/English Canadian value differences: national survey findings. *Canadian Journal of Sociology, 9*(4), 405–428.

BALAKRISHNAN, T.R. (1976). Ethnic residential segregation in the metropolitan areas of Canada. *Canadian Journal of Sociology, 1*(4), 481–498.

_____. (1982). Changing patterns in ethnic residential segregation in the metropolitan areas of Canada. *Canadian Review of Sociology and Anthropology, 19*(1), 92–110.

BELL, D.V.J., & TEPPERMAN, L. (1979). *The roots of disunity: A look at Canadian political culture.* Toronto: McClelland & Stewart.

BLISHEN, B.R. & ATKINSON, T.H. (1982). *Regional and status differences in Canadian values.* Toronto: York University, Institute for Behavioural Research.

CAMPBELL, A. (1980). *The sense of well-being in America: Recent patterns and trends.* New York: McGraw-Hill.

CURTIS, J. (1987). Unpublished tables from 1984 Canada Election Survey.

DAVIS, A., GARDNER, B., & GARDNER, M. (1941). *Deep South: A social anthropological study of caste and class.* Chicago: University of Chicago Press.

EWEN, S. (1976). *Captains of consciousness: Advertising and the social roots of the consumer culture.* New York: McGraw-Hill.

FOOT, D.K. (1982). *Canada's population outlook: Demographic futures and economic challenges*. The Canadian Institute for Economic Policy Series. Toronto: Lorimer.

FUSSELL, P. (1983). *Class*. New York: Ballantine Books.

GARREAU, J. (1981). *The nine nations of North America*. New York: Avon Books.

JAHER, F.C. (1982). *The urban establishment: Upper strata in Boston, New York, Charleston, Chicago and Los Angeles*. Urbana: University of Illinois.

MICHELSON, W. (1977). *Environmental choice, human behavior, and residential satisfaction*. New York: Oxford University Press.

_____. (1985). *From sun to sun: Daily obligations and community structure in the lives of employed mothers and their families*. Totowa, NJ: Rowman & Allanheld.

MITCHELL, A. (1983). *The nine American lifestyles: Who we are and where we are going*. New York: Warner Books.

PINEO, P.C. (1985). Internal migration and occupational attainment. In M. Boyd, J. Goyder, F.E. Jones, H.A. McRoberts, P.C. Pineo, & J. Porter (Eds.), *Ascription and achievement: Studies in mobility and status attainment in Canada* (pp. 479–512). Ottawa: Carleton University Press.

QUALITY OF LIFE SURVEY. (1981). Unpublished raw data from large survey of life satisfaction conducted at the Institute for Behavioural Research, York University, Toronto.

RAINWATER, L., COLEMAN, R.P., & HANDEL, G. (1962). *Workingman's wife: Her personality, world and life style*. New York: Macfadden-Bartell Books.

REED, P. (1976). *Life style as an element of social logic: Patterns of activity, social characteristics, and residential choice*. Unpublished doctoral dissertation, University of Toronto, Department of Sociology.

ROBINSON, J.P., & CONVERSE, P.E. (1972). The impact of television on mass media usage: a cross-national comparison. In A. Szalai (Ed.). *The use of time: Daily activities of urban and suburban populations in twelve countries* (pp. 197–212). The Hague: Mouton.

ROBINSON, J.P., CONVERSE, P.E., & SZALAI, A. (1972). Everyday life in twelve countries. In A. Szalai, (Ed.) *The use of time: Daily activities of urban and suburban populations in twelve countries* (pp. 113–144). The Hague: Mouton.

STATISTICS CANADA (1982). *Census families in private households: 1981 census of Canada* (Catalogue No. 92–905). Ottawa: Supply & Services.

_____. (1987). *Current demographic analysis: Report on the demographic situation in Canada, 1986* (Catalogue No. 91–209E). Ottawa: Supply & Services.

SZALAI, A., (Ed.). (1972). *The use of time: Daily activities of urban and suburban populations in twelve countries*. The Hague: Mouton.

THOMAS, K., & BURCH, T.K. (1985).   Household formation in Canada and the United States, 1900-1901 to 1970-1971: Trends and regional differentials. *Canadian Studies in Population*, *12*(2), 159-182.

VARGA, K. (1972).   Marital cohesion as reflected in time budgets. In A. Szalai (Ed.), *The use of time: Daily activities of urban and suburban populations in twelve countries* (pp. 357-376). The Hague: Mouton.

VEBLEN, T. (1934).   *The theory of the leisure class*. New York: Modern Library.

WARNER, L.W., & MEEKER, M., & EELLS, K. (1960).   *Social class in America*. New York: Harper Torchbooks.

WISTER, A.V., & BURCH, T.K. (1983).   Fertility and household status of older women in Canada, 1981. *Canadian Studies in Population*, *10*, 1-14.

Chapter Eight

What You Want and Get: *closing the gap*

Recapitulation

This book has argued that desires are patterned: different kinds of people want different things out of life. Life satisfaction is also patterned: some kinds of people are more satisfied than others. Further, satisfactions with particular domains are also patterned: some people get the most life satisfaction from their work, others from their marriage, and so on.

This patterning proves that social science has something to teach us about the conduct of everyday life. Without patterning, we could not hope to explain people's values, feelings, and behaviours. If explanation were impossible, the management of our feelings and behaviours would also be impossible. Then advice to choose in one way rather than another would be useless, since choice and change would not lie within our grasp.

But some choice and change *are* within our grasp, if we understand the forces that shape our lives, that make the patterns we observe. This book has discussed a variety of forces that shape our satisfaction with life in general and within particular life domains. Further, it has revealed two main problems people encounter in their search for satisfaction: downward accommodation, or the willingness to settle for a Fool's Paradise; and an inability to close the gap between what they want and what they get.

Fool's Paradise   Many people live in a Fool's Paradise. For these people, key elements in achieving satisfaction are conformity to the dominant cultural goals (that is, common or non-extraordinary wants), limited information, low expectations, and having as much as the next person.

These people find conformity satisfying in itself. The less they know about the choices available to them, the higher their satisfaction rises. Other things being equal, their ignorance is blissful. The lower their aspirations (wants) fall, the less often a gap opens up between their aspirations and achievements. They know little about alternative possible lives, so they can be happy with their own lives.

It is easy to get into Fool's Paradise. For many, it is simply part of the "pragmatic acceptance" of inequality that we discussed in Chapter 2, in relation to "incapacitation." What we want and get from life are beyond our control, largely determined by our position in the class structure. Other factors—such as age, education, and gender—also play a role. In general, everyday experiences make it likely we will know little, want little, get little. So we learn to value what we *do* get.

Social class is more influential in some areas of choice than others. Educational and career choices are obviously tied to class of origin. Marriage is less strongly tied to class of origin, but generally people marry within their own social class. Parenting behaviour is even more distantly related to social class of origin, but given the costs of bearing and raising children, the experience of parenthood will be very different for people of different social classes. Finally, where and how you live are also related to social class.

In each of these areas, what we get and what we want from life are often well matched. Social class both limits what we are likely to get and prepares us for this by limiting what we are likely to want. As a result, most adults have limited—and, in a sense, realistic—aspirations based on well-founded expectations about likely events and circumstances. When life disappoints them, people make small changes and lower their aspirations. They divert their attention from what they do not have to what they do have. They find substitute satisfactions rather than fixate on what is missing.

Because of this congruence between what they want and what they get, and the resulting "pragmatic acceptance," most people are unlikely to fight for major social changes that might give them more of what they started out wanting. A lack of politicization is common even among the most deprived—for example, the poor and unemployed. This is another way in which the class structure perpetuates itself.

However, many people *are* aware of a gap between what they want and what they get. They do not live in a Fool's Paradise, yet seem unable to do anything about it. They face the second of two problems they encounter in search of satisfaction.

Inability to Close the Gap   Two kinds of dissatisfaction or unhappiness might be called Real Hell and Fool's Hell (Michalos, 1987, p. 45).

Fool's Hell is a state of dissatisfaction or unhappiness based on poorly founded information. Othello is miserable because he believes, incorrectly, that Desdemona has been unfaithful. Joe is miserable because he thinks his large nose will prevent him from getting dates with beautiful women. Sally is miserable because she thinks an off-colour story she told at work is going to hinder her chances for promotion. Alfred is miserable because he thinks he might have a serious medical problem but is afraid to see a doctor to find out if he is right.

Each of these people in Fool's Hell is a little bit tragic and a little bit ridiculous. Each is unhappy but could be happier, even happy, by getting accurate information about some matter of vital importance. Instead, they remain unhappy and, worse, may take actions that end up making themselves even unhappier. The wisdom of getting out of Fool's Hell needs little further discussion.

Real Hell is a different kettle of fish. Consider the well-informed political radical who has spent a lifetime fighting injustice, yet sees that much injustice remains. That person has good reason to feel dissatisfied or unhappy with the state of the world and people's failure to improve it substantially. Yet there is also reason to feel satisfied for having fought to the limit of his or her capacities in a good cause. Will that person accept the seemingly inevitable and become satisfied with what has been accomplished, rather than remaining dissatisfied with what has *not* been accomplished? Or will that person fight on, in hopes of trading Real Hell for Real Paradise?

Many of the same class-based factors that limit what you get out of life—closure, incapacitation, and decoupling—limit your ability to close the gap between what you want and what you get. Closure denies the most deprived of resources for an assault on social order. The poorest in any society lack the money and organization to mobilize against the rich. Incapacitation denies the most deprived a sense of competence they need for the sustained attack on a more powerful foe. Decoupling denies them the channels of informal influence through which they might seek major changes more subtly than by frontal assault.

Thus, the very means by which the rich and powerful get what they want—class closure, a sense of political competence and efficacy, and wide contacts with others in positions of power and authority—are least available to the poor in our own and other industrial societies.

Encompassing, sustaining, and reproducing this inequality is a world view, or ideology, that supports the way things are. The observed congruence between what people want and what they get sustains a belief that people get what they want out of life. This ideology blames the victims: it holds people responsible for what they do not get and treats the privileged as though they were rewarded for personal merit. By this reckoning, the deprived "deserve" their plight because they have failed to organize their lives properly: failed to get the right education, the right job, the right marriage, and so on.

Of course, many people *do* organize their lives badly and suffer for it. Yet rich people who organize their lives badly are less likely to suffer. Further, even the most effective personal organization is only a temporary solution to the problem of unequal opportunity in our society. In determining life outcomes, unequal opportunity is much more important than personal organization. As we have seen, this results from a class structure that starts people at vastly different levels of competitiveness. Thus, in the long run, the solution to dissatisfaction and hardship must be sought through changes to the class structure, not through better personal organization.

This book does not argue for accommodation to a Fool's Paradise, nor for strenuous individual solutions that, in the long run, cannot solve the problem most of us face. It argues instead for a Real Paradise. You will remember that, in a Real Paradise, people seek the best information about what is possible, push the possible to its limit, and try to live with the result. This book supports the old maxim that "Man [*sic*] is the measure of all things," which means that people should idealize what is possible, not imaginary, then seek the ideal.

What is possible is what *is*, what *has been*, and what shows signs of *becoming*. A systematic understanding of the past and present is key to understanding and acting upon the future. Our understanding of what is possible will undoubtedly change with time and new evidence. But present evidence, though incomplete and imperfect, is better than ignorance.

Before considering the more effective collective solutions, we shall examine individual solutions to a gap between what people want and what people get.

Individual Solutions

In chapter after chapter, we have found no simple answer to the question "Do people get what they want, or do they learn to want what they get?" In most cases, the answer is mixed. Generally, people get some of what they want, and what they want is shaped by social structure: hence, by what they are likely to get anyway. In that sense, choice is illusory.

But it is not just an illusion. People do make many important choices in life: what kind of career to pursue, whether and whom to marry, whether to have children, where and how to live, and so on. Even in so restricted a domain as education, choice exists. Gender, place of residence, and socio-economic status are powerful determinants of educational attainment. But even if half the education a person actually gets is statistically explained by these powerful forces, another half is not.

Many other factors—for example, the influence of peers, mentors, and the mass media—shape educational choice, each exerting a very small influence. Beyond that, an area of uncertainty and idiosyncrasy remains. Sociologist Christopher Jencks (Jencks *et al*. 1977) calls this region "luck," for lack of a better word. Some people are lucky enough to get profitable, satisfying, or good outcomes, however we want to measure them.

At present, we cannot say that people generally get what they want or generally do not. We must study the question domain by domain, issue by issue. Likewise, we cannot validly generalize about whether people usually learn to want what they get. Previous chapters have shown that sometimes people learn to want what they get—the love people feel for a mate, child, or place of residence illustrates this—and sometimes they do not—job dissatisfaction and divorce illustrate that. In every realm, people accommodate as they get older; but even this is only a tendency, not a certainty.

Other factors also affect the ways people adapt. Some people have less opportunity to change situations, rather than accommodate. For example, although neither solution is highly satisfying, a woman with several young children and few job skills will find it harder to leave a bad marriage than adapt to it. Further, some personalities will prove more adaptable than others. People with a strong sense of mastery and control over their environment will find it easier to adapt to a situation *or* change it than people who feel powerless, alienated, and without choice. Again, we are far from knowing all the factors that influence people's ability to get what they want, or change what they get.

But on one matter the evidence is less ambiguous. Most people are only moderately satisfied with their lives, in whole or in part: they are not in a paradise of any kind. Either they have not gotten all they wanted, or have not learned to want all they have gotten. If we were to examine an average person's life cycle, we would surely find periods of non-accommodation. Most people fall out of accommodation at some times in their lives. And some people— for example, strong political conservatives or radicals—are likely to go through their entire adult lives in a state of non-accommodation, or Real Hell. What do these unaccommodated people do about it?

Proposal One: Merton's Contribution   American sociologist Robert Merton (1957a) redefined Durkheim's (1893/1965, 1897/1951) concept of *anomie* to analyse the consequences of a gap, a "disjuncture," between what people want and what they can get by legitimate means. Considering anomie a result of the disjuncture between "culture goals" and "institutionalized means," Merton examined the variety of "modes of individual adaptation" to this problem.

Merton argued that Americans are faced with the demand that they accept society's culture goals, especially the goal of material success. People are raised to value success very highly and to evaluate themselves and others in terms of the material success they achieve in life. And for some, the conforming or "institutionalized" roads to success—a higher education and a job or career—are open for travel and lead to suitable rewards.

For others—the one in nine who descended from black slaves or the one in two who could not vote until two decades into this century—equal opportunity in the competition for material success has been slow in coming. In Canada and the United States, job discrimination and unequal access to higher education persist today. How do people adapt to the inadequacy of "institutionalized means?"

Logically, only so many adaptations are possible. People might continue to accept both the culture goals and institutionalized means: to conform to social expectations even if they are not paying off. Or they might retain a belief in the culture goals while rejecting the institutionalized means: Merton called these adaptors "innovators." They might reject the culture goals but retain a belief in the institutionalized means: if so, they are "ritualists." They might reject both the culture goals *and* institutionalized means, becoming "retreatists." Finally, they might replace both the culture goals and institutionalized means with substitute goals and means: doing so makes them "rebels," in Merton's terms (see Figure 8.1).

Merton's often-cited analysis documents each type of adaptation and its various forms: for example, the innovator as robber baron and racketeer, the ritualist as bureaucrat, the retreatist as tramp and drug addict, the rebel as political activist.

His analysis denies that multiple goals exist within a given individual, that significant subcultures exist within the population as a whole, and that multiple legitimate or nearly legitimate ways of "making it" are accepted in American society. Merton's theory suggests a uniformity of goals and means that belies the variety of American society.

This deficiency was demonstrated most dramatically when American social scientists Richard Cloward and Lloyd Ohlin (1960), building on Merton's theory, suggested dealing with crime among young people by offering poor youths more access to legitimate means of upward mobility. Put into practice by a series of social programs in the 1960s, this theory was invalidated by the evidence that poor young people did not seem to want the lives being offered

Modes of Adaptation	Culture Goals	Institutionalized Means
Conformity	+	+
Innovation	+	−
Ritualism	−	+
Retreatism	−	−
Rebellion	±	±

FIGURE 8.1 Merton's typology of adaptations to anomie. (Source: *Merton, 1957a, p. 140.*)

them. Other goals—excitement, pleasure, risk-taking—beckoned; other means of getting by were more appealing than a nine-to-five job. This and other research on subcultures has suggested that people are motivated by a variety of goals, not merely material success by means of an Anglo-Saxon middle-class lifestyle.

Even in North America, material success is not everything to everyone. Many people prefer family, romance, and community life. Chapter 1 showed that there is no evidence of a single, essential, or universal set of human concerns.

Because of this flaw, Merton's theory gives us little help in understanding rebellion, conflict, and change, except as responses to limited opportunity for material advancement. Yet many would claim that those involved in the popular movements of the last 30 years—civil rights marchers, black city-burners, anti-war protesters, feminists, gay rights activists, native peoples, environmentalists, and others—were actually concerned with justice, human dignity, and the future of humanity. Merton's theory cannot explain why these protests happened, or when they did, or how they did, or who participated—often, prosperous middle-class people with a stake in conformity—and with what result for the individuals involved or for society.

Merton's single-minded focus on material goals also produces a moral equivalence between robber barons and alcoholics, racketeers and civil rights marchers. Saints and mass murderers are "the same" because they are both deviant, both adaptors to anomie. This viewpoint completely misses the hidden dynamic—the reason one person becomes a saint and the other a mass murderer. It fails to explain why some women became suffragettes in the early part of this century, and others did not. It also fails to explain how Martin Luther King's "adaptation to anomie" helped change American society, while Charles Manson's did not.

Finally, social life today—whether conformist, ritualist, retreatist, innovative, or rebellious—is increasingly collective life. The chief actors in a large, modern society—those who act out anomie and seek remedies—are organized groups, not individuals as in Merton's theory. We must look elsewhere for an adequate theory of conformity, accommodation, and deviance.

Proposal Two: Westhues's Contribution   A recent formulation by Canadian sociologist Kenneth Westhues (1982) deals with many of the flaws in Merton's theory by standing it on its head. Unlike

Merton, Westhues sees conformity, not deviance, as the problem that needs solving. Merton sees people as needing better chances of reward for conformity; and for Merton, a more stable society is the goal. Westhues believes people need more chances for non-conformity. Because he sees "vice in conformity, virtue in deviance," more social justice is Westhues's goal. Thus Westhues equates deviance with "liberation," implying that our society is enslaved and conformity is the shape of that slavery.

At first glance, this reformulation of Merton's theory is just as easily dismissed. Surely deviance *per se* is no better than conformity *per se*, and change is no better than persistence. To argue otherwise is to imply that there is nothing worth preserving in our society, just as to hold Merton's position is to imply that there is nothing wrong with it. Each extreme oversimplifies our picture of society.

Westhues does remedy some of the problems in Merton's theory, though. First, his analysis is less focused on material success than Merton's. Second, it is more complex. For example, Westhues's typology of "generic forms of liberation, or deviance" contains eight types of non-conformity, not four as in Merton's model. It distinguishes between types of liberation that (1) retreat from expectations or attack them; (2) individuals or groups try to carry out; and (3) deviate mildly or severely from conformity (see Figure 8.2).

The basic condition for non-conformity, innovation, deviation, or liberation—all equated by Westhues—is a gap between previous learning and present experience. Old ideas, expectations, and practices fail to serve people well in new situations. Ten secondary conditions evidently contribute to or create this gap: migration, membership in a deprived class, class mobility, intermarriage, social dislocation, Jewish identity, liberal schooling, intellectual occupations, a diverse environment, and catastrophe.

The outlets people choose for expressing discontent are conditioned by three main principles in Westhues's scheme: (1) people withdraw when they cannot attack; (2) signs of weakening invite attack; and (3) the available tools condition how people misbehave.

Westhues points to one central strain in our system: the value placed on creativity (a culture goal) and the limited, diminished, and diminishing opportunity for innovation (Westhues, 1982, p. 463). We gear our children up to create; then capitalism denies most of them the legitimate opportunity to do so. No wonder they go to shopping malls and get into trouble, Westhues laments. Evidently, Westhues has taken Merton's framework and substituted

Degree	Withdrawal		Attack	
	Individual	Collective	Individual	Collective
Mild	Sleeping on the job Daydreams, fantasies Loafing Media opiates Occasional drunkenness Marijuana smoking Many illnesses	Escapist entertainment Sectarian religion Cults	Personal twists and new wrinkles in the performance of conventional roles "I'll do it my way" Minor innovations	Fads, crazes Under capitalism, marginally new products of private companies Reformist social movements
Severe	Refusing to settle down A hermit's life Habitual drunkenness Narcotic addiction Psychosis Suicide	Countercultural movements Utopian communities	Invention in science and technology Boldly original art New philosophic work New forms of human organization Religious prophecy	Under capitalism, major new products of private companies Revolutionary social movements Mass migrations

FIGURE 8.2 Westhues's typology of forms of liberation, or deviance. (Source: *Westhues, 1982, p. 433.*)

"creativity" for "material success" as the chief motivating force, the goal everyone wants to maximize. (Class structure remains the central factor limiting access to legitimate means of attaining the culture goal.)

In making this translation, Westhues's work perpetuates two of the problems with Merton's theory: the assumed uniformity of goals, and the moral equivalence of wonderful innovating acts (for example, inventing a polio vaccine) and horrible innovating acts (for example, establishing death camps). Perhaps creativity (or deviance, or innovation) really is a more elevated goal than material success. Still, the research we reviewed earlier shows that neither is a major life concern of adult Canadians.

But Westhues has taken us farther than Merton, nonetheless. First, he has extended our understanding of the conditions that promote (or free up) non-conforming behaviour, specifying the groups and situations in society that are particularly likely to spawn non-conformity. We still lack knowledge of the social-psychological process that makes one person innovate while another in the same situation conforms.

More important, Westhues emphasizes the difference between individual and collective acts of non-conformity. Collective mobilization is not only a condition under which individuals can each act with greater effect: it enables different *kinds* of non-conforming behaviour. Social movements, cults, and experimental communities are qualitatively different from individual adaptations to anomie, and they also carry a greater potential for changing society.

However, Westhues ultimately fails because, like Merton, he focuses on a single goal he assumes people are trying to attain. This makes his analysis less than completely helpful for people whose goal is not deviance (or creativity) in its own right.

Proposal Three: Various Individual Solutions   Chapter 2 introduced four concepts—closure, incapacitation, decoupling, and scarcity—to explain the limits on people's opportunity. Remedies for these limitations fall into two categories, individual and collective, as we have seen. These remedies can be applied to closing any gap between wants and achievements you may be encountering. They do not presuppose a particular want, as Merton's and Westhues's analyses have done. Limited space, however, does not permit a full discussion of the way each remedy applies to each problem of dissatisfaction. You will have to translate these solutions to your own problems yourself. What follows are merely examples.

As an individual, you may best solve the problem of *closure* by getting whatever credentials allow entry into the group you hope to spend your life in. Chapter 3 showed that higher education is the single best investment you can make if your goals are material, and perhaps even if they are creative.

However, Chapter 2 showed that racial and ethnic discrimination continue to limit people's opportunity to gain entry into many lines of activity. For example, members of discriminated-against groups may not do as well in work settings controlled by other ethnic groups as they would by remaining within their own ethnic community, even with less education. The decision to be made here, a complex one, depends on several factors: the actual extent of discrimination against your ethnic or racial group; the probability of a significant reduction in that discrimination during your lifetime; the range of attractive occupational opportunities within your own racial or ethnic community; and the probability of a significant increase in occupational opportunities within your group during your lifetime.

Alone, you can do little to influence any of these factors. As an individual you can only choose between getting a higher education (and possibly cutting yourself off from your ethnic community) or getting less education (and cultivating ties to your ethnic community). The first choice risks discrimination outside the community; the second limits opportunities for career selection and advancement within the community. Your contribution to a collective solution, to be discussed shortly, will be much more important.

You can solve the problem of personal *incapacitation* by changing the way you think about yourself: not an easy task, but one that a great many people manage to accomplish. This is partly what the major social movements of our time—for example, feminism, native rights, and gay rights—are all about. Learn more about the history of your incapacitation as a member of a despised or belittled group. Discuss this condition with others, find mentors, and seek role models: people who are otherwise just like you—women, native people, gays—who have done what others lead you to believe you cannot do. Most important of all, reject the victim-blaming ideology that you may be whipping yourself with. You have enough problems without being your own worst enemy.

Again, individual solutions are less likely to succeed than collective ones. For people to see that women, for example, can succeed in activities previously believed to be outside their competence requires that women be given a chance. Forcing open new opportunities often requires collective mobilization by an excluded group. Again, personally contributing to a collective solution may be the most important thing you can do, though admittedly results may take a long time in coming.

You can solve the problem of *decoupling* by cultivating and making use of your social networks. This is the way people find good jobs (Chapter 2) and sometimes mates (Chapter 5). To improve the size and heterogeneity of your network, acquaint yourself with people who have larger and "better" networks: people who are themselves mobile and widely acquainted, are (typically) higher-status, or operate within institutions that encourage interpersonal contact.

Social institutions that break down traditional gender, class, and ethnic barriers to interpersonal contact include institutions of higher education and government. Thus, higher education and involvement in civic affairs are doubly beneficial: they allow both self-improvement and increased connection with others. Unfortunately, both higher education and civic involvement sometimes run counter to the goals of participation in your own community, especially if that community is institutionally complete. Here, wrong individual choices are potentially most costly. Try to become a "cosmopolitan" member of your community, with feet in both camps (Merton, 1957b). This connects both you and your community into the larger, outside networks of influence and opportunity.

Finally, you cope individually with real *scarcity* by helping to produce more of what people need; adjusting your thinking downward from the imaginary to the possible; and creatively seeking alternatives to scarce goods. It is the human ability to do this that has kept our species alive for a million years.

The danger here lies in confusing scarcity with maldistribution, considering scarcity beyond remedy, or lowering our heads rather than raising the bridge. French demographer Alfred Sauvy (1969, p. 391) has called this excessively accommodating approach the "Malthusian Spirit . . . a state of mind characterised by the fear of excess—faced with two quantities that need adjusting, it tends to lower the highest instead of boosting the lowest. It is the opposite of courage and generosity." The "Malthusian" is a person who, facing a dinner party with too little food for the guests, wants to get rid of guests rather than get more food.

If apparent scarcity is really maldistribution, or a temporary shortage that could be remedied through innovation and higher productivity, collective remedies are called for. But such collective remedies will call for individual commitments to collective solutions and a patient acceptance of the effects these solutions will have on individual lives.

Collective Solutions

We have repeatedly claimed the superiority of collective solutions to individual solutions. An ideal collective solution will have two main characteristics: it will operate within the realm of the truly possible; and it will tie the advancement of collective well-being to the advancement of individual well-being.

As we have stressed repeatedly, only the realm of the possible is of interest to sociology. One of the earliest social scientists, Thomas Malthus, states this position in the following way: "A writer may tell me that he thinks man will ultimately become an ostrich. I cannot properly contradict him. . . . [But] till the probability of so wonderful a conversion can be shown, it is surely lost time and lost eloquence to expatiate on the happiness of man in such a state" (Malthus, 1798/1959). And so it is with all solutions social science might propose: we must leave poetry to the poets and fantasy to the dreamers, and consider only what seems truly possible.

As to the second criterion, we should give greatest emphasis to solutions that simultaneously serve both the individual and the collectivity. Only solutions that serve the collective interest are likely to endure, but only solutions that promise to increase individual well-being are likely to motivate strong individual effort over the long haul. Ideally, then, solutions that serve both will produce the most change and the most benefit, and will survive.

Let us now consider some proposals for collectively solving the problems raised in this book.

Proposal One: Marx's Contribution   Most religions teach that humble aspirations (goals) are the best way of dealing with life in this world; greater rewards will come in the next life. Such humility allows the most religious people in our society to get the most satisfaction out of life (Quality of Life survey, 1981). But this kind of accommodation to inequality led Karl Marx (1844/1963) to call religion the "opium of the people." An opiate dulls the pain of living; and under certain hopeless conditions, taking opiates is the only sensible course of action.

Marx held that religious opiates are not really necessary—indeed, are counterproductive—because hopelessness about the future is unwarranted. He maintained that all history is the record of struggles that overturned the ruling classes or ruined the contenders in the process. Better the brief pain associated with revolution—something like the pain of giving birth—than the drawn-out pain of living in an unjust, alienating society, he argued.

Marx (1888/1955) contended that a revolution that eliminated ruling classes forever by eliminating private property—by putting the means of production in the hands of the state—would bring better conditions for all. With the eventual "withering away" of the state, communism would end history as we have known it, for it would end social classes and class conflict.

There are two problems with this formulation: one logical, the other empirical. First, a reading of history that shows that every society of any size has had a class structure and a ruling class would *not* lead sociologists to the confident conclusion that a society with no class structure and no ruling class is truly possible. Rather, it would lead in the opposite direction: in the direction perhaps most often associated with the name of Robert Michels (1962), who enunciated the "iron law of oligarchy."

This principle, based on a socialist's study of the German socialist party—a sympathetic observer studying a radically democratic organization—holds that in every social grouping a dominant group will struggle to perpetuate its power, whatever its original ideology. That is, inequality is inevitable in human groupings, whatever their size or the members' ideology.

Empirically, Michels's "iron law" has not proven completely unbreakable. For example, a sociological study of the International Typographical Union, a democratic printers' union in the United States, has revealed some of the conditions under which oligarchy can be prevented or minimized (Lipset, Trow, & Coleman, 1963). So not every organization or society must be oligarchic. Yet the oligarchic organizations in our own society and elsewhere far outnumber the democratic ones. At best, we can only allow the chance that Marx was right about the possibility of a fully democratic society. It remains far from a foregone conclusion.

Second, the premise that history can end with a democratic, class-free society is also thrown into doubt by a lack of evidence that communist revolutions have actually succeeded in bringing about such a society. In the century since Marx's *Communist Manifesto*, a number of groups have experimented with communism. Some attempts have been utopian or anarchistic, based in a small community or region (see Hobsbawm, 1959; Kanter, 1972). Except for Israeli kibbutzim and Hutterite communities, they have all failed or been overturned after varying periods of time, for a variety of reasons: for example, an insufficient material base, inadequate planning, demographic pressures within, and attacks from outside. Even the relatively successful kibbutzim and Hutterite communities have suffered serious losses of population, due to defections by native-borns.

Other attempts to sustain communal equality have been more thorough. But contrary to Marx's expectation that revolutions would bring equality, they have produced new kinds of inequality. Whether the new inequalities are wider or narrower, more or less benevolent, than those they replaced must be studied case by case: in the Soviet Union, China, Albania, Cuba, Viet Nam, Nicaragua, and so on. In every instance, however, rule based on ownership of the means of production has merely been replaced by political and bureaucratic control.

In many places, communism has greatly reduced material inequality and the worst effects of such inequality. The inequality that remains—rule by a political elite, or "vanguard of the proletariat," as Lenin called it—may only be temporary. It may end when the people have fully accepted socialist goals and no longer seek to subvert communism. Moreover, the tight control government exercises in such societies may be a response to efforts made by capitalist nations to overthrow communism.

The communist alternative has proven more attractive in some parts of the world than in others. In particular, the potential benefits of capitalism and liberalism have meant little to most twentieth-century Third World peoples. They consider European nations unsuitable models to emulate, since they carry the stigma of colonialism. Further, "free enterprise" seems less likely to succeed quickly and painlessly in the Third World than large-scale economic planning. "One of the outstanding attractions of communism to Asian and African eyes [is] that it [offers] the underdeveloped peoples a blueprint for development" (Barraclough, 1967, p. 223).

On the other hand, some would argue that material inequality can be significantly reduced without communism, as it has been in the democratic socialist countries of Scandinavia and, to a smaller degree, within certain advanced capitalist countries. Moreover, many people in the industrial capitalist countries—and not simply the very rich and powerful—may not want to give up private property in favour of communism. Values justifying acquisitiveness and "free enterprise" seem to arise whenever and wherever personal acquisition becomes possible. People offered the chance for personal acquisition and upward mobility appear, almost without fail, to seize that opportunity.

Finally, many believe the excesses of control under communism are not just temporary. They may be due to an overcentralization of planning and too few countervailing forces within the country. Supporters of liberal democracy argue that an open competition of ideas and interests produces solutions most satisfactory to the largest number.

Political participation by a large middle class and large, highly mobilized interest groups—political parties, consumer groups, women's and native rights groups, and other such associations—prevents uncontested rule in Western countries. Communist societies tend to lack a large middle class and large interest groups that can freely express their opinions. This absence allows political leaders to make potentially dangerous and harmful decisions almost unopposed.

This book has devoted chapter after chapter to showing that liberal democracy does *not* give people an equal chance to get what they want out of life. So it would be satisfying to believe that communism could do so. However, the current evidence on this question is ambiguous at best. Attaining more satisfaction for more people may be truly possible in Canadian society, and communism may be the best means of doing it. But equally, it may not be. Moreover, the costs in human life of a wrong guess are enormous.

People get killed in revolutions. I need much more supporting evidence before I can vote for revolution.

We have been unable to demonstrate that Marx's proposed solutions lie within the realm of the possible, or that they satisfactorily link the advancement of collective and individual interests. But that is not to say that socialist solutions would also fail to meet our needs. Indeed, any solutions that will help equalize income and power may be beneficial. Let us turn, then, to some truly possible solutions and see whether they meet our requirements.

Proposal Two: Various Collective Solutions   In every instance of limited opportunity, wholly individual solutions are available, but they are "quick fixes" with temporary effects. Though the process may be difficult and slow, in the long run your ability to get more opportunity is greater as part of a collectivity. But if we rule out the revolutionary option, what remains? Again, what follows is merely schematic. It would be impossible, given the space available, to apply all these proposed remedies to all of people's varied dissatisfactions.

Two collective solutions to *closure* are truly possible. One is legislation and social action that would make discrimination against people like you more difficult. To bring this about requires banding together with others who are discriminated against, joining forces across social barriers of ethnicity, class, gender, and region where necessary. The result will be a more assimilated, less discriminatory society.

A second solution is to mobilize within your own group— whether class, ethnic, religious, regional, or so on—to increase institutional completeness. This has the effect of establishing closure in your own favour to counter the closure that is used against you. It is discrimination on your behalf. Many Canadian groups and regions are using this tactic today.

Not the least of these are class-based political parties, unions, lobbies, and associations. The New Democratic Party, for example, has enjoyed considerable success in promoting legislation that protects workers, consumers, and other relatively powerless groups in society.

Group mobilization that is *not* based on social class is somewhat more problematic. First, it escalates the level of intergroup conflict without eliminating the underlying conditions that gave rise to it. Second, it narrows people's field of vision and makes them less available to solve problems that cut across groups: international problems of peace and scarcity, national problems of cultural unity and political or economic independence, and problems of class and gender inequality, among others. The first solution—a frontal collective assault on privilege—is the only one that will benefit everyone in the long run.

Incapacitation can be eliminated by education and re-education; the schools and mass media are key vehicles for such a change. As already noted, the strengthening of individual identities is best done collectively, since nothing changes people's minds more than the evidence that change is possible. The benefits of slow, incremental change are seriously limited (Kanter, 1977). For example, a sole woman given the opportunity to "model" executive capabilities in a large organization is under unusual pressures to succeed "on behalf of all women" and will be judged by criteria quite unlike those applied to men. Confusion will arise between the unique characteristics of the individual and the characteristics of the "type" she represents.

For this reason, we really do not learn what excluded groups can do until we see large numbers of group members performing in commonplace, emotionally neutral situations. Achieving this requires legislation that ensures inclusion for as many representatives of a social "type" as may seek it. Laws against discrimination not only break down traditional structures of closure, but also reduce incapacitation and decoupling. Again, such laws will not be passed and enforced without collective mobilization.

Decoupling can be remedied by building bridges among social collectivities that currently have little connection: for example, among racial, ethnic, regional, and occupational groups. Typically, increased communication between the leaders of these collectivities has been the key to success. But anyone can increase connections by participating in broad-based activities and organizations.

Finally, material *scarcity* can be reduced by producing more of what people want and need, which means an international commitment to economic growth and redistribution. In turn, this may mean first breaking the monopolies that restrict productivity as well as sharing.

These proposals for dealing with dissatisfaction are collective, not individual, and are firmly rooted in the realm of the truly possible. However, they do not systematically address the question of how people might link the advancement of their own interests with those of society as a whole. Such an approach would be ideal, if we agree with C. Wright Mills that the flip side of a personal trouble is a public issue—or, stated otherwise, that personal troubles are shared and socially structured. It is to that question of linkage that we now turn.

Proposal Three: Linking Individual and Collective Solutions
Both Merton and Westhues discuss why gaps arise between what people want and what they get. But each discussion ultimately fails because it is "essentialist": it seeks the single goal people are attempting to attain. Chapter 1 showed that no such single goal exists. Moreover, each theory fails because it implies a moral equivalence among varieties of adaptation. Merton's paradigm goes further in this respect than Westhues's, for Merton's sole concern is with social order while Westhues's is with social justice.

Let us consider a different approach, which takes satisfaction as the goal to be attained. By its nature, satisfaction is attainable in many ways—individual and collective, short-term and long-term—and in many life domains. All people seek satisfaction, but people do not all seek the same satisfactions, much less seek satisfaction in the same ways.

Throughout the book we have discovered gaps between what people want and what they get: call this anomie (following Merton), or a discrepancy between aspirations and achievements (following Michalos). Such gaps produce dissatisfaction, which people try to reduce. People seek greater satisfaction by lowering their expectations or increasing their achievements, or both; moreover, they can do this individually or collectively.

In some cases accommodation is almost inevitable. No alternative is truly possible, at least at present. For example, we have no means of prolonging human life indefinitely. It would be foolish to remain perpetually dissatisfied over this state of affairs, however distraught we may feel about the expected or experienced death of a loved one. Life must go on. So here reducing dissatisfaction through accommodation is justified, sensible, and moral.

In other cases, non-accommodating solutions are truly possible. Imagine that your loved one is going to die because you cannot afford costly nursing care and medical treatment. Such care and treatment might prolong life for another 10, 20, or 30 years; other people's lives *are* being prolonged by such a treatment. Should you accommodate to that situation, in order to reduce your dissatisfaction? If another solution to the problem is truly possible, you should not. Instead, you should pursue both individual and collective strategies for changing the situation, not accommodating to it.

Moreover, in some circumstances increasing your satisfaction harms no one else and may even help others. For example, your enjoyment of a sunny day is not diminished by my enjoyment of it. We may even enhance each other's enjoyment. And your opportunity to find satisfaction as a composer of opera music is not imperilled by my desire to write stories or lyrics: in fact, we can make operas together. In this case, our satisfaction is complementary or symbiotic. In some circumstances, then, individual solutions to the gap between wants and achievements are independent; in others, they are interdependent, maximized through collective effort or co-operation.

But in a great many cases, one person's satisfaction is dependent on someone else's dissatisfaction: this situation is sometimes called a zero-sum game. For every winner there is at least one loser. This fact leads to what Calabresi (1976) calls "tragic choices"—those in which no solution is equally satisfying for everyone, whatever choice is made. He gives as examples the allocation of scarce medical technology (for example, kidney dialysis machines) to equally needy patients, or the drafting of soldiers into a wartime army.

Since creating a winner means also creating a loser, people engaged in tragic choosing are constantly searching for new, more generally accepted principles of allocation. No principle can succeed in appearing just for long. Yet certain principles are more obviously unjust than others. Almost everyone would agree that allocating scarce life-prolonging equipment, or exempting young people from the military draft, on the basis of income would be unjust. It would amount to a market in lives: the rich live, the poor die. In fact, under conditions of pay-as-you-go medical care and draft exemptions for college students—both of which have existed in the United

States in recent times—such an injustice has prevailed. Not surprisingly, people have sought alternatives.

Obviously it is desirable to find solutions that give the most people the most satisfaction possible, even in zero-sum situations. But can it be done? Imagine the following scenario. You are faced with a dissatisfying gap between what you want and what you are getting. Closing that gap is truly possible. Many strategies for doing so, both individual and collective, are available. Further, imagine that your actions might affect other people's well-being adversely. To improve your well-being unilaterally, you must worsen someone else's well-being. To avoid doing so requires the co-operative search for a solution.

Figure 8.3 displays the logically possible solutions, following Merton's paradigm (see Figure 8.1) in format. But unlike Merton, we are concerned with the possible combinations of individual and collective well-being that various strategies might further.

You may choose to *accommodate*—do nothing, either individually or collectively, about your dissatisfaction. Simply lower your aspirations and get used to wanting what you have gotten.

Another solution is to *mythologize*—lower your aspirations, and maybe even urge others to lower theirs. But do not simply accommodate. Make up elaborate explanations, for yourself and others, about why the current situation is better than any other. Mythologizers do this by denying the importance of well-being in principle, by saying that "suffering is good for people." They mystify the character of accommodation by saying that "people don't know when they are really well off." And they use paradoxes to distract attention from the problem at hand, saying things like "Less is really more," "Bad is really good," "The universe is inside you," or "Life is only a dream, reality lies elsewhere."

Adaptation	Your strategy furthers . . .	
	Individual Well-being	*Collective Well-being*
Co-operate	+	+
Sacrifice	−	+
Self-indulge	+	−
Accommodate	−	−
Mythologize	±	±

FIGURE 8.3 Adaptations to a gap between what you want and get.

A third solution is to pursue personal goals at the expense of others; that is, to *self-indulge*. This strategy achieves more individual satisfaction, but not more (and possibly less), collective satisfaction. There are the same number of winners and losers as before, but now you are a winner and someone else is a loser. More important is the fact that this solution allows the original problem of unequal satisfaction—whether due to scarcity or mal-distribution—to remain unchallenged. Someone else will have to challenge and change it, or others will continue to suffer from it.

In fact, we can distinguish two kinds of self-indulgence, which we might call "parasitic" and "productive," respectively. Parasitic self-indulgence merely takes what you have and gives it to me. No more is created in the transaction, and the range of inequality may even be widened. Productive self-indulgence uses the system to produce more for me, while leaving you what you already have; here too, the range of inequality may be widened.

Indeed, the purpose of self-indulgence is self-advancement at the expense of other groups and individuals. This is not to be confused with co-operative redistribution, whose purpose is a broad-based equalization of rewards. We shall consider that option (as "co-operation") shortly.

Another solution, the exact opposite of self-indulgence, is *sacrifice*. Here, no effort is made to maximize individual well-being and every effort is aimed at maximizing collective well-being through collective strategies. However, here too we can distinguish between "productive" and "unproductive" sacrifice. Unproductive sacrifice gives you some of what I have, reducing the inequality between us, but no more is created. Productive sacrifice uses the system to produce more than before, and the new product is used to reduce the inequality between us.

A final adaptation might be called *co-operation*. Good citizens combine individual and collective strategies to pursue individual and collective goals. They seek to gain greater satisfaction without hurting anyone else and, if possible, while helping someone else. This is done by co-operating with others in the search for a solution.

An example may illustrate how this works. Recall from Chapter 6 that parents of young children are very short of free time, and mothers are more deprived than fathers. Imagine that in the Jones family, Mr. Jones (Gord) is dissatisfied because he only has three hours a day to relax. Mrs. Jones (Sheila) is also dissatisfied, and she only has one hour a day to relax. Gord wants to close the gap between what he has and what he wants.

He can accommodate by simply shutting his eyes to the situation: by waiting for the children to grow up and leave home. Or he can mythologize about the nobility of hard work and how, in days to come, he will be rewarded for his unstinting efforts on his children's behalf. He may even tell Sheila that she is a "real woman" and he thinks he will keep her. In both scenarios, Gord retains three hours of rest and Sheila one hour.

On the other hand, Gord may reduce his own dissatisfaction by exploiting his wife: he may pass on a few of his chores, so that he now has four hours of rest a day and she has none. This is the "unproductive" form of exploitation. Or Gord may figure out a way of reducing the household workload through better planning, so that he has two more hours of rest a day. Now, he has five hours and Sheila still has one: the domestic inequality ratio has widened to 5-to-1 from an original 3-to-1. This is productive exploitation: "productive" in the sense that it has improved the domestic system, but "exploitation" in the sense that inequality has widened as a result.

Gord may also reduce his own dissatisfaction by reducing the household workload through better planning, and pass on some of the benefit to his wife. Imagine that his plan has freed up two hours a day. If he takes one free hour and Sheila takes the other, each will have gained more rest and the level of domestic inequality ratio will also have narrowed, to 2-to-1 from an original 3-to-1. This co-operative adaptation does not produce equality, but it increases the well-being of both spouses: that is, the collective well-being.

Finally, Gord may choose to sacrifice his own immediate well-being in the interests of Sheila's greater well-being, domestic equality and, thereby, collective well-being. He may value this on principle or because he believes it will lead to greater marital harmony. In either case, he may sacrifice unproductively (giving up one free hour a day to Sheila) or productively (keeping his three hours and "finding" two more for Sheila through better planning). Both strategies create an equality of free time in the household.

As we have seen in this example, sacrifice and co-operation are potentially system-changing adaptations, while accommodation, mythologizing, and exploitation are system-preserving ones.

System-changing adaptations require attention to collective well-being and, often, collective action. Thus, the most effective individual strategies are linked to collective strategies, and they are bound to change the system of inequality in society or in a household.

To use these strategies we must be alert to the ways individual problems and collective problems are related. Second, we must be aware of what is truly possible, and seek satisfaction in that realm. On the other hand, we can allow ourselves to feel satisfied with accommodation when faced with the truly impossible. If given the opportunity to make truly possible changes, satisfaction is warranted when we have actively sought to make them through co-operation or sacrifice. By this scheme of thinking, exploitation never justifies satisfaction, since it preserves and even worsens the problem many people are facing.

Following the same reasoning, you should not feel dissatisfied if you have "fought the good fight"—co-operated or sacrificed. Under these conditions, you are not to blame for failing to achieve the truly possible, nor for giving in to existing circumstance. More likely than not, you have enjoyed the fight, and you may want to fight on. What, generally, should people do to close the gap between what they have and what they want, particularly when this gap is the result of structured social inequality? How should they think about the problem?

Steps to Real Paradise

Prescribing lives for other people is risky, even foolhardy. This book will not tell you what the Good Life is, nor specifically how to find it. But implied in all that has come before is a method for thinking about your own life if you want to make it more satisfying. Though I recognize its many faults, I cannot think of a better method, so I offer it for your consideration. Use it if it seems useful.

First, *analyse your own state of mind and present course of action*. What do you want, and are you getting it—or likely to get it by the course you are presently following? Do people customarily get that outcome when they do what you are doing? Are you so different from the rest that you can expect a different outcome? Are there other outcomes, offered by other courses of action, that might prove even more satisfying? How likely are you to change your mind about what you want, but find yourself locked in by the decisions you are taking now? Can you think of a plan that would work toward your present goal but leave the door open for changes if you change your mind?

Second, *analyse the relationship between your present course of action and the outcome you desire*. If the desired outcome is unlikely, is that because of a personal deficiency or a structured inequality in society: a private trouble or a public issue? Are you prevented from taking another course of action that is likelier to produce the results you want? If so, is that because of a personal deficiency or structured inequality?

Third, *analyse the contours of "the possible."* Would it be harder to change your present course of action to one that will likely produce the desired outcome, or to change the likelihood that your present course of action will yield the desired outcome? Which change is most possible in general? That is, which change are people already making most successfully? Which change is becoming more likely to succeed?

Fourth, *analyse the strategies that are available*, where change is demonstrably possible. *How* are people making the changes that are already succeeding, or increasingly likely to succeed? Is it through individual actions or collective actions; and what kinds of actions are they? Are they occurring in places (and times) similar to our own, or very different ones? How does this similarity (or difference) reflect on their usefulness in our own society today?

Fifth, *analyse your ability and willingness to undertake these strategies*. Given the possibility of their success, are you—the person you are today—able to use these strategies? If not, how would you have to change yourself to be able to use them in the future? Would you, for example, have to shift your concerns from a focus on short-term goals to a focus on long-term goals? Or from a preference for individual solutions to an acceptance of collective solutions? How would such shifts affect your social relations, or your attainment of other goals that may also attract you? Can you tolerate the consequences of these shifts?

Sixth, *analyse the steps you must take to actually carry out these changes*. Given your ability to shift to new, more successful strategies, what should you do first? Is there a group to join? A credential to gain? A commitment to make? Do you need more money or free time to make these changes—and if so, how can

you get them? Are you able and willing to wait until you have
the information, contacts, time, or money you need to carry out
this new strategy?

Seventh, *analyse the alternative, do-nothing strategy*. If you
cannot demonstrate to your own satisfaction that change is possible; or, if possible in general, that it is possible for a person
like you; or, if possible for a person like you, that it is possible
through a means you can accept; or, if possible through a means
you can accept, that it is possible given your personal resources,
then you are opting for resignation—for accommodation. Can you
imagine living with this choice in future, or will you regret having
done nothing? If accommodation means that from now on, you
will have to want what you can get, and what you will get is
not what you currently want, can you see yourself accepting that
state of affairs? If not, go back to Step Number Two.

Concluding Remarks

In case you haven't noticed, this book has been about one of social
science's classic concerns: namely, the relationship between consciousness and social structure. I have aimed to discuss this
complicated issue in relatively simple terms. Accordingly, I have
translated issues of consciousness—values, perceptions, aspirations, and expectations, among others—into questions of "what
you want," and translated issues of social structure—limits on
your ability to choose freely among desired alternatives—into
questions of "what you get." Thus, the book has been, on the
surface, about the relationship between what you want and what
you get.

We have noted the congruence, for most people at most ages,
between what they want and what they get. Two alternative
explanations of this congruence are possible. One is the explanation offered by liberal ideology which argues that people generally get what they want if they approach the matter correctly. The
other, a sociological explanation, argues that people are more likely
to bring their desires into conformity with what is possible while
preserving the illusion of choice. We have noted that, in fact, most
people do both. As well, they consider and often carry through
strategies for closing the gap.

In a modern society, people want choice and the knowledge
that they have choices to make. Life without choice is demoralizing,

deadening. People who think they have no choices fail to make choices when they are truly available, or make bad choices when several possibilities are offered. In fact, we all have some choices to make in life, and have to practise making them well. This book has urged you to choose wisely, carefully, and with awareness.

This is *not* to argue that your choice is unlimited; in fact, it argues the opposite. If choice were unlimited, wrong choices would have no important consequences; you could always make a right choice that remedied the wrong one you had made earlier. But in fact, your present choices are limited by past choices as well as by the choices other people are making and by factors such as the class structure, which are not, in any real sense, chosen by most of us at all.

Without the possibility of choice, however constrained, morality has no meaning. Morality means taking responsibility for your actions. People are not always responsible for the direction their life has taken, for they are not always in control. When they are, sometimes they are not aware of choosing, or their range of choices may be so small as to offer no real choice at all. Still, if we want to preserve the framework of a moral society we must preserve individuals' responsibility, and opportunity, to choose as freely and wisely as they possibly can.

All choice is constrained or limited, and we typically act to satisfy, not optimize, our desires. No other type of action makes sense. Yet even well-informed people vary in what they believe to be possible. This book has not aimed to make you set your sights lower, to get you to make the easiest or most popular choices. Rather, it has aimed to make you aware of choosing and of the limits placed on your choosing, and to make you ask whether our society could be better—freer, fairer, more moral—than it is today.

In Chapter 1, we learned that a Real Paradise has two elements: moral sensibility and a knowledge of the possible. Moral sensibility demands an awareness of what a "worthwhile life" and a "good society" might look like. Few people besides philosophers are encouraged to think about these questions; many think they are non-scientific and therefore merely speculative or idiosyncratic concerns.

Yet making a good society and a worthwhile life presupposes planning, both individual and collective, which in turn presupposes conceiving of the goal. Whether the desired goal should be "the greatest satisfaction for the greatest number" or something else is beyond the scope of this book. But the question should not be dismissed from consideration simply because it challenges the tools of analysis currently at our disposal.

"Good information" is something we *can* do something about more readily. We know a lot about the forces that limit the information people have at their disposal. According to the multiple discrepancies theory (discussed in Chapter 1), people set low goals for themselves because they make modest comparisons, comparisons with others like themselves. They judge the possible from their own history and the life histories of others just like them. More and better information about the attainability of other lives might lead to behavioural change—both individual and collective— that would make people's desires a reality.

We all need to seek better information about what is truly possible. Sociology is, in one sense, the study of the possible, since it is the study of what already is: lives that certain individuals, groups, or societies are already living. We are less readily manipulated into downward accommodation when we know that alternatives are possible, even if they are difficult and require collective, long-term thinking.

In closing, then, this book carries no simple message. It is not intended to convince you to accept *or* reject your life, but rather to encourage you to question it. Question your life more systematically, with information and awareness. Above all, recognize that as human beings we all make choices, however constrained. The future we shall choose, individually and collectively, and the best means for achieving that future are yet to be determined. How well you construct your own future will demonstrate whether you have understood the purpose of this book.

References

BARRACLOUGH, G. (1967).   *An Introduction to Contemporary History.* Harmondsworth: Penguin.

CALABRESI, G. (1976).   *Tragic Choices.* New York: W.W. Norton.

CLOWARD, R., & OHLIN, L. (1960). *Delinquency and opportunity.* New York: Free Press.

DURKHEIM, E. (1951). *Suicide: A study of sociology.* J. Spaulding & G. Simpson (Trans.). New York: Free Press. (Original work published 1897)

_____. (1965). *The division of labor in society.* New York: Free Press. (Original work published 1893)

HOBSBAWM, E.J. (1959). *Primitive rebels: Studies in archaic forms of social movement in the 19th and 20th centuries.* New York: Norton.

JENCKS, C. *et al.* (1977). *Who gets ahead?: The determinants of economic success in America.* New York: Basic Books.

KANTER, R.M. (1972). *Commitment and community: Communes and utopias in sociological perspective.* Cambridge: Harvard University Press.

_____. (1977). *Men and women of the corporation.* New York: Basic Books.

LIPSET, S.M., TROW, M., & COLEMAN, J. (1963). *Union democracy: The internal politics of the international typographical union.* Garden City, NY: Anchor Books, Doubleday.

MALTHUS, T.R. (1959). *Population: The First Essay.* Foreword by K.E. Boulding. Ann Arbor: University of Michigan Press. (Original work published 1798)

MARX, K. (1955). *The Communist Manifesto.* In S.H. Beer (Ed.). New York: Appleton Century-Crofts. (Original work published in 1888)

_____. (1963). In T.B. Bottomore & M. Rubel (Eds.), *Selected Writings in Sociology and Social Philosophy.* Texts transl. by T.B. Bottomore. Harmondsworth: Penguin. (Original work published 1844)

MERTON, R.K. (1957a). Social structure and anomie. In his *Social Theory and Social Structure* (Rev. ed., pp. 131-160). New York: Free Press.

_____. (1957b). Patterns of influence: Local and cosmopolitan influentials. In his *Social Theory and Social Structure* (Rev. ed., pp. 387-420). New York: Free Press.

MICHALOS, A.C. (1987). *Final Progress Report on Global Report on Student Well-being: Applications of multiple discrepancies theory.* Guelph: University of Guelph.

MICHELS, R. (1962). *Political Parties.* New York: Free Press.

QUALITY OF LIFE SURVEY. (1981). Unpublished raw data from large survey of life satisfaction conducted at the Institute for Behavioural Research, York University, Toronto.

SAUVY, A. (1969). *General theory of population.* Christopher Campos (Trans.). New York: Basic Books.

VEBLEN, T. (1934). *The theory of the leisure class.* New York: Modern Library.

WEBER, M. (1974). *The protestant ethic and the spirit of capitalism.* London: George Allan & Unwin.

WESTHUES, K. (1982). *First Sociology.* New York: McGraw-Hill.

Appendix

Note to Instructors: *Suggestions for Using* Choices and Chances *in the Classroom*

This book is intended to supplement the general textbook you are assigning in your introductory course. To that end, this book can be used in a number of different ways. Some of these suggested uses include the following:

1. A brief introduction to sociology: two-semester course

   Assign this book as the first one students will read, to provide an overview of many of the concepts and concerns they will later encounter in lectures and other readings.

2. A brief introduction to sociology: one-semester course

   Assign this book as the central text in your course, and supplement it with readings in sociology (monographs, research papers, selected textbook chapters) and newspaper articles.

3. The basis of a book review or critical essay

   Ask students to write a critical review of the book. Such a review may compare this book with other books, or one chapter's findings with another's; or reanalyse the data presented in this book from the standpoint of a given theoretical approach (for example, symbolic interactionism, Marxism, structural functionalism).

4. A source of ideas for essay topics

   Suggest that students find their topics (and some references) for a major paper or essay among the issues and debates discussed in this book.

5. A running supplement to your textbook

Match individual chapters of this book with one or more chapters of the textbook you have assigned. Some of the possible match-ups are suggested below:

Life Choices Chapter	Suggested Textbook Chapter
1. What you want	Introduction to sociology Culture Socialization Aging/life cycle
2. What you get	Stratification/inequality Social roles/structure Ethnic/race relations Ideology
3. Educational choices	Education
4. Career choices	Work Industrial sociology Economic sociology Formal organizations
5. Single or married	Marriage and family Gender relations
6. Childless or parent	Marriage and family Population/demography
7. Location and lifestyle	Urban sociology Communities Lifestyles Mass media
8. What you want and get	Political sociology Social movements Deviance and control Social change

Index

To the owner of this book:

We are interested in your reaction to *Choices and Chances: Sociology for Everyday Life* by Lorne Tepperman

1. What was your reason for using this book?

   ☐ university course   ☐ continuing education course
   ☐ college course   ☐ personal interest
                                       ☐ other (specify)

2. In which school are you enrolled? _____

3. Approximately how much of the book did you use?
   ☐ ¼   ☐ ½   ☐ ¾   ☐ all

4. What is the best aspect of the book?

5. Have you any suggestions for improvement?

6. Is there anything that should be added?

- -

Fold here

Tape shut